Book 4 – Fixed Income and Derivatives

SCHWESERNOTES™ 2018 LEVEL II CFA® BOOK 4: FIXED INCOME AND DERIVATIVES

Published in 2017 by Kaplan, Inc.

Printed in the United States of America.

ISBN: 978-1-4754-5981-4

Readings and Learning Outcome Statements

Readings

The following material is a review of the Fixed Income and Derivatives principles designed to address the learning outcome statements set forth by CFA Institute.

Study Session 12

Reading Assignments
Fixed Income and Derivatives, CFA Program Curriculum, Volume 5, Level II (CFA Institute, 2017)

Study Session 13

Reading Assignments
Fixed Income and Derivatives, CFA Program Curriculum, Volume 5, Level II (CFA Institute, 2017)

Study Session 14

Reading Assignments
Fixed Income and Derivatives, CFA Program Curriculum, Volume 5, Level II (CFA Institute, 2017)

Learning Outcome Statements (LOS)

The CFA Institute Learning Outcome Statements are listed below. These are repeated in each topic review; however, the order may have been changed in order to get a better fit with the flow of the review.

Study Session 12

The topical coverage corresponds with the following CFA Institute assigned reading:

35. The Term Structure and Interest Rate Dynamics

The candidate should be able to:

a. describe relationships among spot rates, forward rates, yield to maturity, expected and realized returns on bonds, and the shape of the yield curve. (page 1)
b. describe the forward pricing and forward rate models and calculate forward and spot prices and rates using those models. (page 3)
c. describe how zero-coupon rates (spot rates) may be obtained from the par curve by bootstrapping. (page 6)
d. describe the assumptions concerning the evolution of spot rates in relation to forward rates implicit in active bond portfolio management. (page 8)
e. describe the strategy of riding the yield curve. (page 11)
f. explain the swap rate curve and why and how market participants use it in valuation. (page 12)
g. calculate and interpret the swap spread for a given maturity. (page 14)
h. describe the Z-spread. (page 16)
i. describe the TED and Libor-OIS spreads. (page 17)
j. explain traditional theories of the term structure of interest rates and describe the implications of each theory for forward rates and the shape of the yield curve. (page 18)
k. describe modern term structure models and how they are used. (page 21)
l. explain how a bond's exposure to each of the factors driving the yield curve can be measured and how these exposures can be used to manage yield curve risks. (page 23)
m. explain the maturity structure of yield volatilities and their effect on price volatility. (page 25)

The topical coverage corresponds with the following CFA Institute assigned reading:

36. The Arbitrage-Free Valuation Framework

The candidate should be able to:

a. explain what is meant by arbitrage-free valuation of a fixed-income instrument. (page 34)
b. calculate the arbitrage-free value of an option-free, fixed-rate coupon bond. (page 35)
c. describe a binomial interest rate tree framework. (page 36)
d. describe the backward induction valuation methodology and calculate the value of a fixed-income instrument given its cash flow at each node. (page 38)
e. describe the process of calibrating a binomial interest rate tree to match a specific term structure. (page 39)
f. compare pricing using the zero-coupon yield curve with pricing using an arbitrage-free binomial lattice. (page 41)

g. describe pathwise valuation in a binomial interest rate framework and calculate the value of a fixed-income instrument given its cash flows along each path. (page 43)
h. describe a Monte Carlo forward-rate simulation and its application. (page 44)

STUDY SESSION 13

The topical coverage corresponds with the following CFA Institute assigned reading:

37. Valuation and Analysis: Bonds with Embedded Options

The candidate should be able to:

a. describe fixed-income securities with embedded options. (page 55)
b. explain the relationships between the values of a callable or putable bond, the underlying option-free (straight) bond, and the embedded option. (page 56)
c. describe how the arbitrage-free framework can be used to value a bond with embedded options. (page 56)
d. explain how interest rate volatility affects the value of a callable or putable bond. (page 59)
e. explain how changes in the level and shape of the yield curve affect the value of a callable or putable bond. (page 60)
f. calculate the value of a callable or putable bond from an interest rate tree. (page 56)
g. explain the calculation and use of option-adjusted spreads. (page 60)
h. explain how interest rate volatility affects option adjusted spreads. (page 62)
i. calculate and interpret effective duration of a callable or putable bond. (page 63)
j. compare effective durations of callable, putable, and straight bonds. (page 64)
k. describe the use of one-sided durations and key rate durations to evaluate the interest rate sensitivity of bonds with embedded options. (page 65)
l. compare effective convexities of callable, putable, and straight bonds. (page 67)
m. calculate the value of a capped or floored floating-rate bond. (page 68)
n. describe defining features of a convertible bond. (page 70)
o. calculate and interpret the components of a convertible bond's value. (page 71)
p. describe how a convertible bond is valued in an arbitrage-free framework. (page 73)
q. compare the risk–return characteristics of a convertible bond with the risk–return characteristics of a straight bond and of the underlying common stock. (page 74)

The topical coverage corresponds with the following CFA Institute assigned reading:

38. Credit Analysis Models

The candidate should be able to:

a. explain probability of default, loss given default, expected loss, and present value of the expected loss and describe the relative importance of each across the credit spectrum. (page 92)
b. explain credit scoring and credit ratings. (page 93)
c. explain strengths and weaknesses of credit ratings. (page 95)
d. explain structural models of corporate credit risk, including why equity can be viewed as a call option on the company's assets. (page 95)
e. explain reduced form models of corporate credit risk, including why debt can be valued as the sum of expected discounted cash flows after adjusting for risk. (page 98)
f. explain assumptions, strengths, and weaknesses of both structural and reduced form models of corporate credit risk. (page 99)
g. explain the determinants of the term structure of credit spreads. (page 101)

h. calculate and interpret the present value of the expected loss on a bond over a given time horizon. (page 101)
i. compare the credit analysis required for asset-backed securities to analysis of corporate debt. (page 103)

The topical coverage corresponds with the following CFA Institute assigned reading:
39. Credit Default Swaps
The candidate should be able to:
a. describe credit default swaps (CDS), single-name and index CDS, and the parameters that define a given CDS product. (page 112)
b. describe credit events and settlement protocols with respect to CDS. (page 113)
c. explain the principles underlying, and factors that influence, the market's pricing of CDS. (page 114)
d. describe the use of CDS to manage credit exposures and to express views regarding changes in shape and/or level of the credit curve. (page 117)
e. describe the use of CDS to take advantage of valuation disparities among separate markets, such as bonds, loans, equities, and equity-linked instruments. (page 118)

STUDY SESSION 14

The topical coverage corresponds with the following CFA Institute assigned reading:
40. Pricing and Valuation of Forward Commitments
The candidate should be able to:
a. describe and compare how equity, interest rate, fixed-income, and currency forward and futures contracts are priced and valued. (page 133)
b. calculate and interpret the no-arbitrage value of equity, interest rate, fixed-income, and currency forward and futures contracts. (page 133)
c. describe and compare how interest rate, currency, and equity swaps are priced and valued. (page 147)
d. calculate and interpret the no-arbitrage value of interest rate, currency, and equity swaps. (page 147)

The topical coverage corresponds with the following CFA Institute assigned reading:
41. Valuation of Contingent Claims
The candidate should be able to:
a. describe and interpret the binomial option valuation model and its component terms. (page 166)
b. calculate the no-arbitrage values of European and American options using a two-period binomial model. (page 166)
c. identify an arbitrage opportunity involving options and describe the related arbitrage. (page 174)
d. calculate and interpret the value of an interest rate option using a two-period binomial model. (page 176)
e. describe how the value of a European option can be analyzed as the present value of the option's expected payoff at expiration. (page 166)
f. identify assumptions of the Black-Scholes-Merton option valuation model. (page 178)
g. interpret the components of the Black-Scholes-Merton model as applied to call options in terms of leveraged position in the underlying. (page 179)

h. describe how the Black–Scholes–Merton model is used to value European options on equities and currencies. (page 181)
i. describe how the Black model is used to value European options on futures. (page 182)
j. describe how the Black model is used to value European interest rate options and European swaptions. (page 183)
k. interpret each of the option Greeks. (page 185)
l. describe how a delta hedge is executed. (page 190)
m. describe the role of gamma risk in options trading. (page 192)
n. define implied volatility and explain how it is used in options trading. (page 192)

The topical coverage corresponds with the following CFA Institute assigned reading:

42. Derivative Strategies

The candidate should be able to:

a. describe how interest rate, currency, and equity swaps, futures, and forwards can be used to modify portfolio risk and return. (page 203)
b. describe how to replicate an asset by using options and by using cash plus forwards or futures. (page 205)
c. describe the investment objectives, structure, payoff, and risk(s) of a covered call position. (page 208)
d. describe the investment objectives, structure, payoff, and risk(s) of a protective put position. (page 209)
e. calculate and interpret the value at expiration, profit, maximum profit, maximum loss, and breakeven underlying price at expiration for covered calls and protective puts. (page 210)
f. contrast protective put and covered call positions to being long an asset and short a forward on the asset. (page 212)
g. describe the investment objective(s), structure, payoffs, and risks of the following option strategies: bull spread, bear spread, collar, and straddle. (page 213)
h. calculate and interpret the value at expiration, profit, maximum profit, maximum loss, and breakeven underlying price at expiration of the following option strategies: bull spread, bear spread, collar, and straddle. (page 213)
i. describe uses of calendar spreads. (page 221)
j. identify and evaluate appropriate derivatives strategies consistent with given investment objectives. (page 222)

Getting Started

CFA®

Level II CFA® Exam

Welcome

As the VP of Advanced Designations at Kaplan Schweser, I am pleased to have the opportunity to help you prepare for the CFA® exam. Getting an early start on your study program is important for you to sufficiently **prepare**, **practice**, and **perform** on exam day. Proper planning will allow you to set aside enough time to master the Learning Outcome Statements (LOS) in the Level II curriculum.

Now that you've received your SchweserNotes™, here's how to get started:

Step 1: Access Your Online Tools

Visit **www.schweser.com** and log in to your online account using the button located in the top navigation bar. After logging in, select the appropriate level and proceed to the dashboard where you can access your online products.

Step 2: Create a Study Plan

Create a study plan with the **Study Calendar** (located on the Schweser dashboard) and familiarize yourself with your financial calculator. Check out our calculator videos in the **Candidate Resource Library** (also found on the dashboard).

Step 3: Prepare and Practice

Read your SchweserNotes™ Volumes 1–5

At the end of each reading, you can answer the Concept Checker questions for better understanding of the curriculum.

Attend a Weekly Class

Attend live classes online or take part in our live classroom courses in select cities around the world. Our expert faculty will guide you through the curriculum with a structured approach to help you prepare for the CFA® exam. The Schweser **On-Demand Video Lectures**, in combination with the **Weekly Class**, offer a blended learning approach that covers every LOS in the CFA curriculum.

Practice with SchweserPro™ QBank

Maximize your retention of important concepts by answering questions in the **SchweserPro™ QBank** and taking several **Practice Exams**. Use **Schweser's QuickSheet** for continuous review on the go. (Visit **www.schweser.com/cfa** to order.)

Step 4: Attend a 3-Day, 5-Day, or WindsorWeek™ Review Workshop

Schweser's late-season review workshops are designed to drive home the CFA® material, which is critical for CFA exam success. Review key concepts in every topic, **perform** by working through demonstration problems, and **practice** your exam techniques.

Step 5: Perform

Take a **Live** or **Live Online Schweser Mock Exam** to ensure you are ready to **perform** on the actual CFA® exam. Put your skills and knowledge to the test and gain confidence before the exam.

Again, thank you for trusting Kaplan Schweser with your CFA exam preparation!

Sincerely,

Derek Burkett

Derek Burkett, CFA, FRM, CAIA
VP, Advanced Designations, Kaplan Schweser

The Kaplan Way

Acquire new knowledge through demonstration and examples.

Apply new knowledge through simulation and practice.

Evaluate mastery of new knowledge and identify achieved outcomes.

Visit our website, www.schweser.com/cfa-free-resources, to view all the free materials we have to help you prepare.

Contact us for questions about your study package, upgrading your package, purchasing additional study materials, or for additional information:

888.325.5072 (U.S.) | +1 608.779.8327 (Int'l.)

staff@schweser.com | www.schweser.com/cfa

The following is a review of the Fixed Income: Valuation Concepts principles designed to address the learning outcome statements set forth by CFA Institute. Cross-Reference to CFA Institute Assigned Reading #35.

The Term Structure and Interest Rate Dynamics

Study Session 12

Exam Focus

This topic review discusses the theories and implications of the term structure of interest rates. In addition to understanding the relationships between spot rates, forward rates, yield to maturity, and the shape of the yield curve, be sure you become familiar with concepts like the *z*-spread, the TED spread and the LIBOR-OIS spread. Interpreting the shape of the yield curve in the context of the theories of the term structure of interest rates is always important for the exam. Also pay close attention to the concept of key rate duration.

Introduction

The financial markets both impact and are controlled by interest rates. Understanding the term structure of interest rates (i.e., the graph of interest rates at different maturities) is one key to understanding the performance of an economy. In this reading, we explain how and why the term structure changes over time.

Spot rates are the annualized market interest rates for a single payment to be received in the future. Generally, we use spot rates for government securities (risk-free) to generate the spot rate curve. Spot rates can be interpreted as the yields on zero-coupon bonds, and for this reason we sometimes refer to spot rates as *zero-coupon rates*. A **forward rate** is an interest rate (agreed to today) for a loan to be made at some future date.

Professor's Note: While most of the LOS is this topic review have Describe *or* Explain *as the command words, we will still delve into numerous calculations, as it is difficult to really understand some of these concepts without getting in to the mathematics behind them.*

LOS 35.a: Describe relationships among spot rates, forward rates, yield to maturity, expected and realized returns on bonds, and the shape of the yield curve.

CFA® Program Curriculum, Volume 5, page 6

Spot Rates

The price today of $1 par, zero-coupon bond is known as the discount factor, which we will call P_T. Because it is a zero-coupon bond, the spot interest rate is the yield to maturity of this payment, which we represent as S_T. The relationship between the discount factor P_T and the spot rate S_T for maturity T can be expressed as:

$$P_T = \frac{1}{(1+S_T)^T}$$

The term structure of spot rates—the graph of the spot rate S_T versus the maturity T—is known as the **spot yield curve** or **spot curve**. The shape and level of the spot curve changes continuously with the market prices of bonds.

Forward Rates

The annualized interest rate on a loan to be initiated at a future period is called the **forward rate** for that period. The term structure of forward rates is called the **forward curve**. (Note that forward curves and spot curves are mathematically related—we can derive one from the other.)

We will use the following notation:

$f(j,k)$ = the annualized interest rate applicable on a k-year loan starting in j years.

t = 0 t = j t = j + k

$F_{(j,k)}$ = the forward price of a $1 par zero-coupon bond maturing at time $j+k$ delivered at time j.

$F_{(j,k)}$ = the discount factor associated with the forward rate.

$$F_{(j,k)} = \frac{1}{[1+f(j,k)]^k}$$

Yield to Maturity

As we've discussed, the **yield to maturity** (YTM) or yield of a zero-coupon bond with maturity T is the spot interest rate for a maturity of T. However, for a coupon bond, if the spot rate curve is not flat, the YTM will not be the same as the spot rate.

Example: Spot rates and yield for a coupon bond

Compute the price and yield to maturity of a three-year, 4% annual-pay, $1,000 face value bond given the following spot rate curve: S_1 = 5%, S_2 = 6%, and S_3 = 7%.

Answer:

1. Calculate the price of the bond using the spot rate curve:

$$\text{Price} = \frac{40}{(1.05)} + \frac{40}{(1.06)^2} + \frac{1040}{(1.07)^3} = \$922.64$$

2. Calculate the yield to maturity (y_3):

N = 3; PV = –922.64; PMT = 40; FV = 1,000; CPT I/Y → 6.94
y_3= 6.94%

Note that the yield on a three year bond is a weighted average of three spot rates, so in this case we would expect $S_1 < y_3 < S_3$. The yield to maturity y_3 is closest to S_3 because the par value dominates the value of the bond and therefore S_3 has the highest weight.

Expected and Realized Returns on Bonds

Expected return is the ex-ante holding period return that a bond investor expects to earn.

The expected return will be equal to the bond's yield only when *all three* of the following are true:

- The bond is held to maturity.
- All payments (coupon and principal) are made on time and in full.
- All coupons are reinvested at the original YTM.

The second requirement implies that the bond is option-free and there is no default risk.

The last requirement, reinvesting coupons at the YTM, is the least realistic assumption. If the yield curve is not flat, the coupon payments will not be reinvested at the YTM and the expected return will differ from the yield.

Realized return on a bond refers to the actual return that the investor experiences over the investment's holding period. Realized return is based on actual reinvestment rates.

LOS 35.b: Describe the forward pricing and forward rate models and calculate forward and spot prices and rates using those models.

CFA® Program Curriculum, Volume 5, page 7

The Forward Pricing Model

The **forward pricing model** values forward contracts based on arbitrage-free pricing.

Consider two investors.

Investor A purchases a $1 face value, zero-coupon bond maturing in *j+k* years at a price of $P_{(j+k)}$.

Investor B enters into a *j*-year forward contract to purchase a $1 face value, zero-coupon bond maturing in *k* years at a price of $F_{(j,k)}$. Investor B's cost today is the present value of the cost: $PV[F_{(j,k)}]$ or $P_jF_{(j,k)}$.

Because the $1 cash flows at *j+k* are the same, these two investments should have the same price, which leads to the forward pricing model:

$$P_{(j+k)} = P_jF_{(j,k)}$$

Therefore:

$$F_{(j,k)} = \frac{P_{(j+k)}}{P_j}$$

Example: Forward pricing

Calculate the forward price two years from now for a $1 par, zero-coupon, three-year bond given the following spot rates.

The two-year spot rate, S_2 = 4%.

The five-year spot rate, S_5 = 6%.

Answer:

Calculate discount factors P_j and $P_{(j+k)}$.

$$P_j = P_2 = 1 / (1 + 0.04)^2 = 0.9246$$

$$P_{(j+k)} = P_5 = 1 / (1+0.06)^5 = 0.7473$$

The forward price of a three-year bond in two years is represented as $F_{(2,3)}$

$$F_{(j,k)} = P_{(j+k)} / P_j$$

$$F_{(2,3)} = 0.7473 / 0.9246 = 0.8082$$

In other words, $0.8082 is the price agreed to today, to pay in two years, for a three-year bond that will pay $1 at maturity.

Professor's Note: In the Derivatives portion of the curriculum, the forward price is computed as future value (for j periods) of $P_{(j+k)}$. It gives the same result and can be verified using the data in the previous example by computing the future value of P_5 (i.e., compounding for two periods at S_2). $FV = 0.7473(1.04)^2 = \$0.8082$.

The Forward Rate Model

The **forward rate model** relates forward and spot rates as follows:

$$[1 + S_{(j+k)}]^{(j+k)} = (1 + S_j)^j \, [1 + f(j,k)]^k$$

or

$$[1 + f(j,k)]^k = [1 + S_{(j+k)}]^{(j+k)} / (1 + S_j)^j$$

This model is useful because it illustrates how forward rates and spot rates are interrelated.

This equation suggests that the forward rate $f(2,3)$ should make investors indifferent between buying a five-year zero-coupon bond versus buying a two-year zero-coupon bond and at maturity reinvesting the principal for three additional years.

Example: Forward rates

Suppose that the two-year and five-year spot rates are $S_2 = 4\%$ and $S_5 = 6\%$.

Calculate the implied three-year forward rate for a loan starting two years from now [i.e., $f(2,3)$].

Answer:

$$[1 + f(j,k)]^k = [1 + S_{(j+k)}]^{(j+k)} / (1 + S_j)^j$$

$$[1 + f(2,3)]^3 = [1 + 0.06]^5 / [1 + 0.04]^2$$

$$f(2,3) = 7.35\%$$

Note that the forward rate $f(2,3) > S_5$ because the yield curve is upward sloping.

If the yield curve is upward sloping, [i.e., $S_{(j+k)} > S_j$], then the forward rate corresponding to the period from *j* to *k* [i.e., $f(j,k)$] will be greater than the spot rate for maturity *j+k* [i.e., $S_{(j+k)}$]. The opposite is true if the curve is downward sloping.

LOS 35.c: Describe how zero-coupon rates (spot rates) may be obtained from the par curve by bootstrapping.

CFA® Program Curriculum, Volume 5, page 14

A **par rate** is the yield to maturity of a bond trading at par. Par rates for bonds with different maturities make up the **par rate curve** or simply the **par curve**. By definition, the par rate will be equal to the coupon rate on the bond. Generally, par curve refers to the par rates for government or benchmark bonds.

By using a process called **bootstrapping**, spot rates or zero-coupon rates can be derived from the par curve. Bootstrapping involves using the output of one step as an input to the next step. We first recognize that (for annual-pay bonds) the one-year spot rate (S_1) is the same as the one-year par rate. We can then compute S_2 using S_1 as one of the inputs. Continuing the process, we can compute the three-year spot rate S_3 using S_1 and S_2 computed earlier. Let's clarify this with an example.

Example: Bootstrapping spot rates

Given the following (annual-pay) par curve, compute the corresponding spot rate curve:

Maturity	*Par rate*
1	1.00%
2	1.25%
3	1.50%

Answer:

S_1 = 1.00% (given directly).

If we discount each cash flow of the bond using its yield, we get the market price of the bond. Here, the market price is the par value. Consider the 2-year bond.

$$100 = \frac{1.25}{(1.0125)} + \frac{101.25}{(1.0125)^2}$$

Alternatively, we can also value the 2-year bond using spot rates:

$$100 = \frac{1.25}{(1+S_1)} + \frac{101.25}{(1+S_2)^2} = \frac{1.25}{(1.01)} + \frac{101.25}{(1+S_2)^2}$$

$$100 = 1.2376 + \frac{101.25}{(1+S_2)^2}$$

$98.7624 = \frac{101.25}{(1+S_2)^2}$. Multiplying both sides by $[(1+S_2)^2 / 98.7624]$, we get:

$(1+S_2)^2 = 1.0252$. Taking square roots, we get

$(1+S_2) = 1.01252 \quad S_2 = 0.01252$ or 1.252%

Similarly,

$100 = \frac{1.50}{(1+S_1)} + \frac{1.50}{(1+S_2)^2} + \frac{101.50}{(1+S_3)^3}$. Using the values of S_1 and S_2 computed earlier,

$$100 = \frac{1.50}{(1.01)} + \frac{1.50}{(1.01252)^2} + \frac{101.50}{(1+S_3)^3}$$

$$100 = 2.9483 + \frac{101.50}{(1+S_3)^3}$$

$$97.0517 = \frac{101.50}{(1+S_3)^3}$$

$(1+S_3)^3 = 1.0458$

$(1+S_3) = 1.0151$ and hence $S_3 = 1.51\%$

LOS 35.d: Describe the assumptions concerning the evolution of spot rates in relation to forward rates implicit in active bond portfolio management.

CFA® Program Curriculum, Volume 5, page 20

Relationships Between Spot and Forward Rates

For an upward-sloping spot curve, the forward rate rises as *j* increases. (For a downward-sloping yield curve, the forward rate declines as *j* increases.) For an upward-sloping spot curve, the forward curve will be above the spot curve as shown in Figure 1. Conversely, when the spot curve is downward sloping, the forward curve will be below it.

Figure 1 shows spot and forward curves as of July 2013. Because the spot yield curve is upward sloping, the forward curves lie above the spot curve.

Figure 1: Spot Curve and Forward Curves

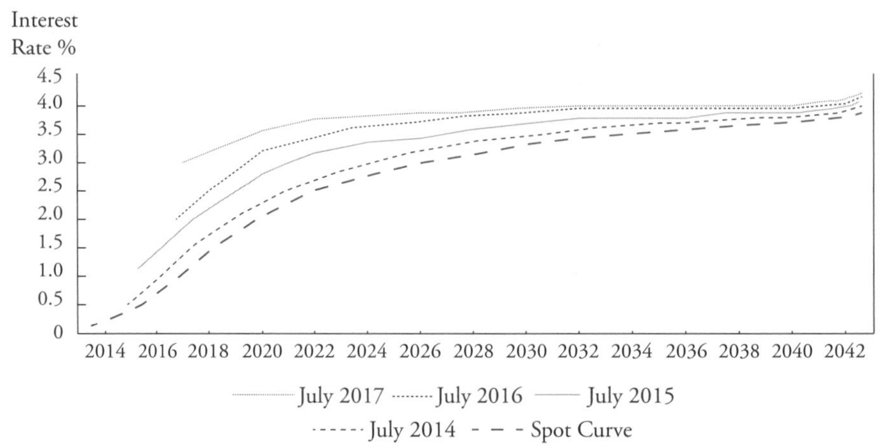

Source: 2016 CFA® Program curriculum, Level II, Vol. 5, page 226.

From the forward rate model:

$$(1 + S_T)^T = (1 + S_1)[1 + f(1,T-1)]^{(T-1)}$$

which can be expanded to:

$$(1 + S_T)^T = (1 + S_1)\ [1 + f(1,1)]\ [1 + f(2,1)]\ [1 + f(3,1)]\ ....\ [1 + f(T-1,1)]$$

In other words, the spot rate for a long-maturity security will equal the geometric mean of the one period spot rate and a series of one-year forward rates.

Forward Price Evolution

If the future spot rates actually evolve as forecasted by the forward curve, the forward price will remain unchanged. Therefore, a change in the forward price indicates that the future spot rate(s) did not conform to the forward curve. When spot rates turn out to be lower (higher) than implied by the forward curve, the forward price will increase (decrease). A trader expecting lower future spot rates (than implied by the current forward rates) would purchase the forward contract to profit from its appreciation.

For a bond investor, the return on a bond over a one-year horizon is always equal to the one-year risk-free rate *if the spot rates evolve as predicted by today's forward curve*. If the spot curve one year from today is not the same as that predicted by today's forward curve, the return over the one-year period will differ, with the return depending on the bond's maturity.

An active portfolio manager will try to outperform the overall bond market by predicting how the future spot rates will differ from those predicted by the current forward curve.

Example: Spot rate evolution

Jane Dash, CFA, has collected benchmark spot rates as shown below.

Maturity	*Spot rate*
1	3.00%
2	4.00%
3	5.00%

The expected spot rates at the end of one year are as follows:

Year	*Expected spot*
1	5.01%
2	6.01%

Calculate the one-year holding period return of a:

1. 1-year zero-coupon bond.
2. 2-year zero-coupon bond.
3. 3-year zero-coupon bond.

Answer:

First, note that the expected spot rates provided just happen to be the forward rates implied by the current spot rate curve.

Recall that:

$$[1 + f(j,k)]^k = [1 + S_{(j+k)}]^{(j+k)} / (1+S_j)^j$$

Hence:

$$[1+f(1,1)]^1 = \frac{(1+S_2)^2}{(1+S_1)} = \frac{(1.04)^2}{(1.03)} \rightarrow f(1,1) = 0.0501 \text{ and}$$

$$[1+f(1,2)]^2 = \frac{(1+S_3)^3}{(1+S_1)} = \frac{(1.05)^3}{(1.03)} \rightarrow f(1,2) = 0.0601$$

1. The price of a one-year zero-coupon bond given the one-year spot rate of 3% is 1 / (1.03) or 0.9709.

   After one year, the bond is at maturity and pays $1 regardless of the spot rates.

   Hence the holding period return = $\left(\frac{1.00}{0.9709}\right) - 1 = 3\%$

2. The price of a two-year zero-coupon bond given the two-year spot rate of 4%:

   $$P_2 = \frac{1}{(1+S_2)^2} = \frac{1}{(1.04)^2} = 0.9246$$

   After one year, the bond will have one year remaining to maturity, and based on a one-year expected spot rate of 5.01%, the bond's price will be 1 / (1.0501) = $0.9523

   Hence, the holding period return = $\left(\frac{0.9523}{0.9246}\right) - 1 = 3\%$

3. The price of three-year zero-coupon bond given the three-year spot rate of 5%:

   $$P_3 = \frac{1}{(1+S_3)^3} = \frac{1}{(1.05)^3} = 0.8638$$

   After one year, the bond will have two years remaining to maturity. Based on a two-year expected spot rate of 6.01%, the bond's price will be 1 / $(1.0601)^2$ = $0.8898

   Hence, the holding period return = $\left(\frac{0.8898}{0.8638}\right) - 1 = 3\%$

Hence, regardless of the maturity of the bond, the holding period return will be the one-year spot rate if the spot rates evolve consistent with the forward curve (as it existed when the trade was initiated).

If an investor believes that future spot rates will be lower than corresponding forward rates, then she will purchase bonds (at a presumably attractive price) because the market appears to be discounting future cash flows at "too high" of a discount rate.

LOS 35.e: Describe the strategy of riding the yield curve.

CFA® Program Curriculum, Volume 5, page 22

"Riding the Yield Curve"

The most straightforward strategy for a bond investor is *maturity matching*—purchasing bonds that have a maturity equal to the investor's investment horizon.

However, with an upward-sloping interest rate term structure, investors seeking superior returns may pursue a strategy called "**riding the yield curve**" (also known as "**rolling down the yield curve**"). Under this strategy, an investor will purchase bonds with maturities longer than his investment horizon. In an upward-sloping yield curve, shorter maturity bonds have lower yields than longer maturity bonds. As the bond approaches maturity (i.e., rolls down the yield curve), it is valued using successively lower yields and, therefore, at successively higher prices.

If the yield curve remains unchanged over the investment horizon, riding the yield curve strategy will produce higher returns than a simple maturity matching strategy, increasing the total return of a bond portfolio. The greater the difference between the forward rate and the spot rate, and the longer the maturity of the bond, the higher the total return.

Consider Figure 2, which shows a hypothetical upward-sloping yield curve and the price of a 3% annual-pay coupon bond (as a percentage of par).

Figure 2: Price of a 3%, Annual Pay Bond

Maturity	*Yield*	*Price*
5	3	100
10	3.5	95.84
15	4	88.88
20	4.5	80.49
25	5	71.81
30	5.5	63.67

A bond investor with an investment horizon of five years could purchase a bond maturing in five years and earn the 3% coupon but no capital gains (the bond can be currently purchased at par and will be redeemed at par at maturity). However, assuming no change in the yield curve over the investment horizon, the investor could instead purchase a 30- year bond for $63.67, hold it for five years, and sell it for $71.81, earning an additional return beyond the 3% coupon over the same period.

In the aftermath of the financial crisis of 2007–08, central banks kept short-term rates low, giving yield curves a steep upward slope. Many active managers took advantage by borrowing at short-term rates and buying long maturity bonds. The risk of such a leveraged strategy is the possibility of an increase in spot rates.

LOS 35.f: Explain the swap rate curve and why and how market participants use it in valuation.

CFA® Program Curriculum, Volume 5, page 24

The Swap Rate Curve

In a plain vanilla interest rate swap, one party makes payments based on a fixed rate while the counterparty makes payments based on a floating rate. The fixed rate in an interest rate swap is called the **swap fixed rate** or **swap rate**.

If we consider how swap rates vary for various maturities, we get the **swap rate curve**, which has become an important interest-rate benchmark for credit markets.

Market participants prefer the swap rate curve as a benchmark interest rate curve rather than a government bond yield curve for the following reasons:

- Swap rates reflect the credit risk of commercial banks rather than the credit risk of governments.
- The swap market is not regulated by any government, which makes swap rates in different countries more comparable. (Government bond yield curves additionally reflect sovereign risk unique to each country.)
- The swap curve typically has yield quotes at many maturities, while the U.S. government bond yield curve has on-the-run issues trading at only a small number of maturities.

Wholesale banks that manage interest rate risk with swap contracts are more likely to use swap curves to value their assets and liabilities. Retail banks, on the other hand, are more likely to use a government bond yield curve.

Given a notional principal of \$1 and a swap fixed rate SFR_T, the value of the fixed rate payments on a swap can be computed using the relevant (e.g., LIBOR) spot rate curve. For a given swap tenor T, we can solve for SFR in the following equation.

$$\sum_{t=1}^{T} \frac{SFR_T}{(1+S_t)^t} + \frac{1}{(1+S_T)^T} = 1$$

In the equation, SFR can be thought of as the coupon rate of a \$1 par value bond given the underlying spot rate curve.

Example: Swap rate curve

Given the following LIBOR spot rate curve, compute the swap fixed rate for a tenor of 1, 2, and 3 years (i.e., compute the swap rate curve).

Maturity	*Spot rate*
1	3.00%
2	4.00%
3	5.00%

Answer:

1. SFR_1 can be computed using the equation:

$$\frac{SFR_1}{(1+S_1)}+\frac{1}{(1+S_1)}=1$$

$$\frac{SFR_1}{(1.03)}+\frac{1}{(1.03)}=1 \rightarrow SFR_1=3.00\%$$

2. SFR_2 can be similarly computed:

$$\frac{SFR_2}{(1+S_1)}+\frac{SFR_2}{(1+S_2)^2}+\frac{1}{(1+S_2)^2}=1$$

$$\frac{SFR_2}{(1.03)}+\frac{SFR_2}{(1.04)^2}+\frac{1}{(1.04)^2}=1 \rightarrow SFR_2=3.98\%$$

3. Finally, SFR_3 can be computed as:

$$\frac{SFR_3}{(1+S_1)}+\frac{SFR_3}{(1+S_2)^2}+\frac{SFR_3}{(1+S_3)^3}+\frac{1}{(1+S_3)^3}=1$$

$$\frac{SFR_3}{(1.03)}+\frac{SFR_3}{(1.04)^2}+\frac{SFR_3}{(1.05)^3}+\frac{1}{(1.05)^3}=1 \rightarrow SFR_3=4.93\%$$

Professor's Note: A different (and better) method of computing swap fixed rates is discussed in detail in the Derivatives area of the curriculum.

LOS 35.g: Calculate and interpret the swap spread for a given maturity.

CFA® Program Curriculum, Volume 5, page 29

Swap spread refers to the amount by which the swap rate exceeds the yield of a government bond with the same maturity.

$$\text{swap spread}_t = \text{swap rate}_t - \text{Treasury yield}_t$$

For example, if the fixed rate of a one-year fixed-for-floating LIBOR swap is 0.57% and the one-year Treasury is yielding 0.11%, the 1-year swap spread is 0.57% – 0.11% = 0.46%, or 46 bps.

Swap spreads are almost always positive, reflecting the lower credit risk of governments compared to the credit risk of surveyed banks that determines the swap rate.

The LIBOR swap curve is arguably the most commonly used interest rate curve. This rate curve roughly reflects the default risk of a commercial bank.

Example: Swap spread

The two-year fixed-for-floating LIBOR swap rate is 2.02% and the two-year U.S. Treasury bond is yielding 1.61%. What is the swap spread?

Answer:

swap spread = (swap rate) – (T-bond yield) = 2.02% – 1.61% = 0.41% or 41 bps

I-SPREAD

The **I-spread** for a credit-risky bond is the amount by which the yield on the risky bond exceeds the swap rate for the same maturity. In a case where the swap rate for a specific maturity is not available, the missing swap rate can be estimated from the swap rate curve using linear interpolation (hence the "I" in I-spread).

Example: I-spread

6% Zinni, Inc., bonds are currently yielding 2.35% and mature in 1.6 years. From the provided swap curve, compute the I-spread.

Swap curve:

Tenor	*Swap rate*
0.5	1.00%
1	1.25%
1.5	1.35%
2	1.50%

Answer:

Linear interpolation:

First, recognize that 1.6 years falls in the 1.5-to-2-year interval.

Interpolated rate = rate for lower bound + (# of years for interpolated rate – # of years for lower bound)(higher bound rate – lower bound rate)/(# of years for upper bound – # of years for lower bound)

$$\text{1.6 year swap rate} =$$

$$\text{1.5-year swap rate} + \frac{0.10\ (\text{2-year swap rate} - \text{1.5-year swap rate})}{0.50}$$

$$= 1.35 + \frac{0.10\ (1.50 - 1.35)}{0.50} = 1.38\%$$

I-spread = yield on the bond – swap rate

= 2.35% – 1.38% = 0.97% or 97bps

While a bond's yield reflects time value as well as compensation for credit and liquidity risk, I-spread only reflects compensation for credit and liquidity risks. The higher the I-spread, the higher the compensation for liquidity and credit risk.

LOS 35.h: Describe the Z-spread.

CFA® Program Curriculum, Volume 5, page 30

The Z-spread

The *Z*-**spread** is the spread that, when added to each spot rate on the default-free spot curve, makes the present value of a bond's cash flows equal to the bond's market price. Therefore, the *Z*-spread is a spread over the entire spot rate curve.

For example, suppose the one-year spot rate is 4% and the two-year spot rate is 5%. The market price of a two-year bond with annual coupon payments of 8% is $104.12. The *Z*-spread is the spread that balances the following equality:

$$\$104.12 = \frac{\$8}{(1+0.04+Z)} + \frac{\$108}{(1+0.05+Z)^2}$$

In this case, the *Z*-spread is 0.008, or 80 basis points. (Plug Z = 0.008 into the right-hand-side of the equation above to reassure yourself that the present value of the bond's cash flows equals $104.12).

The term *zero volatility* in the *Z*-spread refers to the assumption of zero interest rate volatility. *Z*-spread is not appropriate to use to value bonds with embedded options; without any interest rate volatility options are meaningless. If we ignore the embedded options for a bond and estimate the *Z*-spread, the estimated *Z*-spread will include the cost of the embedded option (i.e., it will reflect compensation for option risk as well as compensation for credit and liquidity risk).

Example: Computing the price of an option-free risky bond using Z-spread.

A three-year, 5% annual-pay ABC, Inc., bond trades at a *Z*-spread of 100bps over the benchmark spot rate curve.

The benchmark one-year spot rate, one-year forward rate in one year and one-year forward rate in year 2 are 3%, 5.051%, and 7.198%, respectively.

Compute the bond's price.

Answer:

First derive the spot rates:

$S_1 = 3\%$ (given)

$(1 + S_2)^2 = (1 + S_1)[1 + f(1,1)] = (1.03)(1.05051) \rightarrow S_2 = 4.02\%$

$(1 + S_3)^3 = (1 + S_1)[1 + f(1,1)][1 + f(2,1)] = (1.03)(1.05051)(1.07198) \rightarrow S_3 = 5.07\%$

Value (with *Z*-spread) =

$$\frac{5}{(1.03+0.01)} + \frac{5}{(1.0402+0.01)^2} + \frac{105}{(1.0507+0.01)^3} = 97.33$$

LOS 35.i: Describe the TED and Libor-OIS spreads.

CFA® Program Curriculum, Volume 5, page 32

TED Spread

The "TED" in "**TED spread**" is an acronym that combines the "T" in "*T*-bill" with "*ED*" (the ticker symbol for the Eurodollar futures contract).

Conceptually, the TED spread is the amount by which the interest rate on loans between banks (formally, three-month LIBOR) exceeds the interest rate on short-term U.S. government debt (three-month T-bills).

For example, if three-month LIBOR is 0.33% and the three-month T-bill rate is 0.03%, then:

TED spread = (3-month LIBOR rate) – (3-month T-bill rate) = 0.33% – 0.03% = 0.30% or 30bps.

Because T-bills are considered to be risk free while LIBOR reflects the risk of lending to commercial banks, the TED spread is seen as an indication of the risk of interbank loans. A rising TED spread indicates that market participants believe banks are increasingly likely to default on loans and that risk-free T-bills are becoming more valuable in comparison. The TED spread captures the risk in the banking system more accurately than does the 10-year swap spread.

LIBOR-OIS Spread

OIS stands for overnight indexed swap. The OIS rate roughly reflects the federal funds rate and includes minimal counterparty risk.

The **LIBOR-OIS spread** is the amount by which the LIBOR rate (which includes credit risk) exceeds the OIS rate (which includes only minimal credit risk). This makes the LIBOR-OIS spread a useful measure of credit risk and an indication of the overall wellbeing of the banking system. A low LIBOR-OIS spread is a sign of high market liquidity while a high LIBOR-OIS spread is a sign that banks are unwilling to lend due to concerns about creditworthiness.

LOS 35.j: Explain traditional theories of the term structure of interest rates and describe the implications of each theory for forward rates and the shape of the yield curve.

CFA® Program Curriculum, Volume 5, page 33

We'll explain each of the theories of the **term structure of interest rates**, paying particular attention to the implications of each theory for the shape of the yield curve and the interpretation of forward rates.

Unbiased Expectations Theory

Under the **unbiased expectations theory** or the **pure expectations theory**, we hypothesize that it is investors' expectations that determine the shape of the interest rate term structure.

Specifically, this theory suggests that forward rates are solely a function of expected future spot rates, and that every maturity strategy has the same expected return over a given investment horizon. In other words, long-term interest rates equal the mean of future *expected* short-term rates. This implies that an investor should earn the same return by investing in a five-year bond or by investing in a three-year bond and then a two-year bond after the three-year bond matures. Similarly, an investor with a three-year investment horizon would be indifferent between investing in a three-year bond or in a five-year bond that will be sold two years prior to maturity. The underlying principle behind the pure expectations theory is risk neutrality: Investors don't demand a risk premium for maturity strategies that differ from their investment horizon.

For example, suppose the one-year spot rate is 5% and the two-year spot rate is 7%. Under the unbiased expectations theory, the one-year forward rate in one year must be 9% because investing for two years at 7% yields approximately the same annual return as investing for the first year at 5% and the second year at 9%. In other words, the two-year rate of 7% is the average of the expected future one-year rates of 5% and 9%. This is shown in Figure 3.

Figure 3: Spot and Future Rates

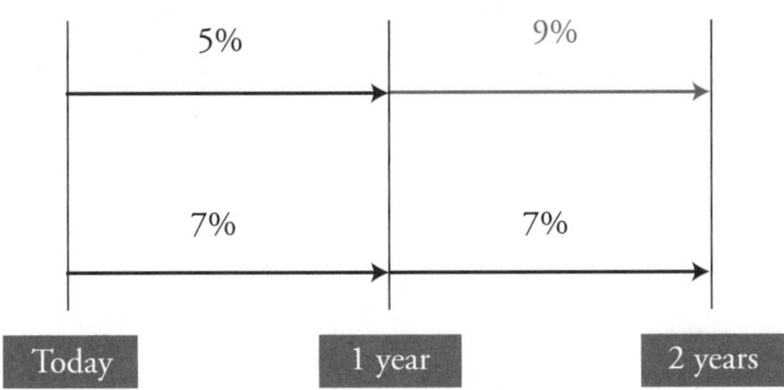

Notice that in this example, because short-term rates are expected to rise (from 5% to 9%), the yield curve will be upward sloping.

Therefore, the implications for the shape of the yield curve under the pure expectations theory are:

- If the yield curve is upward sloping, short-term rates are expected to rise.
- If the curve is downward sloping, short-term rates are expected to fall.
- A flat yield curve implies that the market expects short-term rates to remain constant.

Local Expectations Theory

The **local expectations theory** is similar to the unbiased expectations theory with one major difference: the local expectations theory preserves the risk-neutrality assumption only for short holding periods. In other words, over longer periods, risk premiums should exist. This implies that over short time periods, every bond (even long-maturity risky bonds) should earn the risk-free rate.

The local expectations theory can be shown not to hold because the short-holding-period returns of long-maturity bonds can be shown to be higher than short-holding-period returns on short-maturity bonds due to liquidity premiums and hedging concerns.

Liquidity Preference Theory

The **liquidity preference theory** of the term structure addresses the shortcomings of the pure expectations theory by proposing that forward rates reflect investors' expectations of future spot rates, plus a liquidity premium to compensate investors for exposure to interest rate risk. Furthermore, the theory suggests that this liquidity premium is positively related to maturity: a 25-year bond should have a larger liquidity premium than a five-year bond.

Thus, the liquidity preference theory states that forward rates are *biased* estimates of the market's expectation of future rates because they include a liquidity premium. Therefore, a positive-sloping yield curve may indicate that either: (1) the market expects future interest rates to rise or (2) rates are expected to remain constant (or even fall), but the addition of the liquidity premium results in a positive slope. A downward-sloping yield curve indicates steeply falling short-term rates according to the liquidity theory.

The size of the liquidity premiums need not be constant over time. They may be larger during periods of greater economic uncertainty when risk aversion among investors is higher.

Segmented Markets Theory

Under the **segmented markets theory**, yields are not determined by liquidity premiums and expected spot rates. Rather, the shape of the yield curve is determined by the preferences of borrowers and lenders, which drives the balance between supply of and demand for loans of different maturities. This is called the segmented markets theory because the theory suggests that the yield at each maturity is determined independently of the yields at other maturities; we can think of each maturity to be essentially unrelated to other maturities.

The segmented markets theory supposes that various market participants only deal in securities of a particular maturity because they are prevented from operating at different maturities. For example, pension plans and insurance companies primarily purchase long-maturity bonds for asset-liability matching reasons and are unlikely to participate in the market for short-term funds.

Preferred Habitat Theory

The **preferred habitat theory** also proposes that forward rates represent expected future spot rates plus a premium, but it does not support the view that this premium is directly related to maturity.

Instead, the preferred habitat theory suggests that the existence of an imbalance between the supply and demand for funds in a given maturity range will induce lenders and borrowers to shift from their preferred habitats (maturity range) to one that has the opposite imbalance. However, to entice investors to do so, the investors must be offered an incentive to compensate for the exposure to price and/or reinvestment rate risk in the less-than-preferred habitat. Borrowers require cost savings (i.e., lower yields) and lenders require a yield premium (i.e., higher yields) to move out of their preferred habitats.

Under this theory, premiums are related to supply and demand for funds at various maturities. Unlike the liquidity preference theory, under the preferred habitat theory a 10-year bond might have a higher or lower risk premium than the 25-year bond. It also means that the preferred habitat theory can be used to explain almost any yield curve shape.

LOS 35.k: Describe modern term structure models and how they are used.

CFA® Program Curriculum, Volume 5, page 38

Modern Term Structure Models

Modern interest rate term structure models attempt to capture the statistical properties of interest rates movements and provide us with quantitatively precise descriptions of how interest rates will change.

Equilibrium Term Structure Models

Equilibrium term structure models attempt to describe changes in the term structure through the use of fundamental economic variables that drive interest rates. While equilibrium term structure models can rely on multiple factors, the two famous models discussed in the curriculum, the Cox-Ingersoll-Ross (CIR) model and the Vasicek Model, are both single-factor models. The single factor in the CIR and Vasicek model is the short-term interest rate.

The Cox-Ingersoll-Ross Model

The **Cox-Ingersoll-Ross model** is based on the idea that interest rate movements are driven by individuals choosing between consumption today versus investing and consuming at a later time.

Mathematically, the CIR model is as follows. The first part of this expression is a drift term, while the second part is the random component:

$$dr = a(b - r)dt + \sigma\sqrt{r}dz$$

where:
dr = change in the short-term interest rate
a = speed of mean reversion parameter (a high *a* means fast mean reversion)
b = long-run value of the short-term interest rate
r = the short-term interest rate
t = time
dt = a small increase in time
σ = volatility
dz = a small random walk movement

The $a(b - r)dt$ term forces the interest rate to mean-revert toward the long-run value (b) at a speed determined by the mean reversion parameter (a).

Under the CIR model, volatility increases with the interest rate, as can be seen in the $\sigma\sqrt{r}dz$ term. In other words, at high interest rates, the amount of period-over-period fluctuation in rates is also high.

The Vasicek Model

Like the CIR model, the **Vasicek model** suggests that interest rates are mean reverting to some long-run value.

Mathmatically, the Vasicek model is expressed as:

$$dr = a(b - r)dt + \sigma dz$$

The difference from the CIR model that you will notice is that no interest rate (r) term appears in the second term σdz, meaning that volatility in this model does not increase as the level of interest rates increase.

The main disadvantage of the Vasicek model is that the model does not force interest rates to be non-negative.

Arbitrage-Free Models

Arbitrage-free models of the term structure of interest rates begin with the assumption that bonds trading in the market are correctly priced, and the model is calibrated to value such bonds consistent with their market price (hence the "arbitrage-free" label). These models do not try to justify the current yield curve; rather, they take this curve as given.

The ability to calibrate arbitrage-free models to match current market prices is one advantage of arbitrage-free models over the equilibrium models.

The Ho-Lee Model

The Ho-Lee model takes the following form:

$$dr_t = \theta_t dt + \sigma dz_t$$

where:
θ_t = a time-dependent drift term

The model assumes that changes in the yield curve are consistent with a no-arbitrage condition.

The Ho-Lee model is calibrated by using market prices to find the time-dependant drift term θ_t that generates the current term structure. The Ho-Lee model can then be used to price zero-coupon bonds and to determine the spot curve. The model produces a symmetrical (normal) distribution of future rates.

LOS 35.l: Explain how a bond's exposure to each of the factors driving the yield curve can be measured and how these exposures can be used to manage yield curve risks.

CFA® Program Curriculum, Volume 5, page 45

Managing Yield Curve Risks

Yield curve risk refers to risk to the value of a bond portfolio due to unexpected changes in the yield curve.

To counter yield curve risk, we first identify our portfolio's sensitivity to yield curve changes using one or more measures. Yield curve sensitivity can be generally measured by **effective duration**, or more precisely using **key rate duration**, or a three-factor model that decomposes changes in the yield curve into changes in **level**, **steepness**, and **curvature**.

Effective Duration

Effective duration measures price sensitivity to small *parallel* shifts in the yield curve. It is important to note that effective duration is not an accurate measure of interest rate sensitivity to *non-parallel* shifts in the yield curve like those described by **shaping risk**. Shaping risk refers to changes in portfolio value due to changes in the *shape* of the benchmark yield curve. (Note, however, that parallel shifts explain more than 75% of the variation in bond portfolio returns.)

Key Rate Duration

A more precise method used to quantify bond price sensitivity to interest rates is key rate duration. Compared to effective duration, key rate duration is superior for measuring the impact of nonparallel yield curve shifts.

Key rate duration is the sensitivity of the value of a security (or a bond portfolio) to changes in a single par rate, holding all other spot rates constant. In other words, key rate duration isolates price sensitivity to a change in the yield at a particular maturity only.

Numerically, key rate duration is defined as the approximate percentage change in the value of a bond portfolio in response to a 100 basis point change in the corresponding key rate, holding all other rates constant. Conceptually, we could determine the key rate duration for the five-year segment of the yield curve by changing only the five-year par rate and observing the change in value of the portfolio. Keep in mind that every security or portfolio has a set of key rate durations—one for each key rate.

For example, a bond portfolio has interest rate risk exposure to only three maturity points on the par rate curve: the 1-year, 5-year, and 25-year maturities, with key rate durations represented by $D_1 = 0.7$, $D_5 = 3.5$, and $D_{25} = 9.5$, respectively.

The model for yield curve risk using these key rate durations would be:

$$\frac{\Delta P}{P} \approx -D_1\Delta r_1 - D_5\Delta r_5 - D_{25}\Delta r_{25}$$

$$\frac{\Delta P}{P} \approx -(0.7)\Delta r_1 - (3.5)\Delta r_5 - (9.5)\Delta r_{25}$$

Sensitivity to Parallel, Steepness, and Curvature Movements

An alternative to decomposing yield curve risk into sensitivity to changes at various maturities (key rate duration) is to decompose the risk into sensitivity to the following three categories of yield curve movements:

- **Level** (Δx_L) – A parallel increase or decrease of interest rates.
- **Steepness** (Δx_S) – Long-term interest rates increase while short-term rates decrease.
- **Curvature** (Δx_C) – Increasing curvature means short- and long-term interest rates increase while intermediate rates do not change.

It has been found that all yield curve movements can be described using a combination of one or more of these movements.

We can then model the change in the value of our portfolio as follows:

$$\frac{\Delta P}{P} \approx -D_L\Delta x_L - D_S\Delta x_S - D_C\Delta x_C$$

where D_L, D_S, and D_C are respectively the portfolio's sensitivities to changes in the yield curve's level, steepness, and curvature.

For example, for a particular portfolio, yield curve risk can be described as:

$$\frac{\Delta P}{P} \approx -4\Delta x_L - 5\Delta x_S - 3\Delta x_C$$

If the following changes in the yield curve occurred: $\Delta x_L = -0.004$, $\Delta x_S = 0.001$, and $\Delta x_C = 0.002$, then the percentage change in portfolio value could be calculated as:

$$\frac{\Delta P}{P} \approx -4(-0.004) - 5(0.001) - 3(0.002) = 0.005$$

This predicts a +0.5% increase in the portfolio value resulting from the yield curve movements.

LOS 35.m: Explain the maturity structure of yield volatilities and their effect on price volatility.

CFA® Program Curriculum, Volume 5, page 50

Maturity Structure of Yield Curve Volatilities

Interest rate volatility is a key concern for bond managers because interest rate volatility drives price volatility in a fixed income portfolio. Interest rate volatility becomes particularly important when securities have embedded options, which are especially sensitive to volatility.

The **term structure of interest rate volatility** is the graph of yield volatility versus maturity.

Figure 4 shows a typical term structure of interest rate volatility. Note that, as shown here, short-term interest rates are generally more volatile than are long-term rates.

Volatility at the long-maturity end is thought to be associated with uncertainty regarding the real economy and inflation, while volatility at the short-maturity end reflects risks regarding monetary policy.

Figure 4: Historical Volatility Term Structure: U.S. Treasuries, August 2005–December 2007

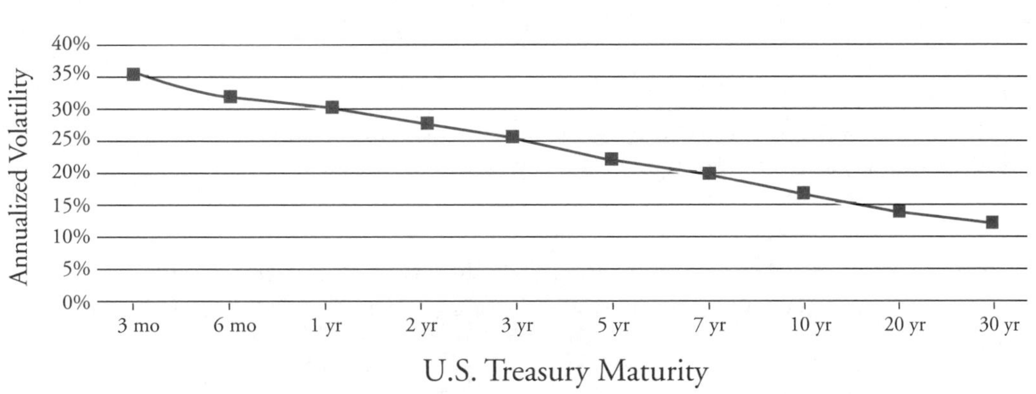

Interest rate volatility at time t for a security with maturity of T is denoted as $\sigma(t,T)$. This variable measures the annualized standard deviation of the change in bond yield.

KEY CONCEPTS

LOS 35.a

The spot rate for a particular maturity is equal to a geometric average of the one-period spot rate and a series of one-period forward rates.

When the spot curve is flat, forward rates will equal spot rates and yields. When the spot curve is upward sloping (downward sloping), forward rate curves will be above (below) the spot curve and the yield for a maturity of *T* will be less than (greater than) the spot rate S_T.

LOS 35.b

The forward *pricing* model values forward contracts by using an arbitrage-free framework that equates buying a zero-coupon bond to entering into a forward contract to buy a zero-coupon bond in the future that matures at the same time:

$$P_{(j+k)} = P_j F_{(j,k)}$$

The forward *rate* model tells us that the investors will be indifferent between buying a long-maturity zero-coupon bond versus buying a shorter-maturity zero-coupon bond and reinvesting the principal at the locked in forward rate $f(j,k)$.

$$[1 + S_{(j+k)}]^{(j+k)} = (1 + S_j)^j \, [1 + f(j,k)]^k$$

LOS 35.c

By using a process called bootstrapping, spot rates (i.e., zero-coupon rates) can be derived from the par curve iteratively—one spot rate at a time.

LOS 35.d

If spot rates evolve as predicted by forward rates, bonds of all maturities will realize a one-period return equal to the one-period spot rate and the forward price will remain unchanged.

Active bond portfolio management is built on the presumption that the current forward curve may not accurately predict future spot rates. Managers attempt to outperform the market by making predictions about how spot rates will change relative to the rates suggested by forward rate curves.

If an investor believes that future spot rates will be lower than corresponding forward rates, then the investor will purchase bonds (at a presumably attractive price) because the market appears to be discounting future cash flows at "too high" of a discount rate.

LOS 35.e

When the yield curve is upward sloping, bond managers may use the strategy of "riding the yield curve" to chase above-market returns. By holding long-maturity rather than short-maturity bonds, the manager earns an excess return as the bond "rolls down the yield curve" (i.e., approaches maturity and increases in price). As long as the yield curve remains upward sloping, this strategy will add to the return of a bond portfolio.

LOS 35.f

The swap rate curve provides a benchmark measure of interest rates. It is similar to the yield curve except that the rates used represent the interest rates of the fixed-rate leg in an interest rate swap.

Market participants prefer the swap rate curve as a benchmark interest rate curve rather than a government bond yield curve for the following reasons:

1. Swap rates reflect the credit risk of commercial banks rather than that of governments.

2. The swap market is not regulated by any government.

3. The swap curve typically has yield quotes at many maturities.

LOS 35.g

We define swap spread as the additional interest rate paid by the fixed-rate payer of an interest rate swap over the rate of the "on-the-run" government bond of the same maturity.

swap spread = (swap rate) – (Treasury bond yield)

Investors use the swap spread to separate the time value portion of a bond's yield from the risk premia for credit and liquidity risk. The higher the swap spread, the higher the compensation for liquidity and credit risk.

For a default-free bond, the swap spread provides an indication of (1) the bond's liquidity and/or (2) possible mispricing.

LOS 35.h

The *Z*-spread is the spread that when added to each spot rate on the yield curve makes the present value of a bond's cash flows equal to the bond's market price. The *Z* refers to zero volatility—a reference to the fact that the *Z*-spread assumes interest rate volatility is zero. *Z*-spread is not appropriate to use to value bonds with embedded options.

LOS 35.i

TED spreads

TED = *T-bill* + *ED* ("ED" is the ticker symbol for the Eurodollar futures contract)

TED spread = (three-month LIBOR rate) – (three-month T-bill rate)

The TED spread is used as an indication of the overall level of credit risk in the economy.

LIBOR-OIS spread

The LIBOR-OIS spread is the amount by which the LIBOR rate (which includes credit risk) exceeds the overnight indexed swap (OIS) rate (which includes only minimal credit risk). The LIBOR-OIS spread is a useful measure of credit risk and an indication of the overall wellbeing of the banking system.

LOS 35.j
There are several traditional theories that attempt to explain the term structure of interest rates:

Unbiased expectations theory – Forward rates are an unbiased predictor of future spot rates. Also known as the *pure expectations theory*.

Local expectations theory – Bond maturity does not influence returns for short holding periods.

Liquidity preference theory – Investors demand a liquidity premium that is positively related to a bond's maturity.

Segmented markets theory – The shape of the yield curve is the result of the interactions of supply and demand for funds in different market (i.e., maturity) segments.

Preferred habitat theory – Similar to the segmented markets theory, but recognizes that market participants will deviate from their preferred maturity habitat if compensated adequately.

LOS 35.k
Modern term structure models are used to predict the shape of the yield curve in order to value bonds and fixed-income derivatives. Two major classes of these modern term structure models are:

1. **Equilibrium term structure models** – Attempt to model the term structure using fundamental economic variables that are thought to determine interest rates.
    a. **the Cox-Ingersoll-Ross model:** $dr = a(b - r)dt + \sigma\sqrt{r}dz$ Assumes the economy has a natural long-run interest rate (b) that the short-term rate (r) converges to.
    b. **the Vasicek model:** $dr = a(b - r)dt + \sigma dz$ Similar to the CIR model, but assumes that interest rate volatility level is independent of the level of short-term interest rates.

2. **Arbitrage-free models** – Begins with observed market prices and the assumption that securities are correctly priced.
    a. **The Ho-Lee model:** $dr_t = \theta_t dt + \sigma dz_t$ Calibrated by using market prices to find the time-dependant drift term θ_t that generates the current term structure.

LOS 35.l
We can measure a bond's exposures to the factors driving the yield curve in a number of ways:

1. **Effective duration** – Measures the sensitivity of a bond's price to *parallel* shifts in the benchmark yield curve.

2. **Key rate duration** – Measures bond price sensitivity to a change in a specific spot rate keeping everything else constant.

3. **Sensitivity to parallel, steepness, and curvature movements** – Measures sensitivity to three distinct categories of changes in the shape of the benchmark yield curve.

LOS 35.m
The maturity structure of yield volatilities indicates the level of yield volatilities at different maturities. This term structure thus provides an indication of yield curve risk. The volatility term structure usually indicates that short-term rates (which are linked to uncertainty over monetary policy) are more volatile than long-term rates (which are driven by uncertainty related to the real economy and inflation). Fixed income instruments with embedded options can be especially sensitive to interest rate volatility.

Concept Checkers

1. When the yield curve is downward sloping, the forward curves are *most likely* to lie:
   A. above the spot curve.
   B. below the spot curve.
   C. either above or below the spot curve.

2. The model that equates buying a long-maturity zero-coupon bond to entering into a forward contract to buy a zero-coupon bond that matures at the same time is known as:
   A. the forward rate model.
   B. the forward pricing model.
   C. the forward arbitrage model.

3. If the future spot rates are expected to be lower than the current forward rates for the same maturities, bonds are *most likely* to be:
   A. overvalued.
   B. undervalued.
   C. correctly valued.

4. The strategy of riding the yield curve is *most likely* to produce superior returns for a fixed income portfolio manager investing in bonds with maturity higher than the manager's investment horizon when the spot rate curve:
   A. is downward sloping.
   B. in the future matches that projected by today's forward curves.
   C. is upward sloping.

5. Which of the following statements about the swap rate curve is *most accurate*?
   A. The swap rate reflects the interest rate for the floating-rate leg of an interest rate swap.
   B. Retail banks are more likely to use the swap rate curve as a benchmark than the government spot curve.
   C. Swap rates are comparable across different countries because the swap market is not controlled by governments.

6. The swap spread for a default-free bond is *least likely* to reflect the bond's:
   A. mispricing in the market.
   B. illiquidity.
   C. time value.

7. Which of the following statements about the *Z*-spread is *most accurate*? The *Z*-spread is the:
   A. difference between the yield to maturity of a bond and the linearly interpolated swap rate.
   B. spread over the Treasury spot curve that a bond would trade at if it had zero embedded options.
   C. spread over the Treasury spot curve required to match the value of a bond to its current market price.

8. The TED spread is calculated as the difference between
   A. the three-month LIBOR rate and the three-month T-bill rate.
   B. LIBOR and the overnight indexed swap rate.
   C. the three-month T-bill rate and the overnight indexed swap rate.

9. Which of the following statements regarding the traditional theories of the term structure of interest rates is *most accurate*?
   A. The segmented markets theory proposes that market participants have strong preferences for specific maturities.
   B. The liquidity preference theory hypothesizes that the yield curve must always be upward sloping.
   C. The preferred habitat theory states that yields at different maturities are determined independently of each other.

10. The modern term structure model that is *most likely* to precisely generate the current term structure is the:
   A. Cox-Ingersoll-Ross model.
   B. Vasicek model.
   C. Ho-Lee model.

11. The *least appropriate* measure to use to identify and manage "shaping risk" is a portfolio's:
   A. effective duration.
   B. key rate durations.
   C. sensitivities to level, steepness, and curvature factors.

12. Regarding the volatility term structure, research indicates that volatility in short-term rates is most strongly linked to uncertainty regarding:
   A. the real economy.
   B. monetary policy.
   C. inflation.

To access other content related to this topic review that may be included in the Schweser package you purchased, log in to your Schweser.com online dashboard. Schweser's OnDemand Video Lectures deliver streaming instruction covering every LOS in this topic review, while SchweserPro™ QBank provides additional quiz questions to help you practice and recall what you've learned.

Answers – Concept Checkers

1. **B** When the yield curve is *upward* sloping, the forward curves will lie above the spot curve. The opposite is true when the yield curve is downward sloping.

2. **B** The forward *pricing* model values forward contracts by using an arbitrage argument that equates buying a zero-coupon bond to entering into a forward contract to buy a zero-coupon bond that matures at the same time:

   $$P_{(j+k)} = P_j F_{(j,k)}$$

   The forward *rate* model tells us that the forward rate *f*(j,k) should make investors indifferent between buying a long-maturity zero-coupon bond versus buying a shorter-maturity zero-coupon bond and reinvesting the principal.

3. **B** If an investor believes that future spot rates will be lower than the current forward rates, then the investor will perceive an opportunity to purchase bonds at an attractive price, as the market is discounting future cash flows at "too high" a discount rate. The bonds are thus undervalued in the market.

4. **C** Fixed income managers will earn an extra return through riding the yield curve if the spot rate curve is upward sloping and remains unchanged over time.

5. **C** The swap market is not controlled by governments, which makes swap rates more comparable across different countries. The swap rate is the interest rate for the *fixed-rate* leg of an interest rate swap. *Wholesale* banks frequently use the swap curve to value their assets and liabilities, while *retail* banks with little exposure to the swap market are more likely to use the government spot curve as their benchmark.

6. **C** The swap spread of a default free bond should provide an indication of the bond's illiquidity—or, alternatively, that the bond is mispriced. Time value is reflected in the government bond yield curve; the swap spread is an additional amount of interest above this benchmark.

7. **C** The *Z*-spread is the constant spread that must be added to the default-free spot curve to match the valuation of a risky bond to its market price. A higher *Z*-spread implies a riskier bond.

8. **A** The TED spread (from *T*-bill and *E*uro*d*ollar) is computed as the difference between the three-month LIBOR rate and the three-month T-bill rate. The LIBOR–OIS spread is the difference between LIBOR and the overnight indexed swap rate (OIS) rates.

9. **A** The segmented markets theory (and the preferred habitat theory) propose that borrowers and lenders have strong preferences for particular maturities. The liquidity preference theory argues that there are liquidity premiums that increase with maturity; however, the liquidity preference theory does not preclude the existence of other factors that could lead to an overall downward-sloping yield curve. The segmented markets theory—not the preferred habitat theory—proposes that yields at different maturities are determined independently of each other.

10. **C** The Ho-Lee model is calibrated by using market prices to find the time-dependant drift term θt that generates the current term structure. (One of the drawbacks of the Vasicek and Cox-Ingersoll-Ross models is that the model prices generated by these models generally do not coincide with observed market prices.)

11. **A** Effective duration is an inappropriate measure for identifying and managing shaping risk. Shaping risk refers to risk to portfolio value from changes in the shape of the benchmark yield curve. Effective duration can be used to accurately measure the risk associated with parallel yield curve changes but is not appropriate for measuring the risk from other changes in the yield curve.

12. **B** It is believed that short-term volatility reflects uncertainty regarding monetary policy while long-term volatility is most closely associated with uncertainty regarding the real economy and inflation. Short-term rates in the volatility term structure tend to be more volatile than long-term rates.

The following is a review of the Fixed Income: Valuation Concepts principles designed to address the learning outcome statements set forth by CFA Institute. Cross-Reference to CFA Institute Assigned Reading #36.

The Arbitrage-Free Valuation Framework

Study Session 12

Exam Focus

This topic review discusses valuation of fixed-income securities using spot rates as well as using the backward induction methodology in a binomial interest rate tree framework. Understand how embedded options impact the suitability of the binomial model or the Monte Carlo simulation method.

The arbitrage-free valuation framework is used extensively in the pricing of securities. The basic principle of the "law of one price" in freely functioning markets drives this analytical framework.

LOS 36.a: Explain what is meant by arbitrage-free valuation of a fixed-income instrument.

CFA® Program Curriculum, Volume 5, page 76

Arbitrage-free valuation methods value securities such that no market participant can earn an arbitrage profit in a trade involving that security. An arbitrage transaction involves no initial cash outlay but a positive riskless profit (cash flow) at some point in the future.

There are two types of arbitrage opportunities: **value additivity** (when the value of whole differs from the sum of the values of parts) and **dominance** (when one asset trades at a lower price than another asset with identical characteristics).

If the principle of value additivity does not hold, arbitrage profits can be earned by **stripping** or **reconstitution**. A five-year, 5% Treasury bond should be worth the same as a portfolio of its coupon and principal strips. If the portfolio of strips is trading for less than an intact bond, one can purchase the strips, combine them (reconstituting), and sell them as a bond. Similarly, if the bond is worth less than its component parts, one could purchase the bond, break it into a portfolio of strips (stripping), and sell those components.

Example: Arbitrage opportunities

The following information is collected

Security	*Current Price*	*Payoff in 1 year*
A	$99	$100
B	$990	$1010
C	$100	$102
D	$100	$103

Securities A and B are identical in every respect other than as noted. Similarly, securities C and D are similar in every other respect.

Demonstrate the exploitation of any arbitrage opportunities.

Answer:

1. Arbitrage due to violation of the value additivity principle:

	Cash Flow	
	t = 0	t = 1
Short 10 units of Security A	+$990	–$1,000
Long 1 unit of Security B	–$990	+$1,010
Net cash flow	-0-	+$10

2. Arbitrage due to the occurrence of dominance:

	Cash Flow	
	t = 0	t = 1
Short 1 unit of Security C	+$100	–$102
Long 1 unit of Security D	–$100	+$103
Net cash flow	-0-	+$1

LOS 36.b: Calculate the arbitrage-free value of an option-free, fixed-rate coupon bond.

CFA® Program Curriculum, Volume 5, page 79

Arbitrage-free valuation of a fixed-rate, option-free bond entails discounting each of the bond's future cash flows (i.e., each coupon payment and the par value at maturity) using the corresponding spot rate.

Example: Arbitrage-free valuation

Sam Givens, a fixed income analyst at GBO Bank, has been asked to value a three-year, 3% annual pay, €100 par bond with the same liquidity and risk as the benchmark. What is the value of the bond using the spot rates provided below?

€ Benchmark Spot Rate Curve:

Year	*Spot Rate*
1	3.00%
2	3.25%
3	3.50%

Answer:

$$\textbf{Bond Value} = \frac{3}{(1.03)} + \frac{3}{(1.0325)^2} + \frac{103}{(1.0350)^3} = €98.63$$

While we can value option-free bonds with a simple spot rate curve, for bonds with embedded options, changes in future rates will affect the probability of the option being exercised and the underlying future cash flows. Thus, a model that allows both rates and the underlying cash flows to vary should be used to value bonds with embedded options. One such model, the binomial interest rate tree framework, is discussed next.

LOS 36.c: Describe a binomial interest rate tree framework.

CFA® Program Curriculum, Volume 5, page 81

The **binomial interest rate tree** framework assumes that interest rates have an equal probability of taking one of two possible values in the next period (hence the term binomial).

Over multiple periods, the set of possible interest rate paths that are used to value bonds with a binomial model is called a binomial interest rate tree. The diagram in Figure 1 depicts a binomial interest rate tree.

Figure 1: Binomial Interest Rate Tree

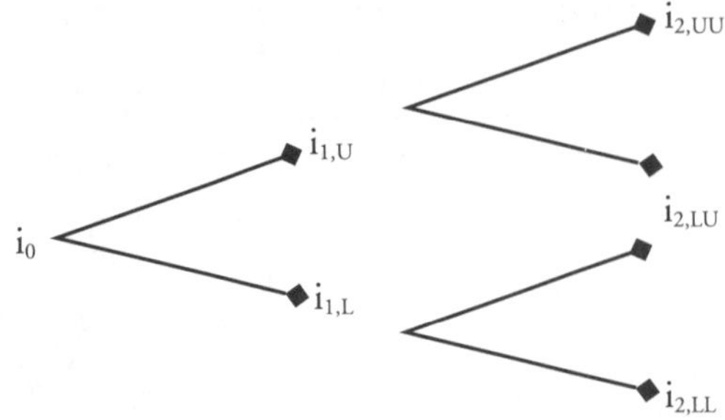

To understand this two-period binomial tree, consider the nodes indicated with the bold dots (◆). A node is a point in time when interest rates can take one of two possible paths, an upper path, *U*, or a lower path, *L*. Now, consider the node on the right side of the diagram where the interest rate $i_{2,LU}$ appears. This is the rate that will occur if the initial rate, i_0, follows the lower path from node 0 to node 1 to become $i_{1,L}$, then follows the upper of the two possible paths to node 2, where it takes on the value $i_{2,LU}$. At the risk of stating the obvious, the upper path from a given node leads to a higher rate than the lower path. In fact,

$$i_{2,LU} = i_{2,LL}\, e^{2\sigma}$$

where:
e $\approx$ 2.7183 (i.e., the base of natural log)
σ = standard deviation of interest rates (i.e., the interest rate volatility used in the model)

Note that an upward move followed by a downward move, or a down-then-up move, produces the same result: $i_{2,LU} = i_{2,UL}$ (the math term for this is lattice).

The interest rates at each node in this interest rate tree are one-period forward rates corresponding to the nodal period. Each forward rate is related to (i.e., is a multiple of) the other forward rates in the same nodal period. Adjacent forward rates (at the same period) are two standard deviations apart. For the first period, there are two forward rates and hence:

$$i_{1,U} = i_{1,L}\, e^{2\sigma}$$

Beyond the first nodal period, non-adjacent forward rates are a multiple of the two standard deviations (depending on how separated the forward rates are).

For example,

$$i_{2,UU} = i_{2,LL}\, e^{4\sigma}$$

The relationship among the set of rates associated with each individual nodal period is a function of the interest rate volatility assumed to generate the tree. Volatility estimates can be based on historical data or can be implied volatility derived from interest rate derivatives.

The binomial interest rate tree framework is a lognormal random walk model with two desirable properties: (1) higher volatility at higher rates and (2) non-negative interest rates.

LOS 36.d: Describe the backward induction valuation methodology and calculate the value of a fixed-income instrument given its cash flow at each node.

CFA® Program Curriculum, Volume 5, page 85

Valuing an Option-Free Bond with the Binomial Model

Backward induction refers to the process of valuing a bond using a binomial interest rate tree. The term "backward" is used because in order to determine the value of a bond today at Node 0, you need to know the values that the bond can take at the Year 1 node. But to determine the values of the bond at the Year 1 nodes, you need to know the possible values of the bond at the Year 2 nodes. Thus, for a bond that has N compounding periods, the current value of the bond is determined by computing the bond's possible values at Period N and working backwards to Node 0.

Because the probabilities of an up move and a down move are both 50%, the value of a bond at a given node in a binomial tree is the average of the present values of the two possible values from the next period. The appropriate discount rate is the forward rate associated with the node.

The following example should make this all clear.

Example: Valuing an option-free bond with the binomial model

A 7% annual coupon bond has two years to maturity. The interest rate tree is shown in the figure below. Fill in the tree and calculate the value of the bond today.

Valuing a 2-Year, 7.0% Coupon, Option-Free Bond

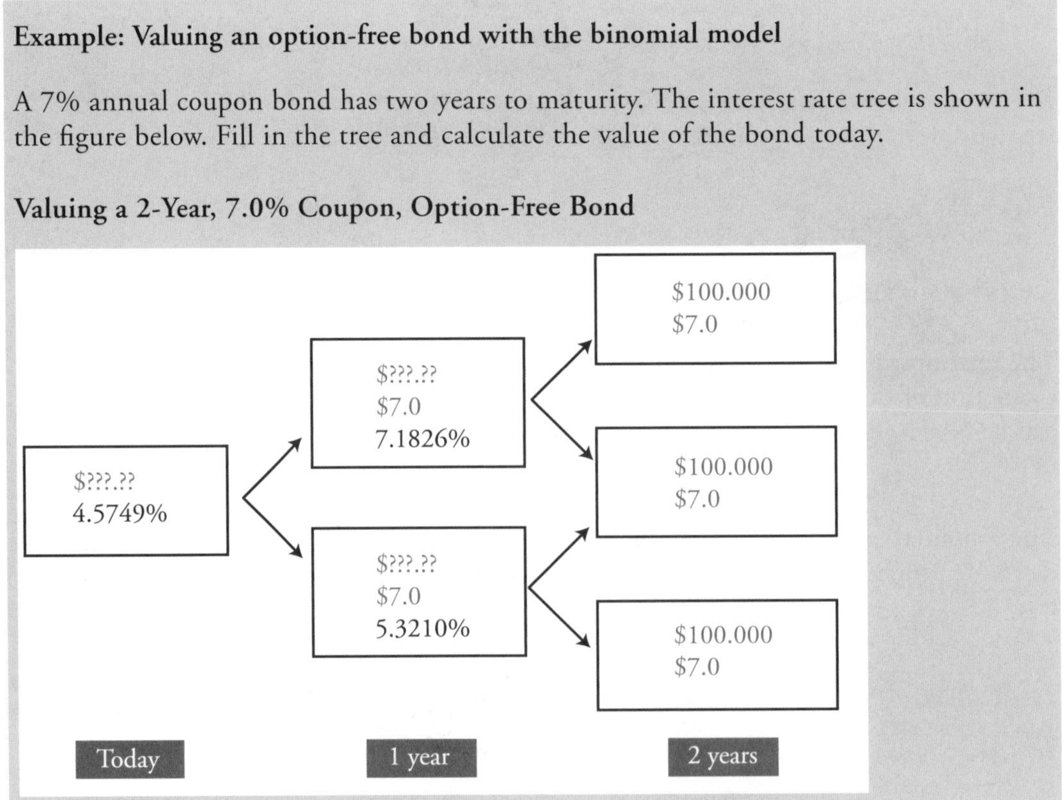

Answer:

Consider the value of the bond at the *upper* node for Period 1 ($V_{1,U}$):

$$V_{1,U} = \frac{1}{2} \times \left[\frac{\$100 + \$7}{1.071826} + \frac{\$100 + \$7}{1.071826} \right] = \$99.830$$

Similarly, the value of the bond at the *lower* node for Period 1 ($V_{1,L}$) is:

$$V_{1,L} = \frac{1}{2} \times \left[\frac{\$100 + \$7}{1.053210} + \frac{\$100 + \$7}{1.053210} \right] = \$101.594$$

Now calculate V_0, the current value of the bond at Node 0.

$$V_0 = \frac{1}{2} \times \left[\frac{\$99.830 + \$7}{1.045749} + \frac{\$101.594 + \$7}{1.045749} \right] = \$102.999$$

The completed binomial tree is shown below:

Valuing a 2-Year, 7.0% Coupon, Option-Free Bond

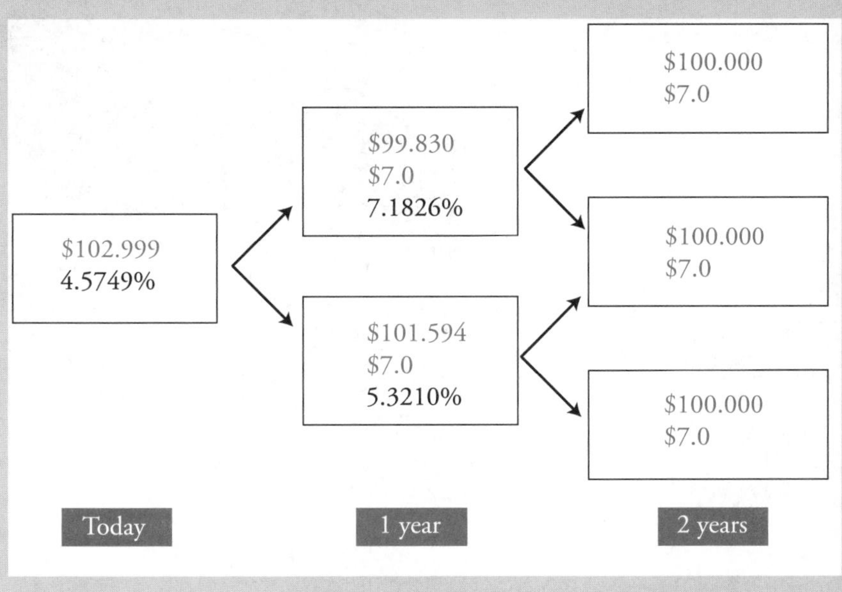

LOS 36.e: Describe the process of calibrating a binomial interest rate tree to match a specific term structure.

CFA® Program Curriculum, Volume 5, page 91

The construction of a binomial interest rate tree is a tedious process. In practice, the interest rate tree is usually generated using specialized computer software. The underlying process conforms to three rules:

1. The interest rate tree should generate **arbitrage-free values** for the benchmark security. This means that the value of bonds produced by the interest rate tree

must be equal to their market price, which excludes arbitrage opportunities. This requirement is very important because without it, the model will not properly price more complex callable and putable securities, which is the intended purpose of the model.

2. As stated earlier, adjacent forward rates (for the same period) are two standard deviations apart (calculated as $e^{2\sigma}$). Hence, knowing one of the forward rates (out of many) for a particular nodal period allows us to compute the other forward rates for that period in the tree.

3. The middle forward rate (or mid-point in case of even number of rates) in a period is approximately equal to the implied (from the benchmark spot rate curve) one-period forward rate for that period.

Example: Binomial interest rate tree

Xi Nguyen, CFA, has collected the following information on the par rate curve, spot rates, and forward rates. Nguyen had asked a colleague, Alok Nath, to generate a binomial interest rate tree consistent with this data and an assumed volatility of 20%. Nath completed a partial interest rate tree shown below.

Maturity	*Par Rate*	*Spot Rate*
1	3%	3.000%
2	4%	4.020%
3	5%	5.069%

Binomial Tree with σ = 20% (One-year Forward Rates)

Time 0	*Time 1*	*Time 2*
3%	5.7883%	B
	A	C
		D

1. Calculate the forward rate indicated by A.

2. Estimate the forward rate indicated by C.

3. Estimate forward rates B and D.

Answer:

1. Forward rate $i_{1,L}$ is indicated by A and is related to forward rate $i_{1,U}$ given as 5.7883%.

$$i_{1,L} = i_{1,U}\,e^{-2\sigma} = (0.057883)\,e^{-(2 \times 0.20)} = 0.0388 \text{ or } 3.88\%$$

2. Forward rate C is the middle rate for Period 3 and hence the best estimate for that rate is the one-year forward rate in two years $f(2,1)$.

   Using the spot rates, we can bootstrap the forward rate:

   $(1 + S_3)^3 = (1 + S_2)^2(1 + f(2,1)) \rightarrow (1.05069)^3 = (1.0402)^2(1 + f(2,1))$
   $\rightarrow f(2,1) = 7.199\%$

3. The forward rates B and D are related to C as follows (note that $C = i_{2,LU}$)

   $D = i_{2,LL} = i_{2,LU}\, e^{-2\sigma} = (0.07198)\ e^{-0.40} = 0.0483$ or 4.83%

   $B = i_{2,UU} = i_{2,LU}\, e^{+2\sigma} = (0.07198)\ e^{+0.40} = 0.1074$ or 10.74%

LOS 36.f: Compare pricing using the zero-coupon yield curve with pricing using an arbitrage-free binomial lattice.

CFA® Program Curriculum, Volume 5, page 93

We have already discussed arbitrage-free valuation of benchmark option-free bonds using the **zero-coupon yield curve** (also known as the spot rate curve). Each known future cash flow is discounted at the underlying spot rate (also known as the zero-coupon yield).

Example: Valuation of option-free bond

Samuel Favre is interested in valuing a three-year, 3% annual-pay Treasury bond. He has compiled the following information on Treasury spot rates:

Treasury Spot Rate Curve

Maturity	*Spot Rate*
1	3.000%
2	4.020%
3	5.069%

Compute the value of the $100 face value option-free bond.

Answer:

$$\text{value of the bond} = \frac{3}{1.03} + \frac{3}{(1.0402)^2} + \frac{103}{(1.05069)^3} = \$94.485$$

For bonds with embedded options, the future cash flows are uncertain as they depend on whether the embedded option will be in the money (and hence exercised). Because the value of the option depends on uncertain future interest rates, the underlying cash flows are also dependent on the same future interest rates. Hence, to value bonds with embedded options, we have to allow for rates to fluctuate. One way to accomplish this is to use the binomial interest rate tree.

Professor's Note: The binomial tree approach can value either option-free bonds or bonds with embedded options. Valuation of bonds with embedded options is covered in the next topic review.

Example: Valuation of an option-free bond using binomial tree

Samuel Favre is interested in valuing the same three-year, 3% annual-pay Treasury bond. The spot rate curve is as before, but this time Favre wants to use a binomial interest rate tree with the following rates:

One-Period Forward Rate in Year

0	*1*	*2*
3%	5.7883%	10.7383%
	3.8800%	7.1981%
		4.8250%

Compute the value of the $100 par option-free bond.

Answer:

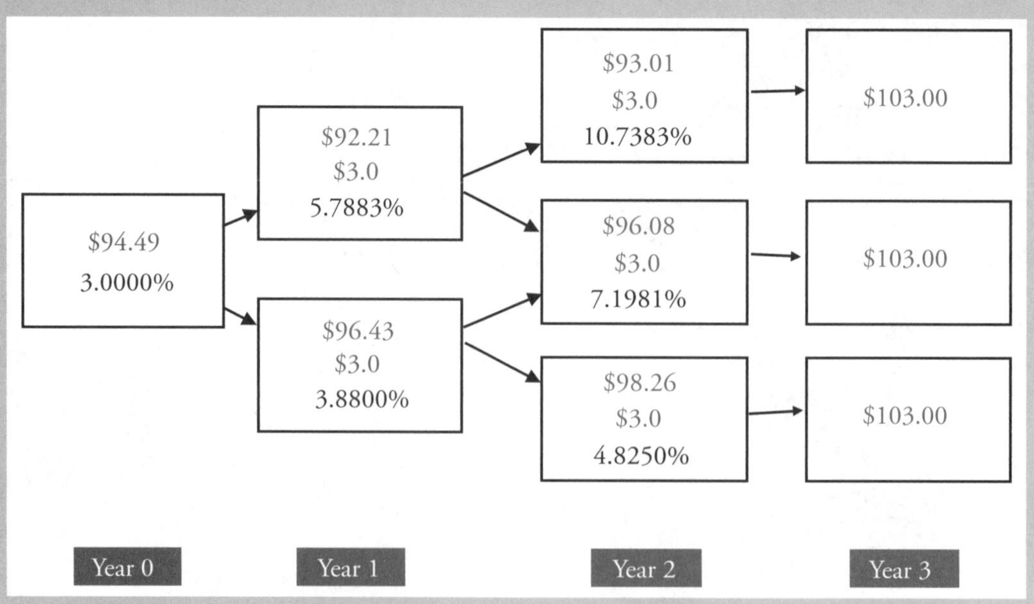

$$V_{2,UU} = \frac{103}{(1.107383)} = \$93.01$$

$$V_{2,UL} = \frac{103}{(1.071981)} = \$96.08$$

$$V_{2,LL} = \frac{103}{(1.048250)} = \$98.26$$

$$V_{1,U} = \frac{1}{2} \times \left[\frac{93.01+3}{1.057883} + \frac{96.08+3}{1.057883}\right] = \$92.21$$

$$V_{1,L} = \frac{1}{2} \times \left[\frac{96.08+3}{1.038800} + \frac{98.26+3}{1.038800}\right] = \$96.43$$

$$V_0 = \frac{1}{2} \times \left[\frac{92.21+3}{1.03} + \frac{96.43+3}{1.03}\right] = \$94.485$$

Note that the underlying interest rate tree in this example was calibrated to generate arbitrage-free values consistent with the benchmark spot rate curve and hence produced the same value for the option-free bond as in the earlier example.

LOS 36.g: Describe pathwise valuation in a binomial interest rate framework and calculate the value of a fixed-income instrument given its cash flows along each path.

CFA® Program Curriculum, Volume 5, page 95

Another mathematically identical approach to valuation using the backward induction method in a binomial tree is the **pathwise valuation** approach. For a binomial interest rate tree with *n* periods, there will be $2^{(n-1)}$ unique paths. For example, for a three-period tree, there will be 2^2 or four paths comprising one known spot rate and varying combinations of two unknown forward rates. If we use the label of *S* for the one-period spot rate and *U* and *L* for upper and lower outcomes, respectively, for forward rates in our binomial framework, the four paths would be SUU, SUL, SLU, and SLL.

Example: Valuation of option-free bond using pathwise valuation

Samuel Favre wants to value the same three-year, 3% annual-pay Treasury bond. The interest rate tree (shown below) is the same as before but this time, Favre wants to use a pathwise valuation approach.

One-period Forward Rate in Year

0	*1*	*2*
3%	5.7883%	10.7383%
	3.8800%	7.1981%
		4.8250%

Compute the value of the $100 par option-free bond.

Answer:

For a three-year bond, there are four potential interest rate paths. The value of the bond for each path is computed as the sum of the present values of each cash flow discounted at its respective path-specified rate. Pathwise valuation discounts cash flows one year at a time using one-year forward rates (similar to backward induction) rather than spot rates.

Path	*Year 1*	*Year 2*	*Year 3*	*Value*
1	3%	5.7883%	10.7383%	$91.03
2	3%	5.7883%	7.1981%	$93.85
3	3%	3.8800%	7.1981%	$95.52
4	3%	3.8800%	4.8250%	$97.55
			Average	$94.49

For example, the value of the bond in Path 1 is computed as:

$$\text{value}_1 = \frac{3}{(1.03)} + \frac{3}{(1.03)(1.057883)} + \frac{103}{(1.03)(1.057883)(1.107383)} = \$91.03$$

LOS 36.h: Describe a Monte Carlo forward-rate simulation and its application.

CFA® Program Curriculum, Volume 5, page 98

Path Dependency

Prepayments on underlying residential mortgages affect the cash flows of a mortgage-backed security. Prepayment risk is similar to call risk in a callable bond. However, unlike call risk, prepayment risk is affected not only by the level of interest rate at a particular point in time, but also by the path rates took to get there.

Consider a mortgage pool that was formed when rates were 6%, then interest rates dropped to 4%, rose to 6%, and then dropped again to 4%. Many homeowners will have refinanced when interest rates dipped the first time. On the second occurrence of 4% interest rates, most homeowners in the pool who were able to refinance would have already taken advantage of the opportunity, leading to lower prepayments than would be observed had 4% interest rates not occurred previously.

An important assumption of the binomial valuation process is that the value of the cash flows at a given point in time is independent of the path that interest rates followed up to that point. In other words, cash flows are not **path dependent**; cash flows at any node do not depend on the path rates took to get to that node. Because of path dependency of cash flows of mortgage-backed securities, the binomial tree backward induction process cannot be used to value such securities. We instead use the Monte Carlo simulation method to value mortgage-backed securities.

A **Monte Carlo forward-rate simulation** involves randomly generating a large number of interest rate paths, using a model that incorporates a volatility assumption and an assumed probability distribution. A key feature of the Monte Carlo method is that the underlying cash flows can be path dependent.

As with pathwise valuation discussed earlier, the value of the bond is the average of values from the various paths. The simulated paths should be calibrated so benchmark interest rate paths value benchmark securities at their market price (i.e., arbitrage-free valuation). The calibration process entails adding (subtracting) a constant to all rates when the value obtained from the simulated paths is too high (too low) relative to market prices. This calibration process results in a **drift adjusted** model.

A Monte Carlo simulation may impose upper and lower bounds on interest rates as part of the model generating the simulated paths. These bounds are based on the notion of mean reversion; rates tend to rise when they are too low and fall when they are too high.

Example: Valuation of option-free bond using Monte Carlo simulation

Samuel Favre is interested in valuing the same three-year, 3% annual-pay Treasury bond as discussed before. Favre wants to use Monte Carlo simulation and has generated the following rate paths.

Monte Carlo Simulation (Drift-adjusted)

Path	*Year 1*	*Year 2*	*Year 3*
1	3%	5.32%	10.59%
2	3%	5.11%	10.33%
3	3%	4.79%	9.89%
4	3%	4.56%	9.10%
5	3%	4.11%	8.22%
6	3%	3.79%	6.54%
7	3%	3.58%	5.11%
8	3%	3.62%	4.11%

Answer:

Valuation using the simulated interest rate paths is shown below:

Path	*Year 1*	*Year 2*	*Year 3*	*Value*
1	3%	5.32%	10.59%	$91.53
2	3%	5.11%	10.33%	$91.91
3	3%	4.79%	9.89%	$92.53
4	3%	4.56%	9.10%	$93.36
5	3%	4.11%	8.22%	$94.47
6	3%	3.79%	6.54%	$96.15
7	3%	3.58%	5.11%	$97.57
8	3%	3.62%	4.11%	$98.42
			Average	$94.49

Where, for example:

$$\text{value}_{\text{path}\,2} = \frac{3}{(1.03)} + \frac{3}{(1.03)(1.0511)} + \frac{103}{(1.03)(1.0511)(1.1033)} = 91.91$$

Note that the interest rates in the above example were calibrated to ensure that the valuation obtained was consistent with market prices (i.e., arbitrage-free) and hence the value obtained is the same as before.

KEY CONCEPTS

LOS 36.a

Arbitrage-free valuation leads to a security value such that no market participant can earn an arbitrage profit in a trade involving that security. In other words, the valuation is consistent with the value additivity principle and without dominance of any security relative to others in the market.

LOS 36.b

Arbitrage-free valuation of fixed-rate, option-free bonds entails discounting each of the bond's future cash flows at its corresponding spot rate.

LOS 36.c

The binomial interest rate tree framework is a lognormal model with two equally likely outcomes for one-period forward rates at each node. A volatility assumption drives the spread of the nodes in the tree.

LOS 36.d

Backward induction is the process of valuing a bond using a binomial interest rate tree. The term backward is used because in order to determine the value of a bond at Node 0, we need to know the values that the bond can take on at nodal period 1, and so on.

LOS 36.e

A binomial interest rate tree is calibrated such that (1) the values of benchmark bonds using the tree are equal to the bonds' market prices, (2) adjacent forward rates at any nodal period are two standard deviations apart and (3) the midpoint for each nodal period is approximately equal to the implied one-period forward rate for that period.

LOS 36.f

Valuation of bonds using a zero-coupon yield curve (also known as the spot rate curve) is suitable for option-free bonds. However, for bonds with embedded options where the value of the option varies with outcome of unknown forward rates, a model that allows for variability of forward rates is necessary. One such model is the binomial interest rate tree framework.

LOS 36.g

In the pathwise valuation approach, the value of the bond is simply the average of the values of the bond at each path. For a *n*-period binomial tree, there are $2^{(n-1)}$ possible paths.

LOS 36.h

The Monte Carlo simulation method uses pathwise valuation and a large number of randomly generated simulated paths. Mortgage-backed securities have path-dependent cash flows on account of the embedded prepayment option. The Monte Carlo simulation method should be used for valuing MBS as the binomial tree backward induction process is inappropriate for securities with path-dependent cash flows.

Concept Checkers

The following information relates to questions 1 to 6.

Dan Green, CFA, is currently working for FIData, a company specializing in the provision of price data for fixed-income instruments.

Green heads a team that inputs raw data into an instructional area on FIData's website. FIData uses these pages to provide hypothetical bond information along with a description of how to read and interpret the information.

One of FIData's customers has questioned whether some of the data used to demonstrate pricing concepts is correct. The customer's email stated, "The prices of the three bonds used are not consistent with each other and hence may not be accurate. If they were, I would be able to make a significant arbitrage profit (i.e., I could secure the current risk free rate of return with zero net investment)." Green thinks the customer is misinformed regarding arbitrage gains, but wants to check the data anyway.

The relevant data for three hypothetical risk free bonds is shown in Figure 1 given that the benchmark yield curve is flat at 1.50%. (FFPQ is an annual-pay bond.)

Figure 1: Bond Pricing Data

Bond Issue	*Maturity*	*Coupon*	*Par ($)*	*Price ($)*
FFPQ	2 years	10%	$1,000	1,170.12
DALO	1 year	0%	$1,000	985.22
NKDS	2 years	0%	$11,000	10,667.28

In another area of the company's instructional website, FIData has an explanation of the binomial interest rate tree framework that its analysts use in their valuation process. All of FIData's models populate a binomial interest rate tree assuming interest rates follow a lognormal random walk.

The webpage makes two statements regarding the assumptions that underpin the construction and population of such trees as shown below.

Assumption 1:

The lognormal model ensures that interest rates are non-negative.

Assumption 2:

The lognormal model ensures a constant volatility of interest rates at all levels of interest rates.

An example of a standard tree used by FIData is given in Figure 2

Figure 2: Binomial Interest Rate Tree

Year 0	*Year 1*
4.5749%	7.1826%
	5.3210%

FIData's website uses rates in Figure 2 to value a two-year, 5% annual-pay coupon bond with a par value of $1,000 using the backward induction method.

1. Green is correct in stating that the customer who sent the email regarding arbitrage gains is misinformed because:
   A. an arbitrage gain always requires a net investment, although this may be small compared to the potential gains.
   B. an arbitrage gain is not constrained by the risk-free rate.
   C. arbitrage gains require a net investment in proportion to returns.

2. Given the three bonds in Figure 1, it is possible to make an arbitrage gain by:
   A. selling 1 FFPQ bond and simultaneously purchasing 10 DALO and 10 NKDS bonds.
   B. selling 10 FFPQ bonds and simultaneously purchasing 1 DALO and 1 NKDS bond.
   C. selling 1 DALO bond and 1 NKDS bond and simultaneously purchasing 10 FFPQ bonds.

3. Which of the following statements regarding the FFPQ bond in Figure 1 is *most likely*?
   A. It is priced above its no arbitrage price.
   B. It is priced at its no arbitrage price.
   C. It is priced below its no arbitrage price.

4. Which of the assumptions regarding the construction of FIData's binomial interest rate trees is *most accurate*?
   A. Assumption 1 only.
   B. Assumption 2 only.
   C. Neither assumption is correct.

5. Using the backward induction method, the value of the 5% annual-pay bond using the interest rate tree given in Figure 2 is *closest* to:
   A. $900.
   B. $945.
   C. $993.

6. When calibrating a binomial interest rate tree to match a specific term structure, which of the following statements is *least accurate*?
   A. Interest rates in the tree should produce an arbitrage-free valuation for benchmark securities.
   B. Adjacent spot rates at each node of the tree are related by the multiplier $e^{2\sigma}$.
   C. The middle forward rate in a period is approximately equal to the implied (from the benchmark spot rate curve) one-period forward rate for that period.

The following information relates to questions 7 to 12.

Farah Dane, CFA, works for Geodesic Investing, a small hedge fund that offers investment services for a handful of clients known personally by the owner, Mike deGrekker. The fund makes few trades, preferring to wait for what it perceives to be arbitrage opportunities before investing. Last year, the fund managed a return of more than 45%, thanks largely to a single transaction on which the company made a profit of $9.4 million.

The transaction, which DeGrekker described as a "valuation farming exercise" involved simultaneously purchasing a government Treasury and selling the corresponding strips for a higher price than the cost of the Treasury.

Dane is currently using a binomial lattice and a pathwise method to value fixed-income bonds in order to identify potential trading opportunities. She has used the binomial lattice shown in Figure 3 to value a three-year, annual pay, 4% coupon risk-free government bond with a par value of $1,000. Her pathwise valuation is also shown.

Figure 3: Binomial Lattice

One-period Forward Rate in Year:

0	*1*	*2*
3%	5.7883%	10.7383%
	3.8800%	7.1981%
		4.8250%

Pathwise Valuation

	Year 1	*Year 2*	*Year 3*	*Value*
Path 1	3%	5.7883%	10.7383%	$937.45
Path 2	3%	5.7883%	7.1981%	$965.92
Path 3	3%	5.7883%	4.8250%	$986.07
Path 4	3%	3.8800%	7.1981%	$982.95
Path 5	3%	3.8800%	4.8250%	$1,003.48
			Average	$975.17

Dane is not satisfied with this method of valuation and has put together a report for deGrekker on the use of the Monte Carlo method, which she feels will lead to more accurate valuations. She quotes the following advantages of using Monte Carlo method:

Advantage 1

The Monte Carlo method will estimate the value of the bond using multiple interest rate paths and hence there is no need to make an assumption about volatility of rates.

Advantage 2

The method could be applied to get more accurate valuations for securities that are interest rate path dependent.

DeGrekker is resistant to the idea as he is concerned about the amount of computing time the model may require. He accepts, however, that the idea of using many paths is attractive. He concedes that, "increasing the number of paths used in the model increases the statistical accuracy of the estimated value and produces a value closer to the true fundamental value of the security."

7. Which of the following statements regarding the valuation of an option-free bond using an arbitrage-free binomial lattice is *most accurate*?
   A. If the binomial lattice is correctly calibrated, it should give the same value for an option-free bond as using the par curve used to calibrate the tree.
   B. The binomial lattice will only produce the same value for an option-free bond as the par curve that was used to calibrate it if the bond is priced at par.
   C. The binomial lattice will only produce the same value for an option-free bond as the par curve that was used to calibrate it if the yield curve is flat.

8. Which of the following statements *most accurately* describes the "valuation farming exercise" undertaken by deGrekker?
   A. DeGrekker used the process of stripping and the law of one price to make an arbitrage gain.
   B. DeGrekker used the process of reconstitution and the principle of no arbitrage to make a risk-free gain.
   C. DeGrekker's profit is not an arbitrage profit as the securities involved are risk free.

9. Which of the following is *most accurate* regarding the value Dane would obtain using the backward induction method as opposed to the pathwise valuation method for the bond in Figure 3?
   A. Both methods would produce the same value.
   B. The pathwise valuation method will give lower values when interest rates are rising because the backward induction method places a higher weighting on earlier cash flows.
   C. The backward induction method will give a different value compared to the pathwise method when the volatility of interest rates is high as the pathwise method uses equal weights.

10. Dane's pathwise valuation is:
    A. correct.
    B. incorrect, as the correct value is lower than $975.17.
    C. incorrect, as the correct value is higher than $975.17.

11. Which of the advantages of the Monte Carlo method stated by Dane is *most accurate*?
    A. Advantage 1 only.
    B. Advantage 2 only.
    C. Neither advantage is correct.

12. DeGrekker's comment on increasing the number of paths is *most likely*:
    A. correct.
    B. incorrect in asserting that a larger number of paths will produce an estimate that is statistically more accurate.
    C. incorrect in asserting that a larger number of paths will produce a value closer to the true fundamental value.

To access other content related to this topic review that may be included in the Schweser package you purchased, log in to your Schweser.com online dashboard. Schweser's OnDemand Video Lectures deliver streaming instruction covering every LOS in this topic review, while SchweserPro™ QBank provides additional quiz questions to help you practice and recall what you've learned.

Answers – Concepts Checkers

1. **B** An arbitrage gain is a risk-free profit and hence requires no net investment. The returns therefore are not simply the risk-free rate. As there is no initial investment, the gains cannot be measures as percentage of initial cost.

2. **B** An up-front arbitrage profit of $38.70 can be earned by selling 10 FFPQ bonds short and purchasing 1 DALO and 1 NKDS bonds as shown below.

Position	*Initial Cash Flow*	*Year 1 Cash Flow*	*Year 2 Cash Flow*
Short 10 FFPQ	$ 11,701.20	$(1,000.00)	$(11,000.00)
Long 1 DALO	$ (985.22)	$ 1,000.00	$ -
Long 1 NKDS	$(10,677.28)	$ -	$ 11,000.00
Net	$38.70	0	0

3. **A** FFPQ is overpriced. Based on the 1.5% benchmark yield, the other two bonds are correctly priced.

Arbitrage-free price = (PV Year 1 Cash Flow) + (PV Year 2 Cash Flow)

	PV Year 1 Cash Flow	*PV Year 2 Cash Flow*	*Arbitrage-Free Price*
FFPQ	98.52	1,067.73	1,166.25
DALO	985.22	0	985.22
NKDS	0	10,677.28	10,677.28

4. **A** A lognormal random walk will ensure non-negativity but will lead to higher volatility at higher interest rates.

5. **C** The value of the 5%, two-year annual pay $1000 par bond is $992.88.

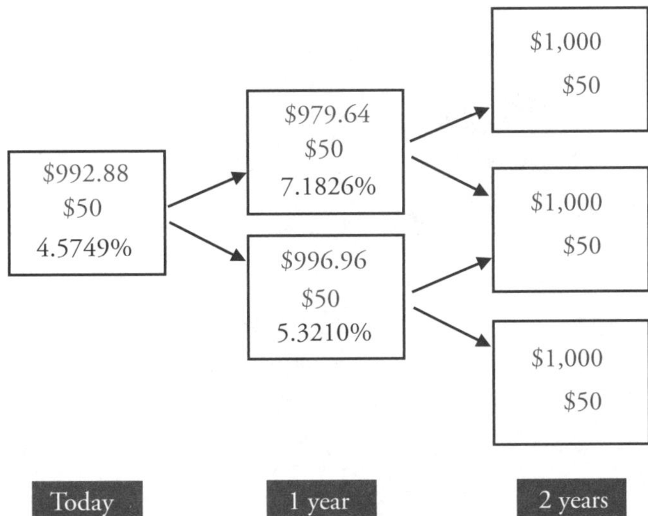

6. **B** The stated multiplier is correct but it is important to note that the rates given at each node of the tree are forward rates not spot rates.

7. **A** A correctly calibrated tree will value the bond at the same price as the par and spot curves used to derive it.

8. **A** DeGrekker purchased the bonds and stripped them into constituent parts before selling them. The strategy involved no initial net investment and yet results in an arbitrage profit.

9. **A** The two methods are identical and will always give the same result.

10. **B** This is a tricky question. There are only four possible paths that Dane should have used. The possible paths are UU (Path 1), UD (Path 2), DU (Path 4), and DD (Path 5). Path 3 isn't a valid path.

Path	*Year 1*	*Year 2*	*Year 3*
Path 1	3%	5.7883%	10.7383%
Path 2	3%	5.7883%	7.1981%
Path 4	3%	3.8800%	7.1981%
Path 5	3%	3.8800%	4.8250%

So the value should be the average of the values for paths 1, 2, 4, and 5. The correct average value is $972.45.

11. **B** Monte Carlo simulation also requires an assumed level of volatility as an input.

12. **C** The larger the number of paths, the more accurate the value in a statistical sense. However, whether the value is closer to the true fundamental value depends on the accuracy of the model inputs.

The following is a review of the Fixed Income: Topics in Fixed-Income Analysis principles designed to address the learning outcome statements set forth by CFA Institute. Cross-Reference to CFA Institute Assigned Reading #37.

Valuation and Analysis: Bonds with Embedded Options

Study Session 13

Exam Focus

This topic review extends the arbitrage-free valuation framework to valuation of bonds with embedded options. Understand the risk/return dynamics of embedded options, including their impact on a bond's duration and convexity. You should also know the adjustment required for the valuation of credit-risky bonds, including the process to estimate an OAS. Finally, understand the terminology and risk/return characteristics of convertibles.

LOS 37.a: Describe fixed-income securities with embedded options.

CFA® Program Curriculum, Volume 5, page 121

Embedded options in a bond allow an issuer to (1) manage interest rate risk and/or (2) issue the bonds at an attractive coupon rate. The embedded options can be a simple call or put option, or more complex options such as provisions for a sinking fund or an estate put.

Simple Options

Callable bonds give the *issuer* the option to call back the bond; the *investor* is *short* the call option. Most callable bonds have a lockout period during which the bond cannot be called. The call option can be a **European-style** option (whereby the option can only be exercised on a single day immediately after the lockout period), or an **American-style** option (whereby the option can be exercised at any time *after* the lockout period), or even a **Bermudan-style** option (whereby the option can be exercised at fixed dates after the lockout period).

Putable bonds allow the *investor* to put (sell) the bond back to the issuer prior to maturity. The *investor* is *long* the underlying put option. A related bond is an **extendible bond**, which allows the investor to extend the maturity of the bond. An extendible bond can be evaluated as a putable bond with longer maturity (i.e., the maturity if the bond is extended). A two-year, 3% bond extendible for an additional year at the same coupon rate would be valued the same as an otherwise identical three-year putable (European style) bond with lockout period of two years.

Complex Options

More complex options include:

- An **estate put** which includes a provision that allows the heirs of an investor to put the bond back to the issuer upon the death of the investor. The value of this contingent put option is inversely related to the investor's life expectancy; the shorter the life expectancy, the higher the value.
- **Sinking fund bonds** (sinkers) which require the issuer to set aside funds periodically to retire the bond (a sinking fund). This provision reduces the credit risk of the bond. Sinkers typically have several related *issuer* options (e.g. call provisions, acceleration provisions, and delivery options).

LOS 37.b: Explain the relationships between the values of a callable or putable bond, the underlying option-free (straight) bond, and the embedded option.

CFA® Program Curriculum, Volume 5, page 126

In essence, the holder of a callable bond owns an option-free (straight) bond and is also short a call option written on the bond. The value of the embedded call option (V_{call}) is, therefore, simply the difference between the value of a straight ($V_{straight}$) bond and the value of the comparable callable bond ($V_{callable}$):

$$V_{call} = V_{straight} - V_{callable}$$

Conversely, investors are willing to pay a premium for a putable bond, since its holder effectively owns an option-free bond plus a put option. The value of a putable bond can be expressed as:

$$V_{putable} = V_{straight} + V_{put}$$

Rearranging, the value of the embedded put option can be stated as:

$$V_{put} = V_{putable} - V_{straight}$$

LOS 37.c: Describe how the arbitrage-free framework can be used to value a bond with embedded options.

LOS 37.f: Calculate the value of a callable or putable bond from an interest rate tree.

CFA® Program Curriculum, Volume 5, pages 127 and 135

The basic process for valuing a callable (or putable) bond is similar to the process for valuing a straight bond. However, instead of using spot rates, one-period forward rates are used in a binomial tree framework. This change in methodology computes the value of the bond at different points in time; these checks are necessary to determine whether the embedded option is in the money (and exercised).

When valuing a callable bond, the value at any node where the bond is callable must be either the price at which the issuer will call the bond (i.e., the call price) or the computed value if the bond is not called, *whichever is lower*. This is known as the call rule. Similarly, for a putable bond, the value used at any node corresponding to a put date must be either the price at which the investor will put the bond (i.e., the put price) or the computed value if the bond is not put, *whichever is higher*. This is known as the put rule.

Professor's Note: Call date and put date in this context vary depending on whether the option is European-, American-, or Bermudan-style.

Example: Valuation of call and put options

Consider a two-year, 7% annual-pay, $100 par bond callable in one year at $100. Also consider a two-year, 7% annual-pay, $100 par bond putable in one year at $100.

The interest rate tree at 15% assumed volatility is as given below.

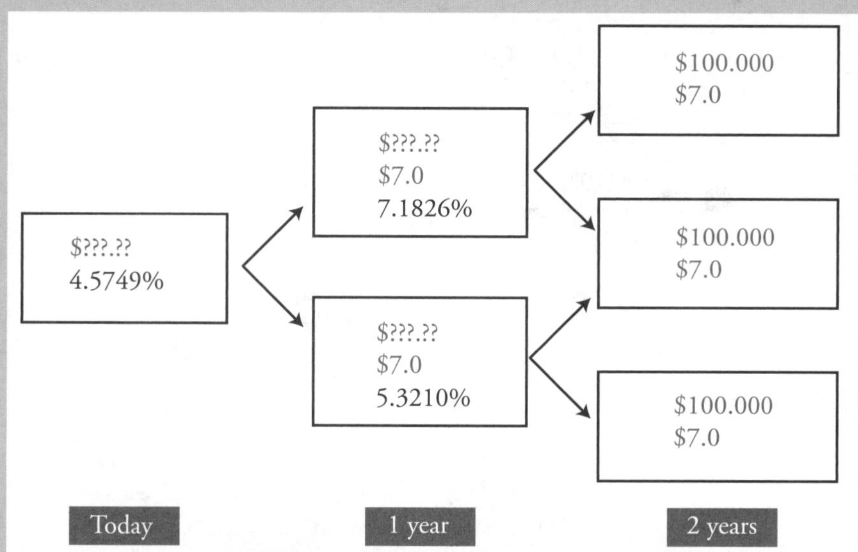

Value the embedded call and put options.

Answer:

Value of the straight (option-free) bond:

Consider the value of the bond at the *upper* node for Period 1, $V_{1,U}$:

$$V_{1,U} = \frac{1}{2} \times \left[\frac{\$100 + \$7}{1.071826} + \frac{\$100 + \$7}{1.071826} \right] = \$99.830$$

Similarly, the value of the bond at the *lower* node for Period 1, $V_{1,L}$, is:

$$V_{1,L} = \frac{1}{2} \times \left[\frac{\$100 + \$7}{1.053210} + \frac{\$100 + \$7}{1.053210} \right] = \$101.594$$

Now calculate V_0, the current value of the bond at Node 0.

$$V_0 = \frac{1}{2} \times \left[\frac{\$99.830 + \$7}{1.045749} + \frac{\$101.594 + \$7}{1.045749} \right] = \$102.999$$

The completed binomial tree is shown below:

Valuing a Two-Year, 7.0% Coupon, Option-Free Bond

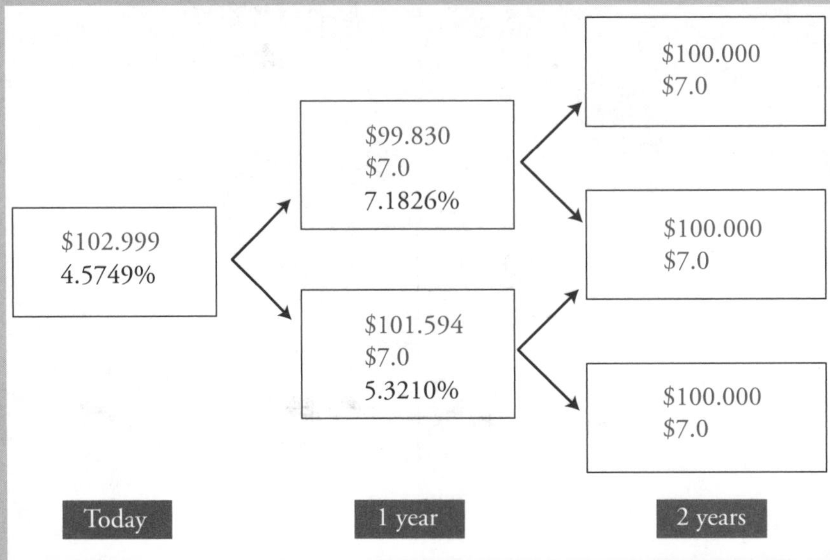

Value of the callable bond:

The call rule (call the bond if the price exceeds $100) is reflected in the boxes in the completed binomial tree, where the second line of the boxes at the one-year node is the lower of the call price or the computed value. For example, the value of the bond in one year at the lower node is $101.594. However, in this case, the bond will be called, and the investor will only receive $100. Therefore, for valuation purposes, the value of the bond in one year at this node is $100.

$V_{1,L}$ = $100

$V_{1,U}$ = (107 / 1.071826) = $99.830

The calculation for the current value of the bond at Node 0 (today), assuming the simplified call rules of this example, is:

$$V_0 = \frac{1}{2} \times \left[\frac{\$99.830 + \$7}{1.045749} + \frac{\$100.00 + \$7}{1.045749} \right] = \$102.238$$

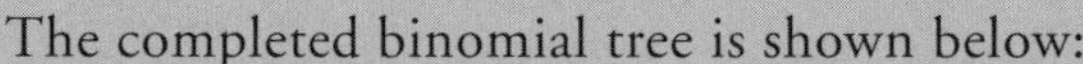

The completed binomial tree is shown below:

Valuing a Two-Year, 7.0% Coupon, Callable Bond, Callable in One Year at 100

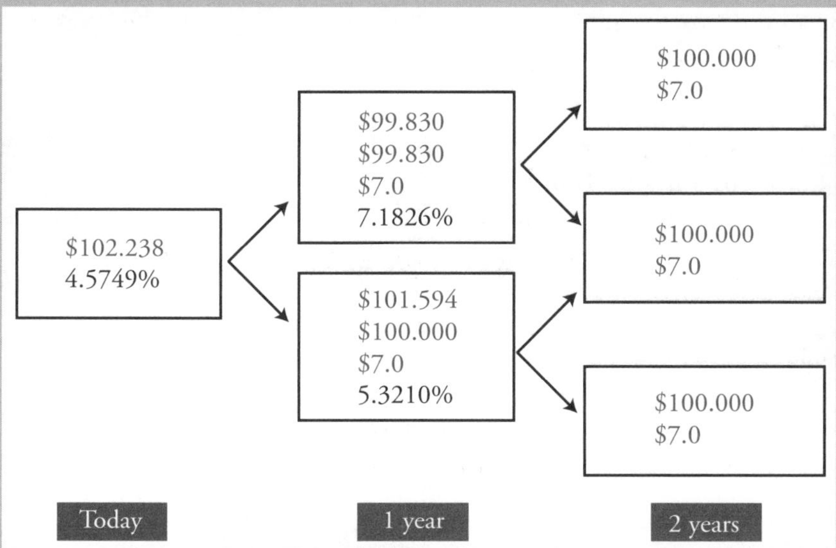

Value of the putable bond:

Similarly, for a putable bond, the put rule is to put the bond if the value falls below $100. The put option would therefore be exercised at the upper-node in year 1 and hence the $99.830 computed value is replaced by the exercise price of $100.

$V_{1,U} = 100$

$V_{1,L} = (107 / 1.053210) = \$101.594$

$$V_0 = \frac{1}{2} \times \left[\frac{100+7}{1.045749} + \frac{101.594+7}{1.045749} \right] = \$103.081$$

Value of the embedded options:

$V_{call} = V_{straight} - V_{callable} = \$102.999 - \$102.238 = \$0.76$

$V_{put} = V_{putable} - V_{straight} = \$103.081 - \$102.999 = 0.082$

LOS 37.d: Explain how interest rate volatility affects the value of a callable or putable bond.

CFA® Program Curriculum, Volume 5, page 130

Option values are positively related to the volatility of their underlying. Accordingly, when interest rate volatility increases, the values of both call and put options increase.

The value of a straight bond is affected by changes in the level of interest rate but is *unaffected* by changes in the *volatility* of interest rate.

When interest rate volatility increases, the value of a callable bond (where the investor is short the call option) decreases and the value of a putable bond (where the investor is long the put option) increases.

LOS 37.e: Explain how changes in the level and shape of the yield curve affect the value of a callable or putable bond.

CFA® Program Curriculum, Volume 5, page 132

Level of Interest Rates

As interest rates decline, the short call in a callable bond limits the bond's upside, so the value of a callable bond rises less rapidly than the value of an otherwise-equivalent straight bond.

As interest rates increase, the long put in a putable bond hedges against the loss in value; the value of a putable bond falls less rapidly than the value of an otherwise-equivalent straight bond.

Call option value is inversely related to the level of interest rates, while put option value varies directly with the level of interest rates.

Shape of the Yield Curve

The value of an embedded call option increases as interest rates decline. When the yield curve is upward sloping (i.e., normal), the more distant one-period forward rates are higher than the one-period forward rates in the near future. Because a higher interest rate scenario limits the probability of the call option being in the money, the value of a call option will be lower for an upward sloping yield curve. As an upward-sloping yield curve becomes flatter, the call option value increases.

The value of a put option increases with interest rates. When the yield curve is upward sloping, the probability of the put option going in the money is higher. Put option value therefore declines as an upward-sloping yield curve flattens.

LOS 37.g: Explain the calculation and use of option-adjusted spreads.

CFA® Program Curriculum, Volume 5, page 144

So far our backward induction process has relied on the risk-free binomial interest rate tree; our valuation assumed that the underlying bond was risk-free. If risk-free rates are used to discount cash flows of a credit risky corporate bond, the calculated value will be too high. To correct for this, a constant spread must be added to all one-period rates in the tree such that the calculated value equals the market price of the risky bond. This constant spread is called the **option adjusted spread** (OAS).

Professor's Note: The OAS is added to the tree after the adjustment for the embedded option (i.e., the node values are adjusted according to the call/put rule). Hence the OAS is calculated after the option risk has been removed.

Example: Computation of OAS

A $100-par, three-year, 6% annual-pay ABC Inc. callable bond trades at $99.95. The underlying call option is a Bermudan-style option that can be exercised in one or two years at par.

The benchmark interest rate tree assuming volatility of 20% is provided below.

One-period forward rates		
Year 0	*Year 1*	*Year 2*
3.000%	5.7883%	10.7383%
	3.8800%	7.1981%
		4.8250%

Compute the OAS on the bond.

Answer:

The value of the bond using the benchmark interest rate tree is $101.77, as shown below.

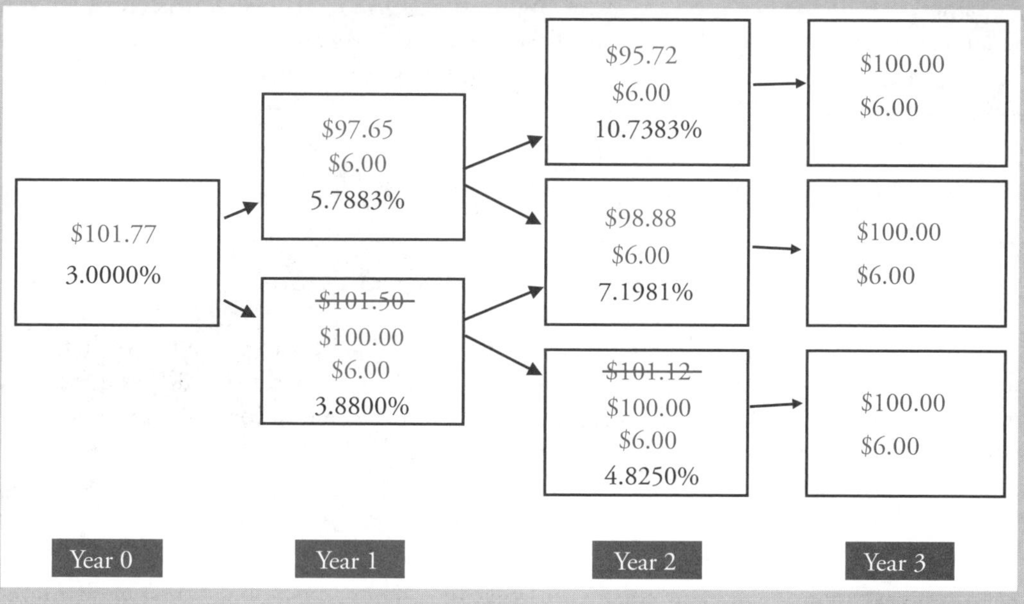

To force the computed value to be equal to the current market price of $99.95, a constant spread (OAS) of 100 bps is added to each interest rate in the tree as shown below:

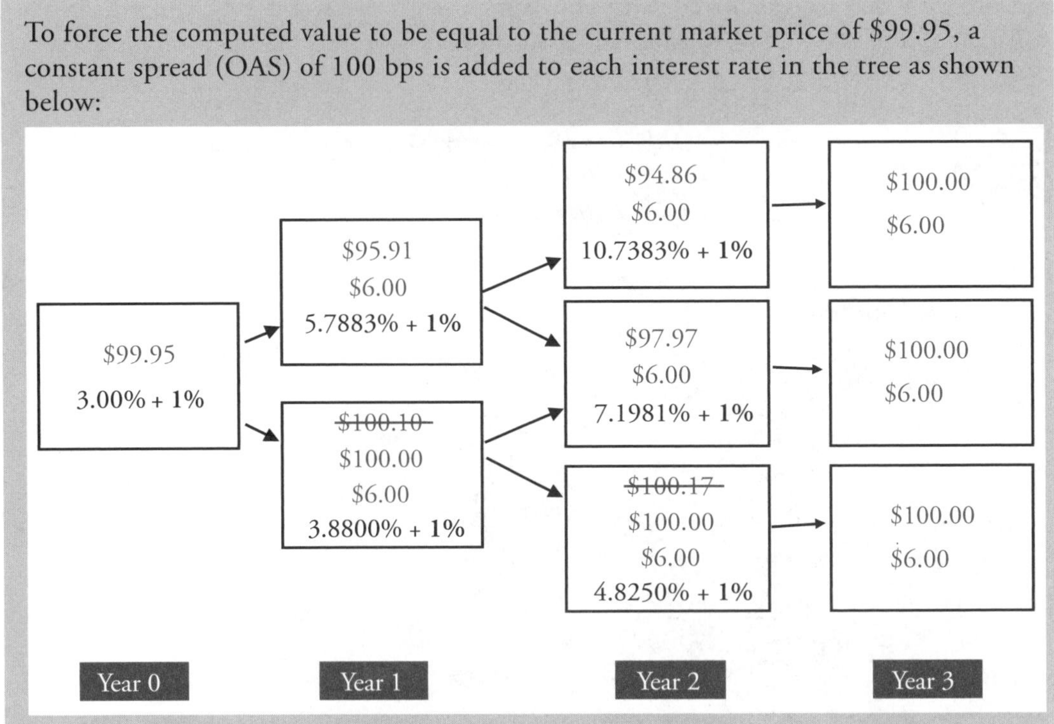

Professor's Note: The OAS computed using the above methodology is the spread implied by the current market price and hence assumes that the bond is priced correctly. Note that the actual estimation of OAS is largely an iterative process and is beyond the scope of the exam.

OAS is used by analysts in relative valuation; bonds with similar credit risk should have the same OAS. If the OAS for a bond is higher than OAS of its peers, it is considered to be undervalued and hence an attractive investment (i.e., it offers a higher compensation for a given level of risk). Conversely, bonds with low OAS (relative to peers) are considered to be overvalued.

LOS 37.h: Explain how interest rate volatility affects option adjusted spreads.

CFA® Program Curriculum, Volume 5, page 145

Consider for a moment the difference between the calculated value of a bond that we obtain from a tree and the bond's actual market price. The greater this difference is, the greater the OAS we would need to add to the rates in the tree to force the calculated value down to the market price.

Consider a 7%, 10-year callable bond of XYZ Corp. trading for $958.

Analyst A assumes a 15% value for future volatility in generating her *benchmark* interest rate tree and calculates the value of the bond as $1,050. She then computes the OAS (the increase in discount rate required to lower the calculated value to the market price of $958) for this bond to be 80 bps.

Analyst B assumes a 20% value for future volatility, and because of higher assumed volatility, the computed value of the bond turns out to be $992. (Note that this is lower than the $1,050 calculated by A—the higher the volatility, the lower a callable bond's value.) The OAS calculated by B is accordingly lower at 54 bps.

Observe that for the same bond, the OAS calculated varied depending on the volatility assumption used.

When we use a higher estimate of volatility to value a callable bond, the calculated value of the call option increases, the calculated value of the straight bond is unaffected, and the *computed value* (not the market price) of the callable bond decreases (since the bondholder is short the option). Hence when the estimated (or assumed) volatility (of benchmark rates) used in a binomial tree is higher, the computed value of a callable bond will be lower—and therefore closer to its true market price. The constant spread that needs to be added to the benchmark rates to correctly price the bond is therefore lower.

To summarize, as the *assumed* level of volatility used in an interest rate tree increases, the computed OAS (for a given market price) for a callable bond decreases. Similarly, the computed OAS of a putable bond increases as the assumed level of volatility in the binomial tree increases.

Figure 1: Relationship Between Volatility and OAS

Assumed Level of Volatility	*Value*				OAS_{CALL}	OAS_{PUT}
	Calls	*Puts*	*Callable*	*Putable*		
High	High	High	Low	High	Low	High
Low	Low	Low	High	Low	High	Low

LOS 37.i: Calculate and interpret effective duration of a callable or putable bond.

CFA® Program Curriculum, Volume 5, page 149

Recall from Level I that:

- Modified duration measures a bond's price sensitivity to interest rate changes, *assuming that the bond's cash flows do not change as interest rates change.*
- The standard measure of convexity can be used to improve price changes estimated from modified duration.

Modified duration and convexity are not useful for bonds with embedded options, however, because the cash flows from these bonds will change if the option is exercised. To overcome this problem, ***effective*** **duration** and ***effective*** **convexity** should be used, because these measures take into account how changes in interest rates may alter cash flows.

The following expressions can be used to compute effective duration and convexity for *any* bond:

$$\text{effective duration} = \text{ED} = \frac{BV_{-\Delta y} - BV_{+\Delta y}}{2 \times BV_0 \times \Delta y}$$

$$\text{effective convexity} = \text{EC} = \frac{BV_{-\Delta y} + BV_{+\Delta y} - (2 \times BV_0)}{BV_0 \times \Delta y^2}$$

where:

Δy = change in required yield, in decimal form

$BV_{-\Delta y}$ = estimated price if yield decreases by Δy

$BV_{+\Delta y}$ = estimated price if yield increases by Δy

BV_0 = initial observed bond price

Calculating effective duration and effective convexity for bonds with embedded options is a complicated undertaking because we must calculate values of $BV_{+\Delta y}$ and $BV_{-\Delta y}$. Here's how it is done:

Step 1: Given assumptions about benchmark interest rates, interest rate volatility, and any calls and/or puts, calculate the OAS for the issue using the current market price and the binomial model.
Step 2: Impose a small parallel shift in the benchmark yield curve by an amount equal to $+\Delta y$.
Step 3: Build a new binomial interest rate tree using the new yield curve.
Step 4: Add the OAS from step 1 to each of the one-year rates in the interest rate tree to get a "modified" tree.
Step 5: Compute $BV_{+\Delta y}$ using this modified interest rate tree.
Step 6: Repeat steps 2 through 5 using a parallel rate shift of $-\Delta y$ to obtain a value of $BV_{-\Delta y}$.

LOS 37.j: Compare effective durations of callable, putable, and straight bonds.

CFA® Program Curriculum, Volume 5, page 153

Both call and put options have the potential to reduce the life of a bond, so the duration of callable and putable bonds will be less than or equal to their straight counterparts.

- Effective duration (callable) ≤ effective duration (straight).
- Effective duration (putable) ≤ effective duration (straight).
- Effective duration (zero-coupon) ≈ maturity of the bond.
- Effective duration of fixed-rate bond < maturity of the bond.
- Effective duration of floater ≈ time (years) to next reset.

While effective duration of straight bonds is relatively unaffected by changes in interest rates, an increase (decrease) in rates would decrease the effective duration of a putable (callable) bond.

LOS 37.k: Describe the use of one-sided durations and key rate durations to evaluate the interest rate sensitivity of bonds with embedded options.

CFA® Program Curriculum, Volume 5, page 154

One-sided Durations

The computation of effective duration discussed earlier relied on computing the value of the bond for equal parallel shifts of the yield curve up and down (by the same amount). This metric captures interest rate risk reasonably well for small changes in the yield curve and for option-free bonds.

For a callable bond, when the call option is at or near the money, the change in price for a decrease in yield will be less than the change in price for an equal amount of increase in yield. The value of a callable bond is capped by its call price: the bond's value will not increase beyond the call price regardless of how low interest rates fall. Similarly, the value of a putable bond is more sensitive to downward movements in yield curve versus upward movements.

For bonds with embedded options, **one-sided durations**—durations that apply only when interest rates rise (or, alternatively, only when rates fall)—are better at capturing interest rate sensitivity than simple effective duration. When the underlying option is at-the-money (or near-the-money), callable bonds will have lower one-sided down-duration than one-sided up-duration; the price change of a callable when rates fall is smaller than the price change for an equal increase in rates. Conversely, a near-the-money putable bond will have larger one-sided down-duration than one-sided up-duration.

Key Rate Duration

Key rate durations or **partial durations** capture the interest rate sensitivity of a bond to changes in yields (par rates) of specific benchmark maturities. Key rate duration is used to identify the interest rate risk from changes in the shape of the yield curve (shaping risk).

The process of computing key rate duration is similar to the process of computing effective duration described earlier, except that instead of shifting the entire benchmark yield curve, only one specific par rate (key rate) is shifted before the price impact is measured.

Figure 2 shows the key rate durations for several 15-year *option-free* bonds, each with a different coupon rate.

Figure 2: Key Rate Durations of Various 15-Year Option-Free Bonds With Different Coupon Rates

Coupon	*Price*	Key Rate Durations					
		Total	*2-year*	*3-year*	*5-year*	*10-year*	*15-year*
1%	$76.12	13.41	–0.05	–0.07	–0.22	–0.45	14.20
2%	$88.06	12.58	–0.03	–0.05	–0.15	–0.27	13.08
3%	$100.00	11.94	0	0	0	0	11.94
5%	$123.88	11.03	0.02	0.1	0.15	0.32	10.44
8%	$159.69	10.18	0.09	0.15	0.32	0.88	8.74

Professor's Note: In these figures the market interest rate is not changing; rather we are considering a number of different bonds that have different coupons.

Figure 3 shows the key rate durations for several 15-year European-style *callable* bonds, each with a different coupon rate (callable in 10 years at par).

Figure 3: Key Rate Durations of Various 15-Year Callable Bonds With Different Coupon Rates

Coupon	*Price*	Key Rate Durations					
		Total	*2-year*	*3-year*	*5-year*	*10-year*	*15-year*
1%	$75.01	13.22	–0.03	–0.01	–0.45	–2.22	15.93
2%	$86.55	12.33	–0.01	–0.03	–0.15	5.67	6.85
3%	$95.66	11.45	0.00	0.00	0.00	6.40	5.05
5%	$112.87	9.22	0.02	0.10	0.15	6.67	2.28
8%	$139.08	8.89	0.09	0.15	0.32	7.20	1.13

Figure 4 shows the key rate durations for several 15-year European-style *putable* bonds, each with a different coupon rate (putable in 10 years at par).

Figure 4: Key Rate Durations of Various 15-Year Putable Bonds With Different Coupon Rates

Coupon	*Price*	Key Rate Durations					
		Total	*2-year*	*3-year*	*5-year*	*10-year*	*15-year*
1%	$77.24	9.22	–0.03	–0.01	–0.45	8.66	1.05
2%	$89.82	9.90	–0.01	–0.03	–0.15	7.23	2.86
3%	$95.66	10.50	0.00	0.00	0.00	5.12	5.38
5%	$123.88	10.70	0.02	0.10	0.15	2.89	7.54
8%	$159.69	10.08	0.09	0.15	0.32	0.45	9.07

The following generalizations can be made about key rates:

1. If an option-free bond is trading at par, the bond's maturity-matched rate is the only rate that affects the bond's value. Its maturity key rate duration is the same as its effective duration, and all other rate durations are zero. In Figure 2, the 3% bond's (i.e., the par bond) 15-year key rate duration is same as the bond's effective duration, and all other rate durations are zero.

2. For option-free bonds not trading at par, the maturity-matched rate is still the most important rate. In Figure 2, the 15-year key rate duration is highest.

3. A bond with a low (or zero) coupon rate may have negative key rate durations for horizons other than its maturity. This is evidenced by some negative key rate durations for 1% and 2% coupon bonds in all three figures.

4. Callable bonds with low coupon rates are unlikely to be called; hence, their maturity-matched rate is their most critical rate (i.e., the highest key rate duration corresponds to the bond's maturity). For the 1% bond in Figure 3, the 15-year key rate duration exceeds all other key rate durations.

5. Keeping everything else (including market interest rates) constant, higher coupon bonds are more likely to be called, and therefore the time-to-exercise rate will tend to dominate the time-to-maturity rate. For the 8% coupon bond in Figure 3, the 10-year key rate duration is highest.

6. Putable bonds with high coupon rates are unlikely to be put and are most sensitive to their maturity-matched rates. For the 8% bond in Figure 4, the 15-year key rate duration is the highest.

7. Keeping everything else (including market interest rates) constant, lower coupon bonds are more likely to be put, and therefore the time-to-exercise rate will tend to dominate the time-to-maturity rate. For the 1% coupon bond in Figure 4, the 10-year key rate duration is highest.

LOS 37.l: Compare effective convexities of callable, putable, and straight bonds.

CFA® Program Curriculum, Volume 5, page 157

Straight bonds have positive effective convexity: the increase in the value of an option-free bond is higher when rates fall than the decrease in value when rates increase by an equal amount. When rates are high, callable bonds are unlikely to be called and will exhibit positive convexity. When the underlying call option is near the money, its effective convexity turns negative; the upside potential of the bond's price is limited due to the call (while the downside is not protected). Putable bonds exhibit positive convexity throughout.

LOS 37.m: Calculate the value of a capped or floored floating-rate bond.

CFA® Program Curriculum, Volume 5, page 160

A floating-rate bond ("floater") pays a coupon that adjusts every period based on an underlying reference rate. The coupon is typically paid in arrears, meaning the coupon rate is determined at the beginning of a period but is paid at the end of that period.

A **capped floater** effectively contains an issuer option that prevents the coupon rate from rising above a specified maximum rate known as the **cap**.

value of a capped floater = value of a "straight" floater – value of the embedded cap

A related floating rate bond is the **floored floater**, which has a coupon rate that will not fall below a specified minimum rate known as the **floor**. In this instance, the embedded option belongs to the investor and offers protection from falling interest rates.

value of a floored floater = value of a "straight" floater + value of the embedded floor

We can use the standard backward induction methodology in a binomial interest rate tree to value a capped or floored floater. As with the valuation of a bond with embedded options, we must adjust the value of the floater at each node to reflect the exercise of an in-the-money option (in this case, a cap or a floor).

Example: Value of a capped and floored floating-rate bond

Susane Albright works as a fixed income analyst with Zedone Banks, NA. She has been asked to value a $100 par, two-year, floating-rate note that pays LIBOR (set in arrears). The underlying bond has the same credit quality as reflected in the LIBOR swap curve. Albright has constructed the following two-year binomial LIBOR tree:

One-period forward rate

Year 0	*Year 1*
4.5749%	7.1826%
	5.3210%

How would we compute the following?

1. The value of the floater, assuming that it is an option-free bond.
2. The value of the floater, assuming that it is capped at a rate of 6%. Also compute the value of the embedded cap.
3. The value of the floater, assuming that it is floored at a rate of 5%. Also compute the value of the embedded floor.

Answer:

1. An option-free bond with a coupon rate equal to the required rate of return will be worth par value. Hence, the straight value of the floater is $100.

2. The value of the capped floater is $99.47, as shown below:

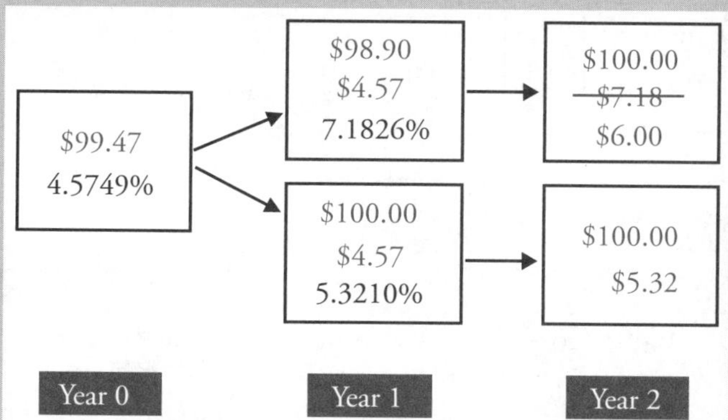

The upper node in year 2 shows the exercise of the cap (the coupon is capped at $6.00 instead of rising to $7.18).

Note that when the option is not in the money, the floater is valued at par.

$V_{1,U}$ = ($100 + $6) / (1 + 0.071826) = $98.90

$V_{1,L}$ = (100 + 5.3210) / (1 + 0.05321) = $100

The year 0 value is the average of the year 1 values (including their adjusted coupons) discounted for one period. In this case, the year 1 coupons require no adjustment, as the coupon rate is below the cap rate.

$$V_0 = \frac{[(98.90 + 4.57) + (100 + 4.57)]/2}{(1.045749)} = \$99.47$$

Thus the value of the embedded cap = $100 – $99.47 = 0.53.

3. The value of the floored floater is $100.41, as shown below:

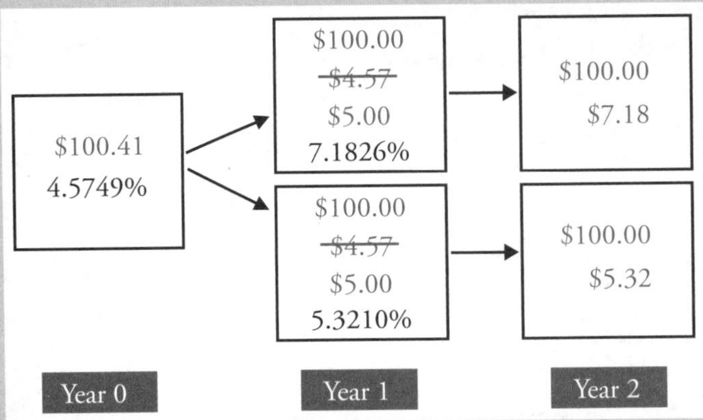

The nodes for year 2 show the coupons for that period (none of the rates are below the floor, and hence the floor is not exercised). Strikethroughs for both nodes in year 1 indicate that the floor was in the money; we replace the LIBOR-rate coupon with a coupon based on the floor strike rate of 5%.

The year 0 value is the average of the year 1 values (including their adjusted coupons) discounted for one period:

$$V_0 = \frac{[(100+5)+(100+5)]/2}{(1.045749)} = \$100.41$$

Thus the value of the embedded floor = $100.41 – $100 = $0.41.

LOS 37.n: Describe defining features of a convertible bond.

CFA® Program Curriculum, Volume 5, page 166

The owner of a **convertible bond** has the right to convert the bond into a fixed number of common shares of the issuer during a specified timeframe (**conversion period**) and at a fixed amount of money (**conversion price**). Convertibles allow investors to enjoy the upside on the issuer's stock, although this comes at a cost of lower yield. The issuer of a convertible bond benefits from a lower borrowing cost, but existing shareholders may face dilution if the conversion option is exercised.

The **conversion ratio** is the number of common shares for which a convertible bond can be exchanged. For example, a convertible bond issued at par with an initial conversion ratio of 10 allows its holder to convert one $1,000 par bond into 10 shares of common stock. Equivalently, the **conversion price** of the bond is $1,000 / 10 shares = $100. For bonds not issued at par, the conversion price is the issue price divided by the conversion ratio. Offer documents will indicate how the initial conversion ratio would be modified to account for corporate actions such as stock splits or stock dividends.

Offer documents may also provide a contingent put option in the event of any change-of-control events such as mergers. Such a contingent put option can be exercised for a specific period of time after the change of control. Alternatively, a lower conversion price may be specified in the event of a change of control. Other put options exercisable during specific periods may also be embedded with a convertible. These put options can be hard puts (i.e., redeemable for cash) or soft puts (i.e., the issuer decides whether to redeem the bond for cash, stock, subordinated debentures, or a combination of the three).

LOS 37.o: Calculate and interpret the components of a convertible bond's value.

CFA® Program Curriculum, Volume 5, page 173

The **conversion value** of a convertible bond is the value of the common stock into which the bond can be converted. The conversion ratio is the number of shares the holder receives from conversion for each bond. Conversion value is calculated as:

conversion value = market price of stock × conversion ratio

The **straight value**, or investment value, of a convertible bond is the value of the bond if it were not convertible—the present value of the bond's cash flows discounted at the return required on a comparable option-free issue.

The **minimum value of a convertible bond** is the greater of its conversion value or its straight value. This must be the case, or arbitrage opportunities would be possible. For example, if a convertible bond were to sell for less than its conversion value, it could be purchased, immediately converted into common stock, and the stock could be sold for more than the cost of the bond.

minimum value of a convertible bond = max (straight value, conversion value)

Example: Calculating the minimum value of a convertible bond

Business Supply Company, Inc. operates retail office equipment stores in the United States and Canada. Consider a BSC convertible bond with a 7% coupon that is currently selling at $985 with a conversion ratio of 25 and a straight value of $950. Suppose that the value of BSC's common stock is currently $35 per share, and that it pays $1 per share in dividends annually. What is this bond's minimum value?

Answer:

The conversion value of this bond is 25 × $35 = $875. Since the straight value of $950 is greater than the conversion value of $875, the bond is worth at least $950.

The market conversion price, or conversion parity price, is the price that the convertible bondholder would effectively pay for the stock if she bought the bond and immediately converted it. The market conversion price is given as:

$$\text{market conversion price} = \frac{\text{market price of convertible bond}}{\text{conversion ratio}}$$

Example: Calculating market conversion price

Compute and interpret the market conversion price of the BSC bond.

Answer:

The market conversion price is: \$985 / 25 = \$39.40. This can be viewed as the stock price at which an investor is indifferent between selling the bond and converting it.

The market conversion premium per share is the difference between the market conversion price and the stock's current market price:

market conversion premium per share
= market conversion price – stock's market price

Example: Calculating market conversion premium per share

Compute and interpret the market conversion premium per share of the BSC bond.

Answer:

Since BSC is selling for \$35 per share, the market conversion premium per share for the BSC bond is: \$39.40 – \$35 = \$4.40. This can be interpreted as the premium that investors are willing to pay for the opportunity to profit should the market price of the stock rise above the market conversion price. This is done with the assurance that even if the stock price declines, the value of the convertible bond will not fall below its straight value.

Market conversion premium per share is usually expressed as a ratio, appropriately called the **market conversion premium ratio**. Its formula is:

$$\text{market conversion premium ratio} = \frac{\text{market conversion premium per share}}{\text{market price of common stock}}$$

Example: Calculating market conversion premium ratio

Compute the market conversion premium ratio of the BSC bond.

Answer:

The BSC bond market conversion premium ratio is:

$$\frac{\$4.40}{\$35} = 12.57\%$$

The convertible bond investor's downside risk is limited by the bond's underlying straight value because the price of a convertible bond will not fall below this value regardless of what happens to the price of the issuer's common stock.

This downside risk is measured by the **premium over straight value**, which is calculated as:

$$\text{premium over straight value} = \left(\frac{\text{market price of convertible bond}}{\text{straight value}}\right) - 1$$

Example: Calculating premium over straight value

Compute and interpret the BSC bond's premium over straight value.

Answer:

The premium over straight value for the BSC bond is:

$$\left(\frac{\$985}{\$950}\right) - 1 = 3.68\%$$

Holding all other factors constant, the greater the premium over straight value, the less attractive the convertible bond.

We need to recognize an obvious flaw with the premium over straight value metric – the straight value is not constant. It varies with changes in interest rate and with the credit spread of the bond.

LOS 37.p: Describe how a convertible bond is valued in an arbitrage-free framework.

CFA® Program Curriculum, Volume 5, page 172

Investing in a noncallable/nonputable convertible bond is equivalent to buying:

- an option-free bond, and
- a call option on an amount of the common stock equal to the conversion ratio.

The value of a noncallable/nonputable convertible bond can be expressed as:

convertible, noncallable bond value = straight value + value of call option on stock

Most convertible bonds are callable, giving the issuer the right to call the issue prior to maturity. Incorporating this feature into the valuation of a convertible bond results in the following expression:

callable convertible bond value = straight value of bond
+ value of call option on stock
– value of call option on bond

To further complicate the situation (just for fun), consider a convertible bond that is both callable and putable. The expression for value then becomes:

callable and putable convertible bond value = straight value of bond
+ value of call option on stock
– value of call option on bond
+ value of put option on bond

LOS 37.q: Compare the risk–return characteristics of a convertible bond with the risk–return characteristics of a straight bond and of the underlying common stock.

CFA® Program Curriculum, Volume 5, page 173

Buying convertible bonds instead of stocks limits downside risk; the price floor set by the straight bond value provides this downside protection. The cost of the downside protection is reduced upside potential due to the conversion premium. Keep in mind though, that just like investing in nonconvertible bonds, convertible bond investors must be concerned with credit risk, call risk, interest rate risk, and liquidity risk.

Consider the following two examples based on our previous BSC example.

Example: Risk and return of a convertible bond, part 1

Calculate the return on the convertible bond and the common stock if the market price of BSC common stock increases to $45 per share.

Answer:

The return from investing in the convertible bond is:

$$\left(\frac{\$45.00}{\$39.40}\right)-1=14.2\%$$

The return from investing directly in the stock is:

$$\left(\frac{\$45.00}{\$35.00}\right)-1=0.2857=28.6\%$$

The lower return from the convertible bond investment is attributable to the fact that the investor effectively bought the stock at the market conversion price of $39.40 per share.

Example: Risk and return of a convertible bond, part 2

Calculate the return on the convertible bond and on the common stock if the market price of BSC common stock falls to $30 per share.

Answer:

Recall that the bond will trade at the greater of its straight value or its conversion value. The conversion value in this scenario is 25 × $30 = $750. Assuming the straight value of the bond does not change, the bond will trade at $950. So, the return from investing in the convertible bond is:

$$\left(\frac{\$950}{\$985}\right)-1 \;=-3.55\%$$

The return from investing directly in the stock is:

$$\left(\frac{\$30}{\$35}\right)-1 \;=-14.29\%$$

The loss is less for the convertible bond investment because we assumed that the straight value of the bond did not change. Even if it had changed, the loss would probably still be less than the loss on the straight stock investment, thus emphasizing how the straight value serves as a floor to cushion a decline, even if it is a moving floor.

The following comparisons can be made between ownership of the underlying stock and the risk-return characteristics of the convertible bond:

- When the stock's price falls, the returns on convertible bonds exceed those of the stock, because the convertible bond's price has a floor equal to its straight bond value.
- When the stock's price rises, the bond will underperform because of the conversion premium. This is the main drawback of investing in convertible bonds versus investing directly in the stock.
- If the stock's price remains stable, the return on a convertible bond may exceed the stock return due to the coupon payments received from the bond, assuming no change in interest rates or credit risk of the issuer.

Sometimes the price of the common stock associated with a convertible issue is so low that it has little or no effect on the convertible's market price, and the bond trades as though it is a straight bond. When this happens, the convertible security is referred to as a *fixed-income equivalent* or a *busted convertible.*

Other times, the price of the stock may be high enough that the price of the convertible behaves as though it is an equity security. When this happens, the convertible issue is referred to as a common stock equivalent. Most of the time, however, it is a *hybrid security* with the characteristics of equity and a fixed-income security.

Bond Analytics

Typical implementation of the binomial-tree models discussed in this topic review involves use of specialized software systems. The outputs of such systems must meet certain minimum qualifications:

1. **Put-call parity**

   Ensure that the option values obtained conform to basic put-call parity:

   C – P = PV(Forward price of the bond on exercise date) – PV(Exercise price)

   where:
   C and P = value of the embedded call and put option respectively.

2. **Option-free bond pricing**

   The valuation of option-free bonds should be independent of the assumed level of volatility used to generate the interest rate tree.

Key Concepts

LOS 37.a
Bonds with embedded options allow issuers to manage their interest rate risk or issue bonds at attractive coupon rates. The embedded options can be simple call or put options, or more complex options such as provisions for sinking fund, estate puts, et cetera.

LOS 37.b
Value of option embedded in a callable or putable bond:

$$V_{call} = V_{straight} - V_{callable}$$

$$V_{put} = V_{putable} - V_{straight}$$

LOS 37.c
To value a callable or a putable bond, the backward induction process and a binomial interest rate tree framework is used. The benchmark binomial interest rate tree is calibrated to ensure that it values benchmark bonds correctly (i.e., that it generates prices equal to their market prices).

LOS 37.d
When interest rate volatility increases, the value of both call and put options on bonds increase. As volatility increases, the value of a callable bond decreases (remember that the investor is short the call option) and the value of a putable bond increases (remember that the investor is long the put option).

LOS 37.e
The short call in a callable bond limits the investor's upside when rates decrease, while the long put in a putable bond hedges the investor against rate increases.

The value of the call option will be lower in an environment with an upward-sloping yield curve as the probability of the option going in the money is low. A call option gains value when the upward-sloping yield curve flattens. A put option will have a higher probability of going in the money when the yield curve is upward sloping; the option loses value if the upward-sloping yield curve flattens.

LOS 37.f
A backwards induction process is used in a binomial interest rate tree framework for valuing a callable (or putable) bond. In the binomial tree, we use one-period forward rates for each period. For valuing a callable (putable) bond, the value used at any node corresponding to a call (put) date must be either the price at which the issuer will call (investor will put) the bond, or the computed value if the bond is not called (put)—whichever is lower (higher).

LOS 37.g
The option adjusted spread (OAS) is the constant spread added to each forward rate in a benchmark binomial interest rate tree, such that the sum of the present values of a credit risky bond's cash flows equals its market price.

LOS 37.h
Binomial trees generated under an assumption of high volatility will lead to higher values for a call option and a corresponding lower value for a callable bond. Under a high volatility assumption, we would already have a lower computed value for the callable bond, and hence, the additional spread (i.e., the OAS) needed to force the discounted value to equal the market price will be lower.

When an analyst uses a lower-than-actual (higher-than-actual) level of volatility, the computed OAS for a callable bond will be too high (low) and the bond will be erroneously classified as underpriced (overpriced).

Similarly, when the analyst uses a lower-than-actual (higher-than-actual) level of volatility, the computed OAS for a putable bond will be too low (high) and the bond will be erroneously classified as overpriced (underpriced).

LOS 37.i

$$\text{effective duration} = \text{ED} = \frac{BV_{-\Delta y} - BV_{+\Delta y}}{2 \times BV_0 \times \Delta y}$$

LOS 37.j

effective duration (callable) $\leq$ effective duration (straight)

effective duration (putable) $\leq$ effective duration (straight)

LOS 37.k
For bonds with embedded options, one-sided durations—durations when interest rates rise versus when they fall—are better at capturing interest rate sensitivity than the more common effective duration. When the underlying option is at (or near) the money, callable (putable) bonds will have lower (higher) one-sided down-duration than one-sided up-duration.

Callable bonds with low coupon rates will most likely not be called and hence their maturity matched rate is their most critical rate (and has the highest key rate duration). As the coupon rate increases, a callable bond is more likely to be called and the time-to-exercise rate will start dominating the time-to-maturity rate.

Putable bonds with high coupon rates are unlikely to be put and are most sensitive to its maturity-matched rate. As the coupon rate decreases, a putable bond is more likely to be put and the time-to-exercise rate will start dominating the time-to-maturity rate.

LOS 37.l
Straight and putable bonds exhibit positive convexity throughout. Callable bonds also exhibit positive convexity when rates are high. However, at lower rates, callable bonds exhibit negative convexity.

LOS 37.m
A capped floater contains an issuer option that prevents the coupon rate on a floater from rising above a specified maximum (i.e., the cap) rate.

value of a capped floater = value of a "straight" floater – value of the embedded cap

A related floating-rate bond is the floored floater where the coupon rate will not fall below a specified minimum (i.e., the floor).

value of a floored floater = value of a "straight" floater + value of the embedded floor

LOS 37.n
The owner of a convertible bond can exchange the bond for the common shares of the issuer. A convertible bond includes an embedded call option giving the bondholder the right to buy the common stock of the issuer.

LOS 37.o
The conversion ratio is the number of common shares for which a convertible bond can be exchanged.

conversion value = market price of stock × conversion ratio

market conversion price = market price of convertible bond/conversion ratio

market conversion premium per share = market conversion price – market price

The minimum value at which a convertible bond trades is its straight value or its conversion value, whichever is greater.

LOS 37.p
The value of a bond with embedded options is determined as the value of the straight bond plus (minus) the value of options that the investor is long (short).

callable and putable convertible bond value = straight value of bond
+ value of call option on stock
– value of call option on bond
+ value of put option on bond

LOS 37.q
- The major benefit from investing in convertible bonds is the price appreciation resulting from an increase in the value of the common stock.
- The main drawback of investing in a convertible bond versus investing directly in the stock is that when the stock price rises, the bond will underperform the stock because of the conversion premium of the bond.
- If the stock price remains stable, the return on the bond may exceed the stock returns due to the coupon payments received from the bond.
- If the stock price falls, the straight value of the bond limits downside risk (assuming bond yields remain stable).

Study Session 13

Concept Checkers

1. Which of the following statements concerning the calculation of value at a node in a binomial interest rate tree is *most accurate*? The value at each node is the:
   A. present value of the two possible values from the next period.
   B. average of the present values of the two possible values from the next period.
   C. sum of the present values of the two possible values from the next period.

2. An increase in interest rate volatility:
   A. increases the value of bonds with embedded call options.
   B. increases the value of bonds with embedded put options.
   C. increases the value of low-coupon bonds with embedded options, but decreases the value of high-coupon bonds with embedded options.

3. The option adjusted spread (OAS) on a callable corporate bond is 73 basis points using on-the-run Treasuries as the benchmark rates in the construction of the binomial tree. The *best* interpretation of this OAS is the:
   A. cost of the embedded option is 73 basis points.
   B. cost of the option is 73 basis points over Treasury.
   C. spread that reflects the credit risk is 73 basis points over Treasury.

4. An analyst has gathered the following information on a convertible bond and the common equity of the issuer.
   - Market price of bond: $925.00
   - Annual coupon: 7.5%
   - Conversion ratio: 30
   - Market price of stock: $28.50
   - Annual stock dividend: $2.15 per share

   The market conversion premium ratio for the convertible bond is *closest* to:
   A. 7.56%.
   B. 7.77%.
   C. 8.18%.

5. Which of the following statements concerning a comparison between the risk and return of convertible bond investing versus common stock investing is *least accurate,* assuming interest rates are stable?
   A. When stock prices fall, the returns on convertible bonds are likely to exceed those of the stock because the convertible bond's price has a floor equal to the straight bond value.
   B. The main drawback of investing in convertible bonds versus direct stock purchases is that when stock prices rise, the convertible bond will likely underperform the stock due to the conversion premium.
   C. Buying convertible bonds instead of direct stock investing limits upside potential to that of buying a straight bond, at the cost of increased downside risk due to the conversion premium.

6. The difference between the value of a callable convertible bond and the value of an otherwise comparable option-free bond is *closest* to the value of the:
   A. call option on the stock minus value of the call option on the bond.
   B. put option on the stock plus value of the call option on the bond.
   C. call option on the stock plus value of call option on the bond.

7. With respect to the value of a callable convertible bond, the *most likely* effects of a decrease in interest rate volatility or a decrease in the underlying stock price volatility are:
   A. both will result in an increase in value.
   B. one will result in an increase in value, the other in a decrease.
   C. both will result in a decrease in value.

Challenge Problems

8. Data on two convertible bonds are shown in the following table.

	Convertible Bond ABC	*Convertible Bond XYZ*
Conversion price	$40	$50
Current stock price	$123	$8

Which factors are *most likely* to influence the market prices of ABC and XYZ: factors that affect equity prices, or factors that affect option-free bond prices?
A. Both will be more affected by equity factors.
B. One will be more affected by equity factors, the other by bond factors.
C. Both will be more affected by bond factors.

9. Ron Hyatt has been asked to do a presentation on how effective duration (ED) and effective convexity (EC) are calculated with a binomial model. His presentation includes the following formulas:

$$\text{effective duration} = \text{ED} = \frac{BV_{-\Delta y} - BV_{+\Delta y}}{2 \times BV_0 \times \Delta y}$$

$$\text{effective convexity} = \text{EC} = \frac{BV_{-\Delta y} + BV_{+\Delta y} - (2 \times BV_0)}{2 \times BV_0 \times \Delta y^2}$$

where:

Δy = change in required yield, in decimal form
$BV_{-\Delta y}$ = estimated price if yield decreases by Δy
$BV_{+\Delta y}$ = estimated price if yield increases by Δy
BV_0 = initial observed bond price

Are Hyatt's formulas for effective duration and effective convexity correctly presented?

A. The formulas are both correct.
B. One formula is correct, the other incorrect.
C. Both formulas are incorrect.

Use the following binomial interest rate tree to answer Questions 10 through 12.

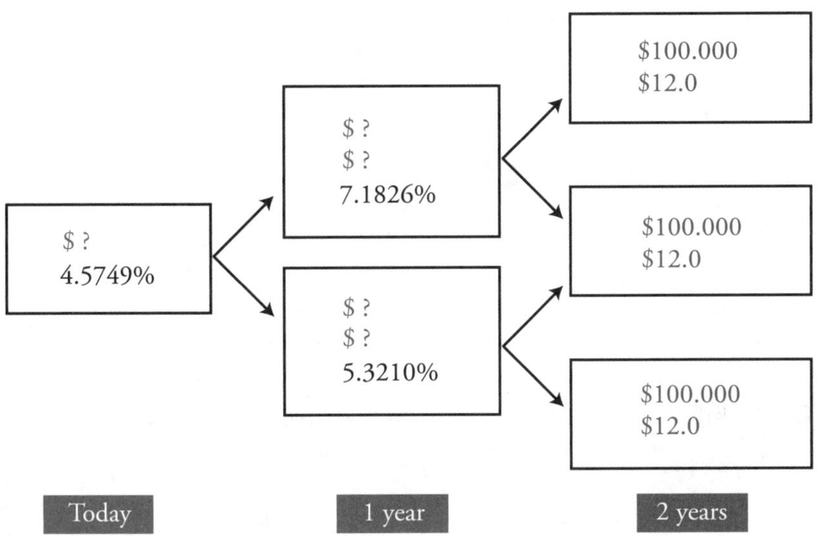

10. The value today of an option-free, 12% annual coupon bond with two years remaining until maturity is *closest* to:
    A. 110.525.
    B. 111.485.
    C. 112.282.

11. The value of the bond and the value of the embedded call option, assuming the bond in Question 10 is callable at $105 at the end of Year 1, are *closest* to:

Callable bond value	Embedded call option value
A. 110.573	1.709
B. 110.573	0.642
C. 111.640	0.642

12. The value of the bond and the value of the embedded put option, assuming the bond in Question 10 is putable at $105 at the end of Year 1, are *closest* to:

Putable bond value	Embedded put option value
A. 112.523	0.241
B. 112.523	1.646
C. 113.928	1.646

Use the following information to answer Questions 13 through 20.

Vincent Osagae, CFA is the fixed income portfolio manager for Alpha Specialists, an institutional money manager. Vanessa Alwan, an intern, has suggested a list of bonds for Osagae's consideration as shown in Figure 1. The benchmark yield curve is currently upward sloping.

Figure 1: Selected Bonds for Consideration

- Bond X, a 3%, 15-year option-free bond.
- Bond Y, a 3%, 15-year callable bond.
- Bond Z, a 3%, 15-year putable bond.

Osagae then turns his attention to a newly issued 4%, 15-year bond issued by Suni Corp. The bond has a Bermudan-style call option exercisable annually at any time after year 4. Osagae computes an OAS of 145 bps for this bond using a binomial interest rate tree. The tree was generated with U.S. Treasury rates and an assumed volatility of 15% which was consistent with historical data. Option markets are currently pricing interest rate options at an implied volatility of 19%.

Every week, Alwan meets with Osagae to discuss what she had learned over the week. At one of their weekly meetings, Alwan makes the following statements about key rate duration:

Statement 1: The highest key rate duration of a low-coupon callable bond corresponds to the bond's time-to-exercise.

Statement 2: The highest key rate duration of a high-coupon putable bond corresponds to the bond's time-to-maturity.

Beth Grange, a senior analyst reporting to Osagae has generated the following two-year LIBOR tree using a 15% volatility assumption:

Figure 2: LIBOR Tree

0	*1*
2.0000%	3.4637%
	2.5660%

Grange has also compiled OAS for two very similar callable corporate bonds as shown in Figure 3.

Figure 3: OAS at 10% Volatility

Bond	*OAS*
A	46 bps
B	34 bps

13. In Figure 1, which bond's embedded option is *most likely* to increase in value if the yield curve flattens?
    A. Bond Y.
    B. Bond Z.
    C. Neither Bond Y nor Bond Z.

14. If Osagae had used implied volatility from U.S. Treasury options to compute the OAS for Suni Corp bond, the estimated OAS would *most likely* have been:
    A. lower than 145 bps.
    B. higher than 145 bps.
    C. equal to 145 bps.

15. Which bond in Figure 1 is *most likely* to have the highest effective duration?
    A. Bond X.
    B. Bond Y.
    C. Bond Z.

16. Regarding Alwan's statements about key rate durations:
    A. only one statement is correct.
    B. both statements are correct.
    C. neither statement is correct.

17. Which bond in Figure 1 is *least likely* to experience the highest increase in value, given a parallel downward shift of 150bps in the yield curve?
    A. Bond X.
    B. Bond Y.
    C. Bond Z.

18. Which bond in Figure 1 is *most likely* to experience an increase in effective duration due to an increase in interest rates?
    A. Bond X.
    B. Bond Y.
    C. Bond Z.

19. In Figure 3, relative to bond A, bond B is *most likely*:
    A. overpriced.
    B. underpriced.
    C. fairly priced.

20. Using the data in Figure 2, the value of a $100 par, two-year, 3% capped floater is *closest* to:
    A. $0.31.
    B. $98.67.
    C. $99.78.

To access other content related to this topic review that may be included in the Schweser package you purchased, log in to your Schweser.com online dashboard. Schweser's OnDemand Video Lectures deliver streaming instruction covering every LOS in this topic review, while SchweserPro™ QBank provides additional quiz questions to help you practice and recall what you've learned.

Answers – Concept Checkers

1. **B** The value at any given node in a binomial tree is the average of the present values of the cash flows at the two possible states immediately to the right of the given node, discounted at the one-period rate at the node under examination.

2. **B** Like ordinary options, the value of an embedded option increases as volatility increases. Furthermore, the arbitrage-free value of an option-free bond ($V_{option\text{-}free}$) is independent of the assumed volatility. This implies that the arbitrage-free value of a callable bond ($V_{callable}$) decreases as volatility increases the value of the embedded call option (V_{call}). This can be seen from the expression for the value of a callable bond:

$$\downarrow V_{callable} = V_{option\text{-}free} - \uparrow V_{call}$$

The value of the putable bond ($V_{putable}$) increases as the assumed volatility increases the value of the embedded put option (V_{put}).

$$\uparrow V_{putable} = V_{option\text{-}free} + \uparrow V_{put}$$

3. **C** Let's construct a table of the risk differences between the issuer's callable bond and on-the-run Treasuries to help us answer this question.

Type of Risk	*Equal?*
Credit	No
Option	Removed by OAS

Therefore, the OAS reflects the credit risk of the corporate callable bond over Treasuries, since option risk has been removed.

4. **C** The market conversion premium per share is the market conversion price per share minus the market price per share. The market conversion price per share is

$\frac{925.00}{30} = \$30.833$, so the conversion premium per share is \$30.833 – \$28.50 = \$2.333.

$$\text{market conversion premium ratio} = \frac{\text{market conversion premium per share}}{\text{market price of common stock}}$$
$$= \frac{2.33}{28.50} = 8.18\%$$

5. **C** Buying convertible bonds in lieu of direct stock investing limits downside risk to that of straight bond investing, at the cost of reduced upside potential due to the conversion premium. (Note that this analysis assumes that interest rates remain stable. Otherwise, the interest rate risk associated with the straight bond investing must be considered.) When stock prices fall, the returns on convertible bonds are likely to exceed those of the stock, because the convertible bond's price has a floor equal to the straight bond value. The main drawback of investing in convertible bonds versus direct stock purchases is that when stock prices rise, the convertible bond is likely to underperform due to the conversion premium. If the stock price remains stable, the return on the bond may exceed the stock's return if the bond's coupon payment exceeds the dividend income of the stock.

6. **A** A bond that is both callable and convertible contains two embedded options: (1) a call option on the stock and (2) a call option on the bond. The investor has a *short* position in the call option on the bond (the issuer has the right to call the bond) and a *long* position in the call option on the stock (the investor has the right to convert the bond into shares of stock). Therefore, the difference in value between the callable convertible bond and the value of the comparable option-free bond to the investor is equal to the value of the call option on the stock minus the value of the call option on the bond.

7. **B** A decrease in interest rate volatility will decrease the value of the embedded short call on the bond (but have no effect on the value of the embedded call on the stock) and increase the value of the convertible bond.

   A decrease in stock price volatility will decrease the value of the embedded call on the stock (but have no effect on the embedded call on the bond) and decrease the value of the convertible bond.

Answers – Challenge Problems

8. **B** ABC has a conversion price much less than the current stock price, so the conversion option is deep in the money. Bond ABC effectively trades like equity and is more likely to be influenced by the same factors that affect equity prices, in general, than the factors that affect bond prices.

   A busted convertible like XYZ, with a stock price significantly less than the conversion price, trades like a bond (that's why a busted convertible is also called a fixed-income equivalent) and is therefore more likely to be influenced by the factors that affect bond prices.

9. **B** The duration formula is presented correctly. The convexity formula is presented incorrectly; the "2" should not appear in the denominator of the convexity formula.

$$\text{effective convexity} = \text{EC} = \frac{BV_{-\Delta y} + BV_{+\Delta y} - (2 \times BV_0)}{BV_0 \times \Delta y^2}$$

10. **C** The tree should look like this:

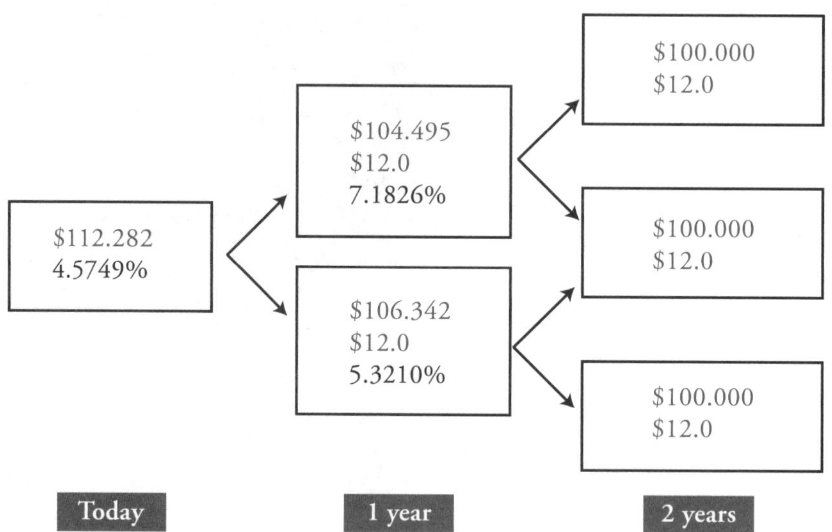

Consider the value of the bond at the upper node for Period 1, $V_{1,U}$:

$$V_{1,U} = \frac{1}{2} \times \left[\frac{\$100 + \$12}{1.071826} + \frac{\$100 + \$12}{1.071826}\right] = \$104.495$$

Similarly, the value of the bond at the lower node for Period 1, $V_{1,L}$ is:

$$V_{1,L} = \frac{1}{2} \times \left[\frac{\$100 + \$12}{1.053210} + \frac{\$100 + \$12}{1.053210}\right] = \$106.342$$

Now calculate V_0, the current value of the bond at Node 0:

$$V_0 = \frac{1}{2} \times \left[\frac{\$104.495 + \$12}{1.045749} + \frac{\$106.342 + \$12}{1.045749}\right] = \$112.282$$

11. **C** The tree should look like this:

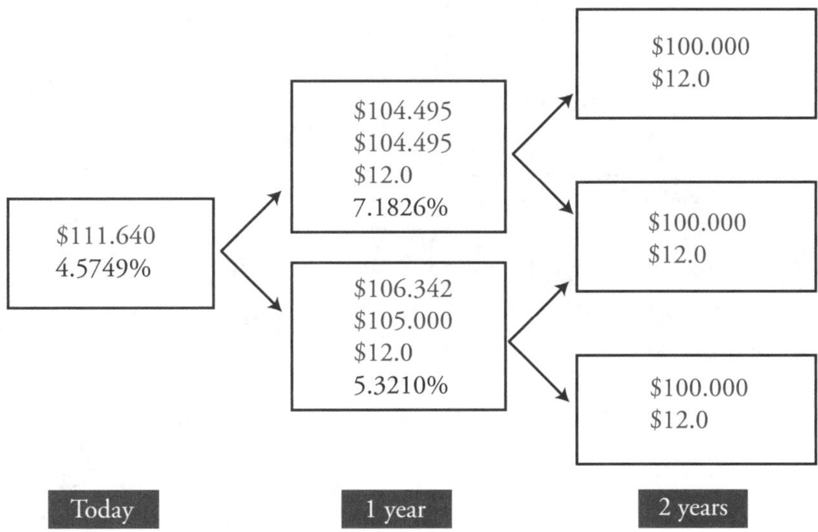

Consider the value of the bond at the upper node for Period 1, $V_{1,U}$:

$$V_{1,U} = \frac{1}{2}\times\left[\frac{\$100+\$12}{1.071826}+\frac{\$100+\$12}{1.071826}\right]=\$104.495$$

Similarly, the value of the bond at the lower node for Period 1, $V_{1,L}$ is:

$$V_{1,L} = \frac{1}{2}\times\left[\frac{\$100+\$12}{1.053210}+\frac{\$100+\$12}{1.053210}\right]=\$106.342$$

Now calculate V_0, the current value of the bond at Node 0:

$$V_0 = \frac{1}{2}\times\left[\frac{\$104.495+\$12}{1.045749}+\frac{\$105.00+\$12}{1.045749}\right]=\$111.640$$

The value of the embedded call option is $112.282 – $111.640 = $0.642.

12. **A** The tree should look like this:

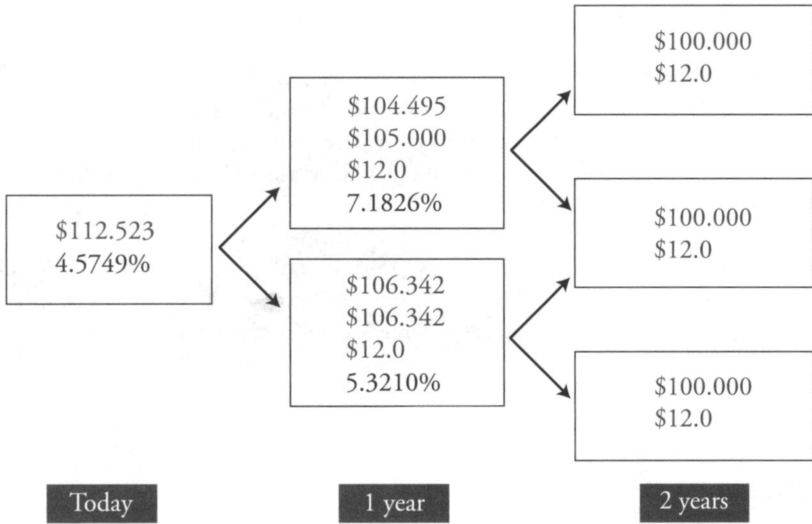

Consider the value of the bond at the *upper* node for Period 1, $V_{1,U}$:

$$V_{1,U} = \frac{1}{2} \times \left[\frac{\$100 + \$12}{1.071826} + \frac{\$100 + \$12}{1.071826} \right] = \$104.495$$

Similarly, the value of the bond at the lower node for Period 1, $V_{1,L}$, is:

$$V_{1,L} = \frac{1}{2} \times \left[\frac{\$100 + \$12}{1.053210} + \frac{\$100 + \$12}{1.053210} \right] = \$106.342$$

Now calculate V_0, the current value of the bond at Node 0:

$$V_0 = \frac{1}{2} \times \left[\frac{\$105.000 + \$12}{1.045749} + \frac{\$106.342 + \$12}{1.045749} \right] = \$112.523$$

The value of the embedded put option is \$112.523 – \$112.282 = \$0.241.

13. **A** When an upward sloping yield curve flattens, call options increase in value while put options decrease in value.

14. **A** When the assumed volatility in a binomial tree increases, the computed value of OAS will decrease. When an analyst uses a lower-than-actual level of volatility like the 15% volatility assumed here, the computed OAS for a callable bond will be too high. Using the 19% implied volatility instead would have resulted in an estimated OAS lower than 145 bps.

15. **A** Straight bonds generally have higher effective durations than bonds with embedded options. Both call and put options have the potential to reduce the life of a bond, so the duration of callable and putable bonds will be less than or equal to that of their straight counterparts.

16. **A** Statement 1 is incorrect. Low-coupon callable bonds are unlikely to be called; hence, their highest key rate duration corresponds to their time-to-maturity. Statement 2 is correct. High coupon putable bonds are unlikely to be put and hence, their highest key rate duration corresponds to their time-to-maturity.

17. **B** Straight and putable bonds exhibit positive convexity at all interest rate levels. The price appreciation for a callable bond due to decline in interest rate is limited due to the call feature; callables exhibit negative convexity at low rates. Hence a decline in rates is least likely to result in best price performance for a callable bond.

18. **B** When interest rates increase, a callable bond becomes less likely to be called (its duration will increase). The put option in a putable bond would be more likely to be exercised in a rising interest rate scenario and hence, the duration of a putable bond would decrease. Duration of an option-free bond would also decrease as interest rate increases (but not as significantly).

19. **A** Relative to bond A, bond B has lower OAS. Given that the two bonds have similar credit risk, bond B offers a lower OAS for the same level of risk as bond A and thus would be considered overpriced. Alternatively, bond A is more attractive (underpriced) relative to bond B.

20. **C** The value of the capped floater is $99.78, as shown below:

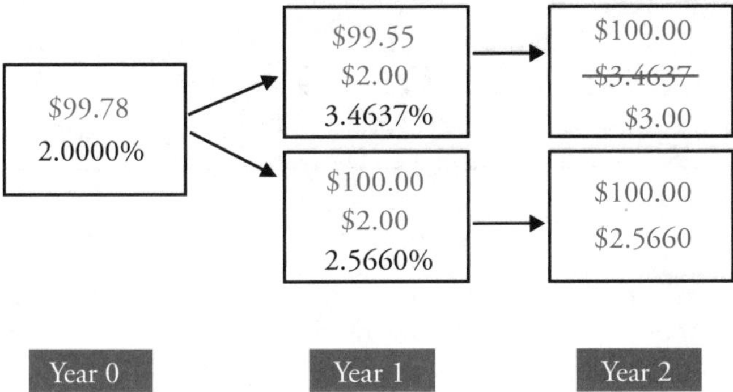

The upper node at Year 2 is subject to the 3% cap, and the coupon is adjusted accordingly.

$V_{1,U}$ = $103 / (1.03467) = $99.55

$V_{1,L}$ = 100 (option is not exercised).

$$V_0 = \frac{[(100+2)+(99.55+2)]/2}{(1.02)} = 99.78$$

The following is a review of the Fixed Income: Topics in Fixed Income Analysis principles designed to address the learning outcome statements set forth by CFA Institute. Cross-Reference to CFA Institute Assigned Reading #38.

Credit Analysis Models

Study Session 13

Exam Focus

This topic review augments credit analysis covered at Level I with newer models of credit analysis including structural models and reduced form models. Be able to differentiate between the two and know the merits and drawbacks of both. Finally, be able to compute the present value of expected loss.

Credit Models

Models of credit analysis seek to evaluate and measure credit risk for risky bonds. Traditional models include credit scoring models and credit rating models. Since the global financial crisis of 2008, newer models of credit analysis take into account the influence of systemic default risk on credit risk measurement.

LOS 38.a: Explain probability of default, loss given default, expected loss, and present value of the expected loss and describe the relative importance of each across the credit spectrum.

CFA® Program Curriculum, Volume 5, page 205

Measures of Credit Risk

Credit risk is the risk associated with losses stemming from the failure of a borrower to make timely and full payments of interest or principal.

Credit metrics:

- **Probability of default**, or *default probability*, is the probability that a borrower (i.e., the bond issuer) fails to pay interest or repay principal when due.
- **Loss given default** refers to the value a bond investor will lose if the issuer defaults. Loss given default can be stated as a monetary amount or as a percentage of a bond's value (principal and unpaid interest). Loss given default varies inversely with the recovery rate.
- **Recovery rate** is the percentage of money received upon default of the issuer.

Loss given default (%) = 100 – recovery rate

- **Expected loss** is equal to the probability of default multiplied by the loss given default. Expected loss can be stated as a monetary value or as a percentage of a bond's value. Expected loss depends on the state of the economy: during boom times, the probability of default as well as loss given default will be lower.

- **Present value of expected loss** is the highest price a hypothetical investor would be willing to pay to an insurer to bear the credit risk of the investment. The present value of expected loss makes two adjustments to the expected loss measure:
    1. Time value adjustment: Future expected losses are discounted to their present value, reflecting that a loss of principal far in the future is less of a concern than a near-term loss.
    2. Risk-neutral probabilities: Adjustment to the probabilities of default is a more complex adjustment that accounts for the risk of the cash flows and is called the *risk premium*. Instead of using the probability of default, we use the risk-neutral probability of default. The difference between actual probabilities of default and risk-neutral probabilities is the adjustment for risk. This process of adjustment of probabilities is similar to risk-neutral valuation of options whereby the probabilities of up and down movements on the stock are not based on expectations of market movements but rather on current stock price equated to the present value (at risk-free interest rate) of future *expected* stock price.

The present value of expected loss is the difference between the value of a credit-risky bond and an otherwise identical risk-free bond. PVEL is the most important of the four metrics discussed.

present value of expected loss = (value of risk-free bond) – (value of credit-risky bond)

The relationship between present value of expected loss (PVEL) and expected loss (EL) can be summarized as follows:

present value of expected loss = expected loss + risk premium – time value discount

or

present value of expected loss – expected loss = risk-premium – time value discount

Hence when the present value of expected loss is greater than expected loss, the risk premium is greater than the time value discount.

The difference between the yield to maturity of a credit-risky zero coupon bond and the yield to maturity of a risk-free zero coupon bond is called the **credit spread** on the credit-risky bond. Credit spread includes measures of probability of default, loss given default, and time value of money (including the adjustment for risk premium as discussed earlier).

LOS 38.b: Explain credit scoring and credit ratings.

CFA® Program Curriculum, Volume 5, page 207

Traditional credit models include credit scoring models and credit ratings. These models provide **ordinal rankings** of credit quality. Ordinal rankings categorize borrowers from highest to lowest risk but do not communicate the *degree* to which the credit risk differs among different ranks.

Credit scoring is used for small businesses and individuals. A higher score indicates better credit quality. FICO is a well-known example of a credit scoring model used in the United States. Characteristics of credit scoring models include:

- Credit scores are ordinal rankings. The credit risk of an individual with a credit score of 900 is not equal to half the credit risk of an individual with a credit score of 450.
- Credit scores are not percentile rankings, and the distribution of credit scores change over time.
- Credit scores do not explicitly take into account current economic conditions; credit scores do not improve with the economy.
- Credit scoring agencies are under pressure from users of credit scores (lenders) to prioritize stability in scores over time (even if it reduces the predictive accuracy of the score).
- Credit scoring does not take into account differing probabilities of default for different loans taken out by the same borrower. For example, an individual is more likely to default on a credit card loan than to default on a mortgage (due to differing consequences for each default); however, the same credit score is considered for both loans.

Credit ratings are issued for corporate debt, asset-backed securities, and government and quasi-government debt.

Figure 1 shows ratings scales used by Standard & Poor's and Moody's Investors Service—two of the major credit rating agencies. Standard & Poor's considers bonds rated BBB– and above to be investment-grade bonds, while Moody's Investors Service considers investment-grade bonds to be those rated Baa3 and above. All other bonds are considered noninvestment-grade bonds, also called speculative-grade or "junk" bonds.

Figure 1: Ratings Scale for Standard & Poor's and Moody's Investors Service

	Moody's Investors Service	Standard & Poor's
Investment Grade	Aaa	AAA
	Aa1	AA+
	Aa2	AA
	Aa3	AA-
	A1	A+
	A2	A
	A3	A-
	Baa1	BBB+
	Baa2	BBB
	Baa3	BBB-

	Moody's Investors Service	Standard & Poor's
Speculative Grade	Ba1	BB+
	Ba2	BB
	Ba3	BB-
	B1	B+
	B2	B
	B3	B-
	Caa1	CCC+
	Caa2	CCC
	Caa3	CCC-
	Ca	CC
	C	D

Credit ratings summarize the results of credit analysis of a borrower in one simple-to-communicate metric. Credit rating agencies arose to take advantage of the significant economies of scale inherent in collection and analysis of credit-related information.

Some rating agencies are compensated by the users of the ratings. In other instances, the borrowers pay for being rated by credit rating agencies. The **issuer-pays** model suffers from an inherent conflict of interest: the rating agency could feel pressure to issue the payer a favorable rating.

Credit rating agencies may also feel pressure to keep their ratings stable over time to reduce debt market volatility. This preference for ratings stability leads lower correlation between credit ratings and default probabilities over time.

LOS 38.c: Explain strengths and weaknesses of credit ratings.

CFA® Program Curriculum, Volume 5, page 212

Strengths of Credit Ratings

- Credit ratings are simple to understand and summarize complex credit analysis in one metric.
- Credit ratings tend to be relatively stable over time, reducing volatility in the debt markets.

Weaknesses of Credit Ratings

- The stability in credit ratings comes at the expense of a reduction in correlation with default probability.
- Ratings do not adjust with the business cycle, even though the probability of default changes with the business cycle.
- In the case of the issuer-pays model, the conflicts of interest may make the ratings less reliable. When an issuer pays a ratings agency for a credit rating, the independence of the rating agency may be compromised. In its pursuit of profits, a rating agency may assign a higher rating to an issuer than the agency otherwise would, resulting in lower reliability of the ratings.

LOS 38.d: Explain structural models of corporate credit risk, including why equity can be viewed as a call option on the company's assets.

CFA® Program Curriculum, Volume 5, page 213

Structural Models

Structural models of corporate credit risk are based on the structure of a company's balance sheet and rely on insights provided by option pricing theory.

Option Analogy

Consider a hypothetical company with assets that are financed by equity and a single issue of zero-coupon debt. The value of the assets at any point in time is the sum of the value of equity and value of debt. Due to the limited liability nature of corporate equity, the shareholders effectively have a call option on the company's assets with a strike price equal to the face value of debt. If at the maturity of the debt, the value of the company's assets is higher than the face value of debt, the shareholders will exercise their call option to acquire the assets (and then pay off the debt and keep the residual). On the other hand, if the value of the company's assets is less than the face value of debt, the shareholders will let the option expire worthless (i.e., default on the debt), leaving the company's assets to the debt holders.

Hence, at time *T* (maturity of debt):

$$\text{Value of stock}_T = \text{Max}\ (0, A_T - K)$$

$$\text{Value of debt}_T = \text{Min}\ (A_T, K)$$

where:
A_T = value of company's assets at time *T* (i.e., at maturity of debt)
K = face value of debt

Based on the above analysis, we can also say that owning risky debt with a face value of *K* is equivalent to owning a risk-free bond with the same face value (*K*) and writing a European put option on the assets of the company with a strike price of *K*. If the value of the assets is greater than the face value of debt, the put option will be out of money and not exercised, and the debt holder will simply receive the face value. If the value of the assets ends up being lower than the face value of debt, the put option will be in the money and will be exercised; the debt holder will receive only the value of the assets.

We can express this relationship as:

value of risky debt = value of risk-free debt – value of put option on company's assets

Valuation

Using the option analogy, the value of debt can be computed as:

$$D_t = A_t N(-d_1) + Ke^{-r(T-t)}N(d_2)$$

Where:
N(.) = cumulative standard normal distribution function

$$d_1 = \frac{\ln\left(\frac{A_t}{K}\right) + r(T-t) + \frac{1}{2}\sigma^2(T-t)}{\sigma\sqrt{T-t}}$$

$$d_2 = d_1 - \sigma\sqrt{T-t}$$

r = continuously compounded risk-free rate
σ = standard deviation of asset returns

Professor's Note: The LOS command word is "Explain."

The first term in the previous equation is the present value of payoff on the company's debt if default occurs. The second term is the present value of payoff if default does not occur.

Risk Measures

Structural models allow us to estimate the components of credit risk: probability of default, expected loss, and present value of expected loss.

$$\text{probability of default} = 1 - N(e_2)$$

where:

$$e_1 = \frac{\ln\left(\frac{A_t}{K}\right) + \mu(T-t) + \frac{1}{2}\sigma^2(T-t)}{\sigma\sqrt{T-t}}$$

$$e_2 = e_1 - \sigma\sqrt{T-t}$$

where:
μ = annual rate of return on company assets.

Then the expected loss is:

$$\text{expected loss} = KN(-e_2) - A_t e^{\mu(T-t)}N(-e_1)$$

The present value of the expected loss is the value of a riskless zero-coupon bond minus the value of the debt:

$$\text{present value of expected loss} = Ke^{-r(T-t)}N(-d_2) - A_tN(-d_1)$$

Input Estimates

Use of structural models requires estimates of μ (expected return on company's assets) and σ^2 (asset return volatility). Regardless of the assumptions (discussed later) of the structural models, a company's assets are not traded and, hence, these parameters are not directly observable; we cannot estimate them using historical data. We can, however, use **implicit estimation techniques** (also known as **calibration**) if the company's stock is traded. This estimation technique is similar to solving for implied stock volatility using market prices for options traded on the stock.

LOS 38.e: Explain reduced form models of corporate credit risk, including why debt can be valued as the sum of expected discounted cash flows after adjusting for risk.

CFA® Program Curriculum, Volume 5, page 221

One of the key assumptions of the structural model is that the assets of the company are traded in the market. This restrictive assumption makes the structural model impractical. **Reduced form models of corporate credit risk** do not impose assumptions on the company's balance sheet, instead they impose assumptions on the output of a structural model. Reduced form models also allow the analyst flexibility to incorporate real world conditions in the model.

Reduced form models allow the input parameters to vary with changing economic conditions.

The value of the debt under a reduced form model is:

$$D_t = \tilde{E}\left(\frac{K}{\prod(1+r_i)}\right)$$

where:
K = face value of debt
Π = product operator (similar to Σ, but the terms are multiplied not added)
i = t to T
$\tilde{E}$ = Expectation operator using risk-neutral probabilities
r_i = Risk-free rate for year i

Note that the risk-free rate is no longer constant under the reduced form model. The risk in the cash flows is accounted for by using risk-neutral probabilities instead of actual probabilities of default.

In an extremely simplified (and unrealistic) scenario where the probability of default per year (λ) and loss given default % (γ) for a zero-coupon bond are constant, the value of a credit-risky zero coupon bond is given by:

$$D_t = Ke^{-\lambda\gamma r(T-t)} = Ke^{-\lambda\gamma(T-t)}P_t$$

where:
P_t = present value (at risk-free rate) of \$1 received at time T

The credit measures are given by:

$\lambda\gamma$ = (probability of default per year) × (loss given default %)

= expected percentage loss per year

Probability of default (over remaining life) = $1 - e^{-\lambda(T-t)}$

$$\text{Expected loss} = K(1 - e^{-\lambda\gamma(T-t)})$$

$$\text{Present value of expected loss} = KP_t - D_t = KP_t(1 - e^{-\lambda\gamma(T-t)})$$

In this simple formulation, the expected loss will always be greater than the present value of expected loss.

Input Estimates

Unlike estimation of inputs for structural models, the inputs for reduced form models can be estimated with historical data using a technique called **hazard rate estimation**. Hazard rate estimation entails estimating probability of a binary event such as default versus no default and can be done using logistic regression.

LOS 38.f: Explain assumptions, strengths, and weaknesses of both structural and reduced form models of corporate credit risk.

CFA® Program Curriculum, Volume 5, page 230

Structural Model

Assumptions of the structural model:

1. The company's assets are traded in a frictionless arbitrage-free market with a time T value that has a lognormal distribution with mean μT and variance $\sigma^2 T$. Under this assumption, the assets have a rate of return of μ% per year. The asset return volatility (σ^2) is also assumed to be constant.

2. The risk-free interest rate (r) is constant over time. This assumption implies that there is no interest rate risk, which is illogical in fixed-income valuation.

3. The company has a simple balance sheet structure with only one class of simple zero-coupon debt.

Strengths of structural models:

1. Allow us to use option pricing theory to understand a company's probability of default and loss given default.

2. The structural model can be estimated using current market prices.

Weaknesses of structural models:

1. Balance sheet cannot be modeled realistically using a single zero-coupon bond, meaning that recovery rates and default probabilities may be inaccurate.

2. Company assets are not actually traded and, hence, their value is not directly observable. Therefore, the practical application of structural models relies on (inaccurate) implicit estimation procedures for model inputs. These inaccuracies result in errors in estimating credit measures.

3. Estimation procedures do not consider the business cycle.

Reduced Form Model

Assumptions of the reduced form model:

1. The company has a zero-coupon bond liability that trades in frictionless and arbitrage-free markets. There is no restriction for other liabilities of the company. This is not a restrictive assumption; other liabilities could be used in lieu of the zero coupon bond.

2. The risk-free interest rate (r) is stochastic (i.e., varies randomly).

3. The state of the economy is stochastic and depends on nonconstant macroeconomic variables.

4. The probability of default depends on the state of the economy and is not constant. This assumption specifically allows for credit risk to vary across the business cycle and also allows for the possibility of systemic default across companies.

5. While the probability of default varies with the state of the economy, whether a particular company actually defaults depends only on company-specific considerations.

6. The recovery rate (hence, loss given default) is also stochastic and depends on the state of the economy.

Strengths of reduced form models:

1. Since model inputs are observable, historical estimation procedures can be used.

2. Credit risk is allowed to fluctuate with the business cycle.

3. Reduced form models do not require specification of the company's balance sheet structure.

Weaknesses of reduced form models:

1. Unless the model has been formulated and backtested properly, the hazard rate estimation procedures (using past observations to predict the future) may not be valid.

Comparison of Different Approaches

The three models for evaluating credit risk (credit ratings, structural models, and reduced form models) have been tested to evaluate their ability to predict the probability with which debt will default.

Of the three, credit ratings have been found to be the least accurate credit risk evaluation approach because they tend to be relatively stable and lag the market.

Reduced form models perform better than structural models due to the flexibility of the hazard rate estimation procedures that reduced form models use. Reduced form models are able to incorporate the business cycle, thus, not being required to make simplifying assumptions about the balance sheet structure.

LOS 38.g: Explain the determinants of the term structure of credit spreads.

CFA® Program Curriculum, Volume 5, page 232

The **term structure of credit spreads** represents the relationship of credit spreads to debt maturity. For term structure purposes, credit spread is the difference between yield on a zero-coupon, credit-risky bond and the yield on a zero-coupon, risk-free bond. In other words, the credit spread is the difference in spot rates for credit-risky bonds and risk-free bonds.

To estimate the credit spread for a specific maturity, one needs to **bootstrap** spot rates using coupon bond prices for both risky bonds and risk-free bonds.

The average credit spread over a specific horizon can then be used as an estimate for expected percentage loss per year on the risky zero-coupon bond.

We should recognize that even though we assumed frictionless markets under both reduced form and structural models, the market for corporate bonds is not frictionless. Therefore, the credit spread as computed *includes* a premium for liquidity risk in addition to credit risk.

LOS 38.h: Calculate and interpret the present value of the expected loss on a bond over a given time horizon.

CFA® Program Curriculum, Volume 5, page 234

As stated earlier, the difference in the value of a risk-free bond and a similar risky bond is the present value of expected loss. This is the maximum amount an investor would pay an insurer to bear the credit risk of the risky bond.

We can estimate the present value of expected loss from credit spread on a risky bond, as demonstrated next.

Professor's Note: The computation of present value of expected loss uses continuously compounded interest rates: $PV = FV \times e^{-rT}$. The negative sign in front of the rate implies that FV is discounted to find PV.

Example: Present value of expected loss

ABC Inc. has a 6% semiannual coupon bond outstanding that is maturing in 3 years. Information on the risk-free rate and credit spread for the next 3 years is given in the following table. Assume all rates are continuously compounded.

Time (yrs)	*Risk-Free Rate*	*Credit Spread*
0.50	0.11%	0.03%
1.00	0.16%	0.07%
1.50	0.21%	0.08%
2.00	0.22%	0.09%
2.50	0.27%	0.09%
3.00	0.31%	0.10%

Compute the present value of expected loss for:

1. The payment due in 2 years.
2. The bond.

Answer:

Time (yrs)	*Risk-Free Rate*	*Credit Spread*	*Total Yield*	*Cash Flow*	*PV(Risk-Free)*	*PV(Risky)*	*Difference*
0.50	0.11%	0.03%	0.14%	30	$29.98	$29.98	$0.00
1.00	0.16%	0.07%	0.23%	30	$29.95	$29.93	$0.02
1.50	0.21%	0.08%	0.29%	30	$29.91	$29.87	$0.04
2.00	0.22%	0.09%	0.31%	30	$29.87	$29.81	$0.05
2.50	0.27%	0.09%	0.36%	30	$29.80	$29.73	$0.07
3.00	0.31%	0.10%	0.41%	1030	$1,020.47	$1,017.41	$3.06
				Total	$1,169.97	$1,166.73	$3.24

The PV(risk-free) is the present value of the cash flow computed using the risk-free rate.

For example, the first coupon payment:

$$\text{PV(risk-free)} = 30e^{-(0.0011)(0.5)} = 29.98$$

$$\text{PV(risky)} = 1{,}030e^{-(0.0041)(3.0)} = 1{,}017.41$$

1. The present value of expected loss for payment due in 2 years = PV(risk-free) – PV(risky) = 29.87 – 29.81 = $0.06.
2. The present value of expected loss for the bond = 1,169.97 – 1,166.73 = $3.24.

Professor's Note: To solve $30e^{-(0.0011)(0.5)}$ *on your BA II Plus, use the following keystrokes:*

0.0011[×]0.5[=][+|–][2ND][LN][×]30[=]

LOS 38.i: Compare the credit analysis required for asset-backed securities to analysis of corporate debt.

CFA® Program Curriculum, Volume 5, page 238

Credit analysis of ABS is different from credit analysis of a corporate bond. In the case of a corporate bond, when the issuer defaults, the cash flows cease and there is a terminal cash flow (based on recovery rate). When one of the constituents of the collateral pool of an ABS defaults, the ABS itself does not default; rather, the ABS distributes whatever cash flow was received during the period to the holders of different ABS tranche securities per the pre-specified distribution waterfall. Hence, the cash flow characteristics of an ABS differ from the cash flow characteristics of a corporate bond.

The credit risk analysis of an ABS entails evaluation of the credit risk of the collateral pool in conjunction with the distribution waterfall. This is best achieved if ABS is viewed as credit derivatives rather than as ordinary bonds. To value an ABS, either a reduced form or a structural model can be used. However, the valuation must incorporate the distribution waterfall of the ABS.

The credit risk metric of probability of default does not apply to an ABS; we instead use the **probability of loss**.

Key Concepts

LOS 38.a
Probability of default is the probability that a borrower (i.e., the bond issuer) fails to pay interest or repay principal when due. Loss given default refers to the value a bond investor will lose if the issuer defaults. Expected loss is equal to the probability of default multiplied by the loss given default.

The present value of expected loss makes two adjustments to the expected loss measure: time value adjustment and use of risk-neutral probabilities instead of default probabilities. The present value of expected loss is the difference in value of a credit-risky bond and an otherwise identical risk-free bond.

Of these credit risk measures, the present value of the expected loss is considered the most important, as the dollar difference in value between a risky and riskless bond most clearly quantifies the credit risk in the risky bond.

LOS 38.b
Credit scoring is used for small businesses and individuals, while credit ratings are used for corporate, government, and ABS debt securities. Both are ordinal rankings, meaning that the securities are ordered from lowest credit risk to highest; however, the differences in ranking do not indicate the degree to which credit risk differs.

LOS 38.c
Credit ratings are simple, summary measures of risk that are easy to communicate. However, the ratings do not adjust with business cycle, and the stability in ratings comes at an expense of reduction in correlation with default probabilities.

LOS 38.d
Structural models of corporate credit risk are based on the structure of a company's balance sheet and rely on insights provided by option pricing theory. Owning risky debt with a face value of K is analogous to owning a risk-free bond with the same face value (K) and writing a European put option on the assets of the company with a strike price of K.

value of risky debt = value of risk-free debt – value of put option on company's assets

An important insight of the structural model is that owning the company's equity is equivalent to holding a European call option on the company's assets.

Because historical asset returns are not available, implicit estimation techniques are needed for input parameters of the structural models.

LOS 38.e

Reduced form models do not impose assumptions on the company's balance sheet, instead they impose assumptions on the output of a structural model. Reduced form models also allow the analyst flexibility to incorporate real world conditions in the model.

The input estimates for reduced form models can be estimated using historical data, which are called **hazard rate estimation**.

LOS 38.f

Assumptions of the structural model:

1. Company's assets are traded in a frictionless market with return μ and variance σ^2.

2. The risk-free interest rate (r) is constant.

3. The company has a simple balance sheet structure.

Strengths of structural models:

1. Provides option analogy to understand probability of default and loss given default and can be estimated using current market prices.

Weaknesses of structural models:

1. Model assumptions of simple balance sheet and traded assets are not realistic.

2. Estimation procedures do not consider business cycle.

Assumptions of the reduced form model:

1. Company has a zero-coupon bond with a maturity at time T, and it trades in frictionless and arbitrage-free markets.

2. The risk-free interest rate (r) and the state of the economy are stochastic. The probability of default and recovery rate is not constant and depends on the state of the economy.

Strengths of reduced form models:

1. Since model inputs are observable, historical estimation procedures can be used.

2. Credit risk is allowed to fluctuate with the business cycle.

3. Reduced form models do not require specification of the company's balance sheet structure.

Weaknesses of reduced form models:

1. Unless the model has been formulated and backtested properly, the hazard rate estimation procedures (using past observations to predict the future) may not be valid.

LOS 38.g
Term structure of credit spreads captures the relationship between credit spread and maturity. Credit spread is the difference between yield on a zero-coupon, credit-risky bond and the yield on a zero-coupon, risk-free bond.

LOS 38.h
Present value of expected loss is the difference between the value of a risk-free bond and the value of a similar risky bond. This is the maximum amount an investor would pay an insurer to bear the credit risk of a risky bond.

We can estimate the present value of expected loss from the credit spread on a risky bond (given the risk-free rate).

LOS 38.i
Credit analysis of ABS differs from credit analysis of corporate bonds because ABS do not default, but they will lose value as defaults occur in the collateral pool. Thus, probability of default does not apply to an ABS; we instead model ABS credit risk using the probability of loss, loss given default, expected loss, and the present value of the loss.

Concept Checkers

Use the following information to answer questions 1 through 9.

Tim Petrovich is the portfolio manager of fixed income securities at Gamma Bank. Petrovich is concerned about the performance of the bank's corporate bond portfolio over the past four years. He feels that the bank's credit analysis models have been inadequate in evaluating the impact of changing market conditions on the bank's investments.

Petrovich evaluates some of the metrics currently being generated by the credit analysis department of the bank. While comparing the metrics, Petrovich makes the following statement:

Statement 1: The expected loss metric and present value of expected loss metric differ only in terms of time value of money and discounting of expected future losses.

Petrovich discusses credit ratings with Steve McGraw, the bank's senior credit analyst. McGraw states that the bank uses S&P's credit ratings, and these ratings divide the credit-risky bond universe into 21 categories with an equal number of issues in each category. The ratings themselves tend to be stable even though default probabilities fluctuate with the business cycle.

Petrovich examines the term structure of credit spreads for one of the bank's holdings. He obtains the data on Aries Corp's 5-year, 3% senior unsecured bonds issued three years ago. Exhibit 1 shows the relevant data.

Exhibit 1: Data on 3% 5-year Aries Corp bonds

Payment Date	*Risk-Free Rate*	*Credit Spread*
30-Sep 20X1	0.15%	0.13%
31-Mar 20X2	0.22%	0.17%
30-Sep 20X2	0.25%	0.18%
31-Mar 20X3	0.27%	0.21%

While discussing credit spreads, McGraw states that the bank uses reduced form models to estimate credit spreads. McGraw points out that one of the limitations of reduced form models is the assumption that the issuer has a simple balance sheet with only one class of coupon debt.

Finally, McGraw states that credit analysis of ABS is different than credit analysis of corporate bonds because (1) the cash flow characteristics of the ABS differs from the cash flow characteristics of corporate bonds, (2) ABS can be viewed as credit derivatives due to distribution the waterfall, and (3) credit analysis of ABS uses probability of default instead of *probability of loss* as a credit risk metric.

1. Petrovich's statement 1 is *most likely:*
   A. correct.
   B. incorrect, because the expected loss computation uses risk-neutral probabilities.
   C. incorrect, because the present value of expected loss also adjusts default probabilities to capture the riskiness of the cash flows (i.e., the risk premium).

2. McGraw's statement about credit ratings is *most likely:*
   A. correct.
   B. incorrect in regards to the stability of credit ratings.
   C. incorrect in regards to the number of issues in each rating category.

3. McGraw's statement about limitation of reduced form model is *most likely:*
   A. correct.
   B. incorrect, as the reduced form model assumes one class of zero-coupon debt.
   C. incorrect, as structural models assume a simple balance sheet.

4. Which of the following *least accurately* describes an assumption of the structural model of credit analysis?
   A. The issuer's assets are traded in frictionless markets.
   B. The issuer's debt is traded in frictionless markets.
   C. The value of the issuer's assets at the time of the maturity of debt has a lognormal distribution.

5. The credit spread in Exhibit 1 *most likely* includes a premium for:
   A. credit risk only.
   B. credit risk and liquidity risk only.
   C. credit risk, liquidity risk, and interest rate risk.

6. Under the structural model, a long position in a debt security can be viewed as equivalent to a long position in:
   A. a risk-free asset and a short position in a European put option on the stock of the issuer.
   B. the assets of the issuer and short position on a risk-free asset.
   C. a risk-free asset and a short position in a European put option on the assets of the issuer.

7. Which of the following statements regarding credit ratings is *least accurate?*
   A. Credit ratings tend to be stable over time, reducing their correlation with default probabilities over the business cycle.
   B. Credit ratings tend to be stable over time, reducing debt market price volatility.
   C. The issuer-pays model provides a strong financial incentive to credit-rating agencies to rate issuer debt accurately.

8. Suppose that the rates given in Exhibit 1 are continuously compounded annual rates. The present value of expected loss for the 3% Aries Corp bond is *closest* to:
   A. $4.31.
   B. $8.55.
   C. $50.13.

9. Which of the differences given by McGraw regarding the credit analysis of ABS versus credit analysis of corporate bonds is *most accurate?*
   A. (1) only.
   B. (1) and (2) only.
   C. (1), (2), and (3).

To access other content related to this topic review that may be included in the Schweser package you purchased, log in to your Schweser.com online dashboard. Schweser's OnDemand Video Lectures deliver streaming instruction covering every LOS in this topic review, while SchweserPro™ QBank provides additional quiz questions to help you practice and recall what you've learned.

Answers – Concept Checkers

1. **C** The expected loss computation uses default probabilities. The present value of expected loss computation uses risk-neutral probabilities reflecting adjustment for risk of the cash flows.

2. **C** McGraw is correct about stability of credit ratings. However, he is incorrect about there being equal number of issues in each rating category.

3. **C** Simple balance sheet structure is an assumption of structural models of credit analysis and not of the reduced form models.

4. **B** Structural models do not make an assumption about the company's debt being traded.

5. **B** Credit spreads computed relative to a risk-free asset include premiums for credit and liquidity risks.

6. **C** A long position in risky debt with a face value of K is analogous to a long position in a risk-free bond with the same face value K, plus a short position in a European put option on the assets of the company with a strike price equal to K.

7. **C** The issuer-pays model in credit ratings introduces a conflict of interest that may distort the accuracy of credit ratings. Under an issuer-pays model, the agency receives income from the same firms that the agency is supposed to accurately rate. This incentivizes the rating agency to award higher ratings to its customers than they deserve.

8. **A**

Payment Date	*Risk-Free Rate*	*Credit Spread*	*Total Yield*	*Time to CF*	*Cash Flow*	*PV (Risk-Free)*	*PV (Risky)*	*Difference*
30-Sep 20X1	0.15%	0.13%	0.28%	0.5	15	$14.99	$14.98	$0.01
31-Mar 20X2	0.22%	0.17%	0.39%	1.0	15	$14.97	$14.94	$0.03
30-Sep 20X2	0.25%	0.18%	0.43%	1.5	15	$14.94	$14.90	$0.04
31-Mar 20X3	0.27%	0.21%	0.48%	2.0	1015	$1,009.53	$1,005.30	$4.23
					Total	$1,054.43	$1,050.13	$4.31

9. **B** Statement (3) is incorrect: credit analysis of ABS uses *probability of loss* instead of *probability of default* as a credit measure.

The following is a review of the Fixed Income: Topics in Fixed Income Analysis principles designed to address the learning outcome statements set forth by CFA Institute. Cross-Reference to CFA Institute Assigned Reading #39.

Credit Default Swaps

Study Session 13

Exam Focus

A credit default swap (CDS) is a contract between two parties in which one party purchases protection from another party against losses from the default of a borrower. For the exam, you should be able to describe CDS, as well as related securities like index CDS. You should know what a credit event is and how the different protocols for settlement work. You should be familiar with the principles and factors that drive market pricing of CDS. Be able to describe how CDS are used to manage credit exposure, and how they can be used to profit from anticipated changes in the credit curve. You should understand how CDS are used for arbitrage to take advantage of relative mispricings of different risky securities.

Credit Default Swaps

A **credit default swap** (CDS) is essentially an insurance contract. If a credit event occurs, the *credit protection buyer* gets compensated by the *credit protection seller*. To obtain this coverage, the protection buyer pays the seller a premium called the **CDS spread**. The protection seller is assuming (i.e., long) credit risk, while the protection buyer is short credit risk. Note that the CDS does not provide protection against market-wide interest rate risk, only against credit risk. The contract is written on a face value of protection called the **notional principal** (or "notional").

Even though the CDS spread should be based on the underlying credit risk of the reference obligation, standardization in the market has led to a fixed **coupon** on CDS products: 1% for investment-grade securities and 5% for high-yield securities. Hence, the coupon rate on the CDS and the actual credit spread may be different. The present value of the difference between the standardized coupon rate and the credit spread on the reference obligation is paid upfront by one of the parties to the contract. For example, a CDS on an investment-grade bond with a credit spread of 75 basis points (bps) would require a premium payment of 100bps (CDS coupon rate) by the protection buyer. To compensate the protection buyer (who pays a higher-than-market premium), the protection seller would then pay upfront to the buyer the present value of 25bps of the notional principal.

For a protection buyer, a CDS has some of the characteristics of a put option—when the underlying performs poorly, the holder of the put option has a right to exercise the option.

The **International Swaps and Derivatives Association** (ISDA), the unofficial governing body of the industry, publishes standardized contract terms and conventions to facilitate smooth functioning of the CDS market.

LOS 39.a: Describe credit default swaps (CDS), single-name and index CDS, and the parameters that define a given CDS product.

CFA® Program Curriculum, Volume 5, page 254

Single-Name CDS

In the case of a single-name CDS, the **reference obligation** is the fixed-income security on which the swap is written, usually a senior unsecured obligation (in the case of a **senior CDS**). The issuer of the reference obligation is called the **reference entity**. The CDS pays off not only when the reference entity defaults on the reference obligation but also when the reference entity defaults on any other issue that is ranked pari passu (i.e., same rank) or higher. The CDS payoff is based on the market value of the **cheapest-to-deliver** (CTD) bond that has the same seniority as the reference obligation.

*Professor's Note: The **cheapest-to-deliver** bond is the debt instrument with the same seniority as the reference obligation but that can be purchased and delivered at the lowest cost.*

Example: Cheapest-to-deliver

Party X is a protection buyer in a $10 million notional principal senior CDS of Alpha, Inc. There is a credit event (i.e., Alpha defaults) and the market prices of Alpha's bonds after the credit event are as follows:

- Bond P, a subordinated unsecured debenture, is trading at 15% of par.
- Bond Q, a five-year senior unsecured debenture, is trading at 25% of par.
- Bond R, a three-year senior unsecured debenture, is trading at 30% of par.

What will be the payoff on the CDS?

Answer:

The cheapest-to-deliver senior unsecured debenture (i.e., same seniority as the senior CDS) is bond Q. The payoff will be the difference between the notional principal and market value of the CTD.

payoff = $10 million – (0.25)($10 million) = $7.5 million.

Index CDS

An *index CDS* covers multiple issuers, allowing market participants to take on an exposure to the credit risk of several companies simultaneously in the same way that stock indexes allow investors to take on an equity exposure to several companies at once. In this case, the protection for each issuer is equal (i.e., equally weighted) and the total notional principal is the sum of the protection on all the issuers.

Example: Index CDS

Party X is a protection buyer in a five-year, $100 million notional principal CDS for CDX-IG, which contains 125 entities. One of the index constituents, company A, defaults and its bonds trade at 30% of par after default.

1. What will be the payoff on the CDS?

2. What will be the notional principal of the CDS after default?

Answer:

1. The notional principal attributable to entity A is $100 million / 125 = $0.8 million. Party X should receive payment of $0.8 million – (0.3)($0.8 million) = $560,000.

2. Post the default event, the remainder of the CDS continues with a notional principal of $99.2 million.

The pricing of an index CDS is dependent on the correlation of default (credit correlation) among the entities in the index. The higher the correlation of default among index constituents, the higher the spread on the index CDS.

LOS 39.b: Describe credit events and settlement protocols with respect to CDS.

CFA® Program Curriculum, Volume 5, page 258

A default is defined as the occurrence of a credit event. Common types of credit events specified in CDS agreements include bankruptcy, failure to pay, and restructuring.

- Bankruptcy: A bankruptcy protection filing allows the defaulting party to work with creditors under the supervision of the court so as to avoid full liquidation.
- Failure to pay: Occurs when the issuer misses a scheduled coupon or principal payment without filing for formal bankruptcy.
- Restructuring: Occurs when the issuer forces its creditors to accept terms that are different than those specified in the original issue. Restructuring is less common in the United States as issuers prefer to go the bankruptcy protection route.

A 15-member group of the ISDA called the **Determinations Committee** (DC) declares when a credit event has occurred. A supermajority vote (at least 12 members) is required for a credit event to be declared.

When there is a credit event, the swap will be settled in cash or by physical delivery. With physical delivery, the protection seller receives the reference obligation (i.e., the bond or loan) and pays the protection buyer the notional amount, as shown in Figure 1.

Figure 1: Physical Settlement on Credit Default Swap After a Credit Event

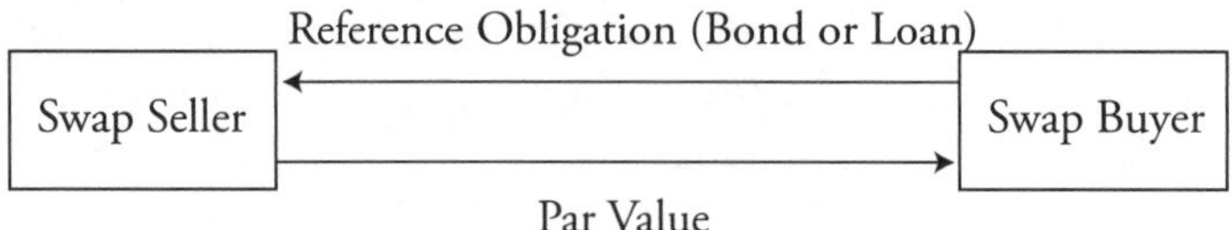

In the case of a cash settlement, the payout amount is the payout ratio times the notional principal. The payout ratio depends on the recovery rate (i.e., the proportion of par that the bond trades at after default) as shown in Figure 2.

payout amount = payout ratio × notional principal

where:
payout ratio = 1 – recovery rate (%)

Figure 2: Cash Settlement on Credit Default Swap After a Credit Event

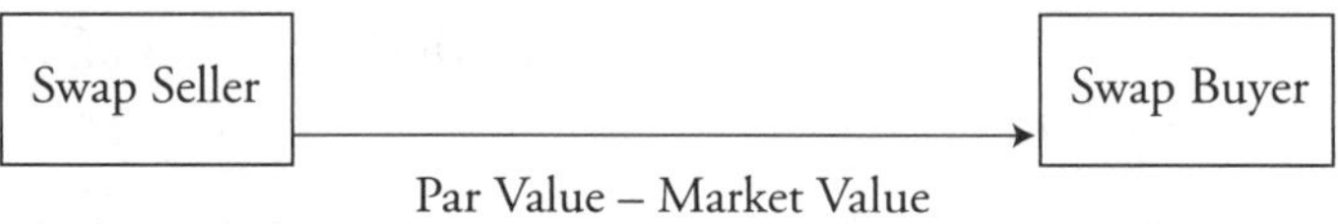

LOS 39.c: Explain the principles underlying, and factors that influence, the market's pricing of CDS.

CFA® Program Curriculum, Volume 5, page 263

The factors that influence the pricing of CDS (i.e., CDS spread) include the probability of default, the loss given default, and the coupon rate on the swap. The CDS spread is higher for higher probability of default and for higher loss given default. For this discussion, we will focus on single-name CDS. However, the principles apply to index CDS as well.

Professor's Note: Candidates are not expected to precisely estimate the credit spread on a CDS. You should understand the factors that influence the spread and the spread's relation to the upfront payment.

Probability of default is the likelihood of default by the reference entity in a given year. However, because the CDS typically covers a multi-year horizon, the probability of default is not constant; the probability of default usually increases over time. For a single-name CDS, when a default occurs, a payment is made by the protection seller to the protection buyer and the CDS ceases to exist. Hence, in the context of a CDS, the probability of default in any given year assumes that no default has occurred in the preceding years. We call the probability of default *given that it has not already occurred* the **conditional probability of default** or **hazard rate**. The credit risk of a reference obligation and hence the cost of protection is proportional to the hazard rate.

Example: Hazard rate

Consider a five-year senior CDS on Xeon Corp. Xeon's hazard rate is 2% and increases by 1% per year.

Compute the survival rate in five years.

Answer:

The hazard rates for the five years are: 2%, 3%, 4%, 5%, and 6%.

Survival rate in five years = (1 – 0.02)(1 – 0.03)(1 – 0.04)(1 – 0.05)(1 – 0.06) = 0.815 or 81.5%

Loss given default is the expected amount of loss in the event that a default occurs. Loss given default is inversely related to the recovery rate. The expected loss for any given period is the hazard rate for that period times the loss given default for that period.

$$(\text{expected loss})_t = (\text{hazard rate})_t \times (\text{loss given default})_t$$

The cash payments made by the protection buyer on the CDS (i.e., the coupon payments) cease when there is a default (i.e., when the CDS terminates). Hence, the expected value of the coupon payments also depends on the hazard rate.

The payments made by the protection buyer to the seller are the **premium leg**. On the other side of the contract, the protection seller must make a payment to the protection buyer in case of a default; these contingent payments make up the **protection leg**.

The difference between the present value of the premium leg and the present value of the protection leg determines the upfront payment.

upfront payment (by protection buyer) = PV(protection leg) – PV(premium leg)

We can approximate the upfront premium as the difference between the CDS spread and the CDS coupon rate, multiplied by the duration of the CDS. Again, the CDS spread is the compensation for bearing the credit risk of the reference obligation.

Professor's Note: Be careful here! The formula uses duration of the CDS and not the duration of the reference obligation.

upfront premium % ≈ (CDS spread – CDS coupon) × duration

which means that:

$$\text{CDS spread} = \frac{\text{upfront premium \%}}{\text{duration}} + \text{CDS coupon}$$

We can also quote the **CDS price** as:

$$\text{price of CDS (per \$100 notional)} \approx \$100 - \text{upfront premium (\%)}$$

Example: Upfront premium and price of CDS

Aki Mutaro, bond portfolio manager for a regional bank, is considering buying protection on one of the bank's high-yield holdings: Alpha Inc. bonds. Ten-year CDS on Alpha bonds have a coupon rate of 5% while the 10-year Alpha CDS spread is 3.5%. The duration of the CDS is 7.

Calculate the approximate upfront premium and price of a 10-year Alpha Inc., CDS.

Answer:

$$\begin{aligned}\text{upfront premium \%} &\approx (\text{CDS spread} - \text{CDS coupon}) \times \text{duration} \\ &= (3.5\% - 5.0\%) \times 7 = -10.5\%\end{aligned}$$

Hence, the protection seller would pay (approximately) 10.5% of the notional to the protection buyer upfront because the CDS coupon is higher than the credit spread.

$$\text{CDS price} = 100 - (-10.5) = \$110.50 \text{ per \$100 notional}$$

Valuation After Inception of CDS

At inception of a CDS, the CDS spread (and the upfront premium) is computed based on the credit quality of the reference entity. After inception, the credit quality of the reference entity (or the credit risk premium in the overall market) may change. This will lead to the underlying CDS having a nonzero value. For example, if the credit spread declines, the protection seller, having locked in a higher credit spread at initiation, would gain.

The change in value of a CDS after inception can be approximated by the change in spread multiplied by the duration of the CDS:

$$\text{profit for protection buyer} \approx \text{change in spread} \times \text{duration} \times \text{notional principal}$$

or

$$\text{profit for protection buyer (\%)} \approx \text{change in spread (\%)} \times \text{duration}$$

Note that the protection buyer is short credit risk and hence benefits (i.e., profit is positive) when credit spreads widen.

The protection buyer (or seller) can unwind an existing CDS exposure (prior to expiration or default) by entering into an offsetting transaction. For example, a protection buyer can remove his exposure to the CDS by selling protection with the same terms as the original CDS and maturity equal to the remaining maturity on the existing CDS. The difference between the upfront premium paid and received should be (approximately) equal to the profit for the protection buyer. This process of capturing value from an in-the-money CDS exposure is called **monetizing** the gain.

LOS 39.d: Describe the use of CDS to manage credit exposures and to express views regarding changes in shape and/or level of the credit curve.

CFA® Program Curriculum, Volume 5, page 273

Credit Curve

The **credit curve** is the relationship between credit spreads for different bonds issued by an entity, and the bonds' maturities. The credit curve is similar to the term structure of interest rates. If the longer maturity bonds have a higher credit spread compared to shorter maturity bonds, the credit curve will be upward sloping. However, if the hazard rate is constant, the credit curve will be flat.

CDS can be used to manage credit exposures of a bond portfolio. For example, in anticipation of declining (increasing) credit spreads, a portfolio manager may increase (decrease) credit exposure in the portfolio by being a protection seller (buyer).

In a **naked CDS**, an investor with no underlying exposure purchases protection in the CDS market. In a **long/short trade**, an investor purchases protection on one reference entity while simultaneously selling protection on another (often related) reference entity. The investor is betting that the difference in credit spreads between the two reference entities will change to the investor's advantage. This is similar to going long (protection seller exposure) in one reference entity bond and simultaneously going short (protection buyer exposure) in the other reference entity bond.

A **curve trade** is a type of long/short trade where the investor is buying and selling protection on the *same* reference entity but with a different maturity. If the investor expects that an upward-sloping credit curve on a specific corporate issuer will flatten, she may take the position of protection buyer in a short maturity CDS and the position of protection seller in a long maturity CDS.

An investor concerned about the credit risk of an issuer in the near term while being more confident of the long-term prospects of the issuer might buy protection in the short-term CDS and offset the premium cost by selling protection in the long-term CDS. An investor who believes that the short-term outlook for the reference entity is better than the long-term outlook can use a curve-steepening trade; buying protection in a long-term CDS and selling protection in a short-term CDS. The investor will profit if the credit curve steepens; that is, if long-term credit risk increases relative to short-term credit risk. Conversely, an investor who is bearish about the reference entity's prospects in the short term will enter into a curve-flattening trade.

LOS 39.e: Describe the use of CDS to take advantage of valuation disparities among separate markets, such as bonds, loans, equities, and equity-linked instruments.

CFA® Program Curriculum, Volume 5, page 277

Uses of CDS

Earning arbitrage profits is another motivation for trading in the CDS market. Differences in pricing between asset and derivative markets, or differences in pricing of different products in the market, may offer potential arbitrage profits.

A **basis trade** is an attempt to exploit the difference in credit spreads between bond markets and the CDS market. Basis trades rely on the idea that such mispricing will be temporary and that disparity should eventually disappear after it is recognized. For example, if a specific bond is trading at a credit spread of 4% over LIBOR in the bond market but the CDS spread on the same bond is 3%, a trader can profit by buying the bond and taking the protection buyer position in the CDS market. If the expected convergence occurs, the trader will make a profit.

Another arbitrage transaction involves buying and selling debt instruments issued by the same entity based on which instruments the CDS market suggests to be undervalued or overvalued.

In a leveraged buyout (LBO), the firm will issue a great amount of debt in order to repurchase all of the company's publicly traded equity. This additional debt will increase the CDS spread because default is now more likely. An investor who anticipates an LBO might purchase both the stock and CDS protection, both of which will increase in value when the LBO eventually occurs.

In the case of an index CDS, the value of the index should be equal to the sum of the values of the index components. An arbitrage transaction is possible if the credit risk of the index constituents is priced differently than the index CDS spread.

Collateralized debt obligations (CDO) are claims against a portfolio of debt securities. A synthetic CDO has similar credit risk exposure to that of a cash CDO but is assembled using CDS rather than debt securities. If the synthetic CDO can be created at a cost lower than that of the cash CDO, investors can buy the synthetic CDO and sell the cash CDO, engaging in a profitable arbitrage.

Key Concepts

LOS 39.a

A credit default swap (CDS) is essentially an insurance contract wherein upon occurrence of a credit event, the credit protection buyer gets compensated by the credit protection seller. To obtain this coverage, the protection buyer pays the seller a premium called the CDS spread. In the case of a single-name CDS, the reference obligation is the fixed income security on which the swap is written. An index CDS covers an equally-weighted combination of borrowers.

LOS 39.b

A default is defined as occurrence of a credit event. Common types of credit events specified in CDS agreements include bankruptcy, failure to pay, and restructuring.

When there is a credit event, the swap will be settled in cash or by physical delivery.

LOS 39.c

The factors that influence the pricing of CDS (i.e., CDS spread) include the probability of default, the loss given default, and the coupon rate on the swap. The CDS spread is higher for a higher probability of default and for a higher loss given default. The conditional probability of default (i.e., the probability of default given that default has not already occurred) is called the hazard rate.

$$(\text{expected loss})_t = (\text{hazard rate})_t \times (\text{loss given default})_t$$

The upfront premium on a CDS can be computed as:

$$\text{upfront payment (by protection buyer)} = \text{PV(protection leg)} - \text{PV(premium leg)}$$

Or approximately:

$$\text{upfront premium} \approx (\text{CDS spread} - \text{CDS coupon}) \times \text{duration}$$

The change in value for a CDS after inception can be approximated by the change in spread multiplied by the duration of the CDS.

$$\text{profit for protection buyer} \approx \text{change in spread} \times \text{duration} \times \text{notional principal}$$

$$\text{profit for protection buyer (\%)} \approx \text{change in spread (\%)} \times \text{duration}$$

LOS 39.d

In a naked CDS, an investor with no exposure to the underlying purchases protection in the CDS market.

In a long/short trade, an investor purchases protection on one reference entity while selling protection on another reference entity.

A curve trade is a type of long/short trade where the investor is buying and selling protection on the same reference entity but with different maturities. An investor who believes the short-term outlook for the reference entity is better than the long-term outlook can use a curve-steepening trade (buying protection in a long-term CDS and selling protection in a short-term CDS) to profit if the credit curve steepens. Conversely, an investor who is bearish about the reference entity's prospects in the short term will enter into a curve-flattening trade.

LOS 39.e

A **basis trade** is an attempt to exploit the difference in credit spreads between bond markets and the CDS market. Basis trades rely on the idea that such mispricings will be temporary and that disparity should eventually disappear after it is recognized.

If a synthetic CDO can be created at a cost lower than that of the equivalent cash CDO, investors can buy the synthetic CDO and sell the cash CDO, producing a profitable arbitrage.

Concept Checkers

Use the following information to answer questions 1 through 6.

Jamshed Banaji, CFA, manages a $400 million bond portfolio for a large public pension fund. Banaji is concerned about volatility in the credit markets and expects credit spreads to widen in the short-term but revert back to current levels over the long-term.

Banaji has flagged two of his holdings for further scrutiny: IDG Corp. and Zeta Corp.

The portfolio currently has $10 million par value of 6% 10-year senior unsecured IDG Corp. bonds. Because he is concerned about IDG's credit risk, Banaji enters into a credit default swap as a protection buyer. Banaji selects a five-year senior CDS for IDG with a coupon rate of 5% and a duration of 4. IDG bonds have a yield-to-maturity of 6.5%. The LIBOR yield curve is flat at 2%.

Banaji is also concerned about the Zeta Corp. bonds that he holds. Zeta's management is planning to pursue a recapitalization plan that involves a large stock buyback program financed by new debt.

1. The *most* appropriate strategy for Banaji, given his expectation about changing credit spreads, is a:
   A. credit curve trade; selling protection in the short-term and purchasing protection in the long-term.
   B. credit curve trade; buying protection in the short-term and selling protection in the long-term.
   C. CDS trade; buying protection in the short-term only.

2. At inception of the CDS for IDG bonds, Banaji is *most likely* to:
   A. receive a premium of $200,000.
   B. pay a premium of $300,000.
   C. receive a premium of $400,000.

3. For this question only, suppose that six months after the inception of the swap, IDG declares bankruptcy. Exhibit 1 shows the market prices of IDG bonds after the company files for bankruptcy.

   Exhibit 1: Market Price of IDG Bonds Post Bankruptcy Filing

Description	*Market Price (%) of Par*
9.5-year 6% senior unsecured	45% of par
5-year 5% senior unsecured	40% of par
5-year 6% subordinated unsecured	30% of par

   If Banaji has a choice of settlement procedure, he is *most likely* to choose:
   A. physical settlement.
   B. cash settlement and the payoff would be $6 million.
   C. cash settlement and the payoff would be $7 million.

4. Which of the following statements about hazard rate is *most* accurate? Hazard rate:
   A. is the probability of default given that default has already occurred in a previous period.
   B. affects both the premium leg as well as the protection leg in a CDS.
   C. is higher for higher loss given default.

5. The most appropriate strategy for Banaji to follow in regard to Zeta Corp. would be to buy Zeta Corp.:
   A. stock and buy CDS protection on Zeta Corp. bonds.
   B. bonds and sell CDS protection on Zeta Corp. bonds
   C. stock and sell CDS protection on Zeta Corp. bonds.

6. The statement "credit spreads are positively related to loss given default and to hazard rate" is *most accurately* described as:
   A. correct.
   B. correct regarding loss given default but incorrect regarding hazard rate.
   C. correct regarding hazard rate but incorrect regarding loss given default.

To access other content related to this topic review that may be included in the Schweser package you purchased, log in to your Schweser.com online dashboard. Schweser's OnDemand Video Lectures deliver streaming instruction covering every LOS in this topic review, while SchweserPro™ QBank provides additional quiz questions to help you practice and recall what you've learned.

Answers – Concept Checkers

1. **B** Banaji expects credit spreads to widen in the short-term; therefore, the appropriate strategy is to buy short-term CDS protection. Similarly, long-term credit spreads are expected to revert back to current levels (narrow) and hence Banaji can sell protection in the long-term CDS. Buying protection only would cost more money (the protection buyer premium is not offset by premium income from selling protection) and does not use Banaji's entire information set and, therefore, is not most appropriate.

2. **A** Credit spread on IDG bonds = yield – LIBOR = 6.5% – 2% = 4.5%

   upfront premium (paid by protection buyer) ≈ (CDS spread – CDS coupon) × duration × notional principal

   = (0.045 – 0.05) × 4 × \$10 million = –\$200,000

   Because the computed value is negative, \$200,000 would be received by Banaji as the protection buyer.

3. **B** The CDS in the question is a senior CDS, hence the reference obligation is a senior unsecured bond. The payoff on the CDS is based on the CTD with same seniority as reference obligation. From the three choices given, the five-year 5% senior unsecured is the cheapest to deliver. Hence, the payoff will be notional principal – market value of the CTD = \$10 million – \$ 4 million = \$6 million.

   Note that physical settlement would not be advantageous to Banaji; the bonds to be surrendered have a market value of \$4.5 million so the implied payoff would be only \$5.5 million (\$10 million – \$4.5 million).

4. **B** Hazard rate is the conditional probability of default given that default has not occurred in previous periods. The hazard rate affects the protection leg: the higher the hazard rate, the higher the expected value of payoffs made by the protection seller upon default. Hazard rate also affects the premium leg because once default occurs, the CDS ceases to exist and premium income would also cease. Loss given default depends on the recovery rate and not on hazard rate (probability of default).

5. **A** Due to leveraged recapitalization of Zeta Corp., it can be expected that the credit spread on Zeta bonds would widen leading to increased value for CDS protection buyer. Additionally, the increase in stock buyback would be expected to increase the value of Zeta stock. Banaji should purchase both the stock and CDS protection, both of which will increase in value when the LBO occurs.

6. **A** Credit spreads are positively related to hazard rates and loss given default, and negatively related to recovery rates.

Self-Test: Fixed Income

You have now finished the Fixed Income topic section. The following self-test will provide immediate feedback on how effective your study of this material has been. The test is best taken timed; allow 3 minutes per subquestion (18 minutes per item set). This self-test is more exam-like than typical Concept Checkers or QBank questions. A score less than 70% suggests that additional review of this topic is needed.

Use the following information for Questions 1 through 6.

Jonathan Song is a CFA candidate who recently took the Level II exam and is currently waiting to receive his test results. Song is also pursuing his MBA at a prestigious Ivy League university. He has accepted a position as an intern at a large brokerage firm in New York for this year's summer break. Over the course of his internship, he will rotate among the different areas of the firm, spending two weeks in each. His current rotation is in the brokerage firm's research department, where he will report to Bill Dixon, a managing director whose group is responsible for bond analytics. Dixon is evaluating all of the interns who rotate through his department this summer to identify possible candidates for future permanent positions at the brokerage firm.

Song has successfully completed several courses in finance and economics, and Dixon seeks to assess Song's knowledge of various concepts that are of specific importance to his group. Dixon decides to focus first on valuation of fixed income securities. To this end, Dixon supplies Song with some fundamental market information. Figure 1 shows paths from a three-year binomial interest rate tree for risk-free securities using current market data.

Figure 1: Benchmark Interest Rate Paths for 3-Year Horizon

Path	*Year 1*	*Year 2*	*Year 3*
1	2%	2.8050%	4.0787%
2	2%	2.8050%	3.0216%
3	2%	2.0780%	3.0216%
4	2%	2.0780%	2.2384%

Dixon wants Song to value three-year, 4% annual pay, $100 face value Zena, Inc., bonds. The bonds have a Bermudan-style call option that can be exercised at par in one and two years. Comparable bonds have an OAS of 100bps. Dixon explains to Song that investments in callable bonds have special interest rate risk considerations. Dixon states, "Callable bonds exhibit negative convexity. When the underlying option is at or near the money, a callable bond will have lower one-sided down-duration than one-sided up-duration."

While discussing spread measures, Song states, "Everything else constant, higher OAS indicates better compensation for risk. However, OAS estimation for callable bonds can be biased upward if the analyst uses too high an estimate of interest rate volatility."

Song says that an analyst could use structural models to analyze credit risk of Zena, Inc., bonds, and that one of the ways to evaluate credit risk is to look at the economic exposure of the equity investors. Specifically, owning equity is similar to owning a European option on the assets of the company.

When Dixon asks about term structure of interest rates, Song mentions that he had attended a seminar on that topic at university the previous semester. While Song could not remember the specific model, he recalled that it had a drift term ensuring mean reversion of rates and a constant level of volatility.

1. Using the information in Figure 1, the value of a three-year, 3% annual-pay benchmark bond under Path 1 and Path 2 is *closest* to:

	Path 1	Path 2
A.	$99.98	$100.15
B.	$100.18	$101.15
C.	$102.32	$103.98

2. Using the information given in the case and in Figure 1, the value of 4% Zena, Inc., callable bond is *closest* to:
   A. $97.12
   B. $100.00
   C. $100.82

3. Dixon's statement about interest rate risk of callable bonds is *most accurately* described as:
   A. correct.
   B. incorrect about convexity.
   C. incorrect about one-sided duration.

4. Song's statement regarding OAS is *most accurately* described as:
   A. correct.
   B. incorrect about higher OAS indicating better compensation for risk.
   C. incorrect about OAS estimation for callable bonds possibly being biased upward.

5. While discussing structural models, the European option that Song discusses is *most likely*:
   A. a conversion option.
   B. a put option.
   C. a call option.

6. The term structure model that Song is referring to is *most likely*:
   A. the Cox-Ingersoll-Ross model.
   B. the Vasicek model.
   C. the Ho-Lee model.

Self-Test Answers: Fixed Income

1. **B** Pathwise valuation discounts each cashflow with its corresponding spot or forward rate. A three-year, 3% annual pay bond would have cash flows of \$3, \$3, and \$103 in years 1, 2, and 3, respectively. The values for each path and the average value is shown below.

Path	*Year 1*	*Year 2*	*Year 3*	*Value*
1	2%	2.8050%	4.0787%	\$100.18
2	2%	2.8050%	3.0216%	\$101.15
3	2%	2.0780%	3.0216%	\$101.85
4	2%	2.0780%	2.2384%	\$102.58
			Average	\$101.44

$$\text{Path 1 value} = \frac{3}{(1.02)} + \frac{3}{(1.02)(1.02805)} + \frac{103}{(1.02)(1.02805)(1.040787)} = 100.18$$

2. **C** The value of a Zena, Inc., callable bond is \$100.82, as shown below. The interest rate tree is updated by adding a constant spread (OAS) of 100bps at each node.

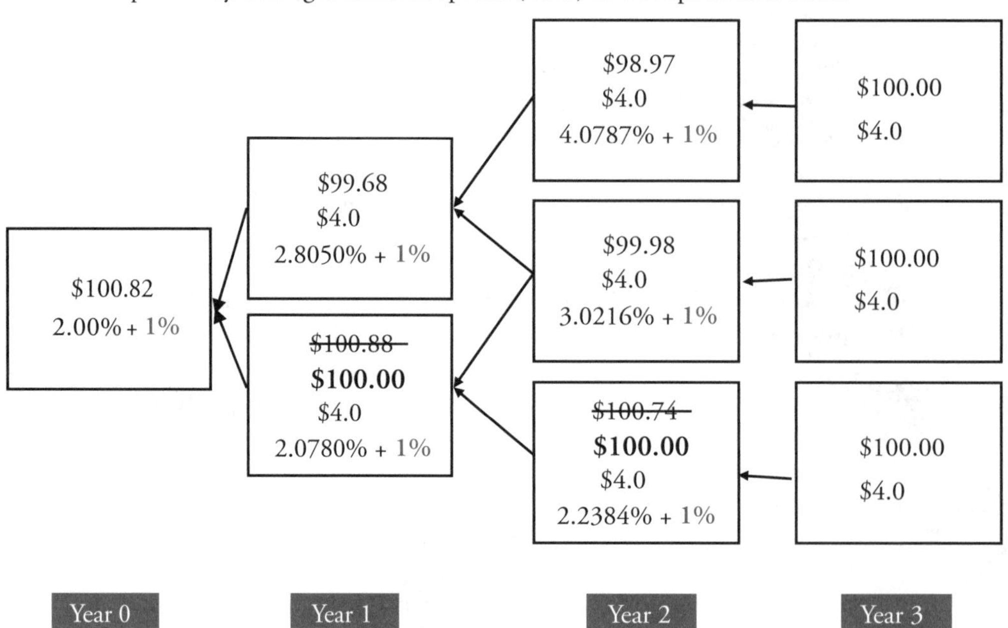

$$V_{2,UU} = \frac{104}{(1.050787)} = \$98.97$$

$$V_{2,UL} = \frac{104}{(1.040216)} = \$99.98$$

$$V_{2,LL} = \frac{104}{(1.032384)} = \$100.74$$

Because at node $V_{2,LL}$ the calculated value > the call price, the call option is exercised and we replace the node value with the call price of \$100.

$$V_{1,U} = \frac{1}{2}\times\left[\frac{98.97+4}{1.038050}+\frac{99.98+4}{1.038050}\right]=\$99.68$$

$$V_{1,L} = \frac{1}{2}\times\left[\frac{99.98+4}{1.03078}+\frac{100+4}{1.03078}\right]=\$100.88$$

Because at node $V_{1,L}$ the calculated value > the call price, the call option is exercised and we replace the node value with call price of $100.

$$V_0 = \frac{1}{2}\times\left[\frac{99.68+4}{1.03}+\frac{100+4}{1.03}\right]=\$100.82$$

3. **A** Dixon is correct about callable bonds exhibiting negative convexity. This occurs when the option is at or near money. Dixon is also correct that when the underlying option is at or near money, for a given decrease in rates, the price appreciation of a callable bond will be lower than loss in value for an equal amount of increase in rates. Hence, the callable bond will have lower one-sided down-duration than one-sided up-duration.

4. **C** Song is correct about higher OAS reflecting higher compensation for risk. Song is incorrect about the relationship between assumed volatility and computed OAS for a callable bond. If the assumed volatility is too high, the computed OAS for a callable bond would be too low, and hence the bias would be on the downside.

5. **C** Equity investors can be thought of as holders of a European call option on the assets of the company with a strike price equal to the face value of debt. At the maturity of debt, if the assets of the company are worth more than the face value of debt, the option is exercised (i.e., debt is paid). However, if the assets are insufficient to pay the debt, due to limited liability of shareholders, the option is allowed to expire (i.e., the company defaults).

6. **B** The drift term to ensure mean reversion of interest rates is a feature of the Cox-Ingersoll-Ross model and the Vasicek model. The Cox-Ingersoll-Ross model has volatility increasing with rates (and hence is not constant). The Vasicek model assumes a constant level of volatility over the period of analysis (i.e., independent of the level of interest rates).

The following is a review of the Derivative Instruments: Valuation and Strategies principles designed to address the learning outcome statements set forth by CFA Institute. Cross-Reference to CFA Institute Assigned Reading #40.

Pricing and Valuation of Forward Commitments

Study Session 14

Exam Focus

This topic review covers the calculation of price and value for forward and future contracts, specifically equity forward contracts, bond forward contracts, currency forwards, and forward (interest) rate agreements. This topic review also covers pricing and valuation of different swaps, including interest rate swaps, equity swaps, and currency swaps. Be able to structure profitable arbitrage transactions should the forward price differs from the no-arbitrage price. There are many formulae in this reading. However, once you realize the fundamental principles of no-arbitrage pricing, the formulae will start becoming somewhat less intimidating. There is a lot of testable material from this four-LOS reading!

Warm-Up: Forward Contracts

The party to the forward contract that agrees to buy the financial or physical asset has a **long forward position** and is called the *long*. The party to the forward contract that agrees to sell/deliver the asset has a **short forward position** and is called the *short*.

We will illustrate the basic forward contract mechanics through an example based on the purchase and sale of a Treasury bill. Note that while forward contracts on T-bills are usually quoted in terms of a discount percentage from face value, we use dollar prices here to make the example easy to follow.

Consider a contract under which Party A agrees to buy a $1,000 face value 90-day Treasury bill from Party B 30 days from now at a price of $990. Party A is the long and Party B is the short. Both parties have removed uncertainty about the price they will pay or receive for the T-bill at the future date. If 30 days from now T-bills are trading at $992, the short must deliver the T-bill to the long in exchange for a $990 payment. If T-bills are trading at $988 on the future date, the long must purchase the T-bill from the short for $990, the contract price.

Typically, no money changes hands at the inception of the contract, unlike futures contracts in which each party posts an initial deposit called the **margin** as a guarantee of performance.

At any point in time, including the settlement date, the party to the forward contract with the negative value will owe money to the other side. The other side of the contract will have a positive value of equal amount. Following this example, if the T-bill price is

$992 at the (future) settlement date, and the short does not deliver the T-bill for $990 as promised, the short has defaulted.

Professor's Note: A video explaining the basics of forward contracts can be found in the online Schweser Candidate Resource Library.

Warm-Up: Forward Contract Price Determination

The No-Arbitrage Principle

The price of a forward contract is *not* the price to purchase the contract because the parties to a forward contract typically pay nothing to enter into the contract at its inception. Here, *price refers to the contract price of the underlying asset under the terms of the forward contract*. This price may be a U.S. dollar or euro price, but it is often expressed as an interest rate or currency exchange rate. For T-bills, the price will be expressed as an annualized percentage discount from face value; for coupon bonds, it will usually be expressed as a yield to maturity; for the implicit loan in a forward rate agreement (FRA), it will be expressed as annualized London Interbank Offered Rate (LIBOR); and for a currency forward, it is expressed as an exchange rate between the two currencies involved. However it is expressed, this rate, yield, discount, or dollar amount is the forward price in the contract.

The price that we wish to determine is the forward price that makes the *values* of both the long and the short positions zero at contract initiation. We will use the *no-arbitrage principle*: there should not be a riskless profit to be gained by a combination of a forward contract position with positions in other assets. This principle assumes that (1) transactions costs are zero, (2) there are no restrictions on short sales or on the use of short sale proceeds, and (3) both borrowing and lending can be done in unlimited amounts at the risk-free rate of interest. This concept is so important that we'll express it in a formula:

forward price = price that prevents profitable riskless arbitrage in frictionless markets

A Simple Version of the Cost-of-Carry Model

In order to explain the no-arbitrage condition as it applies to the determination of forward prices, we will first consider a forward contract on an asset that costs nothing to store and makes no payments to its owner over the life of the forward contract. A zero-coupon (pure discount) bond meets these criteria. Unlike gold or wheat, it has no storage costs; unlike stocks, there are no dividend payments to consider; and unlike coupon bonds, it makes no periodic interest payments.

The general form for the calculation of the forward contract price can be stated as follows:

$$FP = S_0 \times (1 + R_f)^T$$

or

$$S_0 = \frac{FP}{(1 + R_f)^T}$$

where:
FP = forward price
S_0 = spot price at inception of the contract (t = 0)
R_f = annual risk-free rate
T = forward contract term in years

Example: Calculating the no-arbitrage forward price

Consider a 3-month forward contract on a zero-coupon bond with a face value of $1,000 that is currently quoted at $500, and suppose that the annual risk-free rate is 6%. Determine the price of the forward contract under the no-arbitrage principle.

Answer:

$$T = 3/12 = 0.25$$

$$FP = S_0 \times (1 + R_f)^T = \$500 \times 1.06^{0.25} = \$507.34$$

Now, let's explore in more detail why $507.34 is the no-arbitrage price of the forward contract.

Cash and Carry Arbitrage When the Forward Contract Is Overpriced

Suppose the forward contract is actually trading at $510 rather than the no-arbitrage price of $507.34. A short position in the forward contract requires the delivery of this bond three months from now. The arbitrage that we examine in this case amounts to borrowing $500 at the risk-free rate of 6%, buying the bond for $500, and simultaneously taking the short position in the forward contract on the zero-coupon bond so that we are obligated to deliver the bond at the expiration of the contract for the forward price and receive $510.

At the settlement date, we can satisfy our obligation under the terms of the forward contract by delivering the zero-coupon bond for a payment of $510, regardless of its market value at that time. We will use the $510 payment we receive at settlement from the forward contract (the forward contract price) to repay the $500 loan. The total amount to repay the loan, since the term of the loan is three months, is:

$$\text{loan repayment} = \$500 \times (1.06)^{0.25} = \$507.34$$

The payment of $510 we receive when we deliver the bond at the forward price is greater than our loan payoff of $507.34, and we will have earned an arbitrage profit of $510 – $507.34 = $2.66. Notice that this is equal to the difference between the actual forward price and the no-arbitrage forward price. The transactions are illustrated in Figure 1.

Figure 1: Cash and Carry Arbitrage When Forward Is Overpriced

Today		*Three Months From Today*	
Spot price of bond	$500		
Forward price	$510		
Transaction	*Cash flow*	*Transaction*	*Cash flow*
Short forward	$0	Settle short position by delivering bond	$510.00
Buy bond	–$500		
Borrow at 6%	+$500	Repay loan	– $507.34
Total cash flow	$0	Total cash flow = arbitrage profit	+$2.66

Professor's Note: Here's a couple hints to help you remember which transactions to undertake for cash and carry arbitrage: (1) always start with nothing (no cash, no securities), (2) buy underpriced assets and sell overpriced assets ("buy low, sell high"), and (3) take opposite positions in the spot and forward markets. So, if the futures contract is overpriced, you want to take a short position in those futures (which obligates you to sell at a fixed price). Because you go short in the forward market, you take the opposite position in the spot market and buy the asset. You need money to buy the asset, so you have to borrow. Therefore, to set up a cash and carry arbitrage:

forward overpriced:

borrow money ⇒ buy (go long) the spot asset ⇒ go short the asset in the forward market

Reverse Cash and Carry Arbitrage When the Forward Contract Is Underpriced

Suppose the forward contract is actually trading at $502 instead of the no-arbitrage price of $507.34. We reverse the arbitrage trades from the previous case and generate an arbitrage profit as follows. We sell the bond short today for $500 and simultaneously take the long position in the forward contract, which obligates us to purchase the bond in 90 days at the forward price of $502. We invest the $500 proceeds from the short sale at the 6% annual rate for three months.

In this case, at the settlement date, we receive the investment proceeds of $507.34, accept delivery of the bond in return for a payment of $502, and close out our short position by delivering the bond we just purchased at the forward price.

The payment of $502 we make as the long position in the contract is less than investment proceeds of $507.34, and we have earned an arbitrage profit of $507.34 – $502 = $5.34. The transactions are illustrated in Figure 2.

Figure 2: Reverse Cash and Carry Arbitrage When Forward Is Underpriced

Today		*Three Months From Today*	
Spot price of bond	$500		
Forward price	$502		
Transaction	*Cash flow*	*Transaction*	*Cash flow*
Long forward	$0	Settle long position by buying bond	–$502.00
Short sell bond	+$500	Deliver bond to close short position	$0.00
Invest short-sale proceeds at 6%	–$500	Receive investment proceeds	+$507.34
Total cash flow	$0	Total cash flow = arbitrage profit	+$5.34

Professor's Note: In this case, because the forward contract is underpriced, the trades are reversed from cash and carry arbitrage. To set up the reverse cash-and-carry arbitrage:

forward underpriced:

borrow asset ⇒ short (sell) spot asset ⇒ lend money ⇒ long (buy) forward

We can now determine that the no-arbitrage forward price that yields a zero *value* for both the long and short positions in the forward contract at inception is the no-arbitrage price of $507.34.

Professor's Note: This long explanation has answered the question, "What is the forward price that allows no arbitrage?" A very clear understanding here will make what follows easier and will serve you well as we progress to futures, options, and swaps.

Professor's Note: Day count and compounding conventions vary among different financial instruments. There are three variations used in the CFA curriculum:

- *All LIBOR-based contracts, such as FRAs, swaps, caps, floors, etc:*
    - *360 days per year and simple interest*
    - *Multiply "r" by days/360*
- *Equities, bonds, currencies, and stock options:*
    - *365 days per year and periodic compound interest*
    - *Raise (1+r) to an exponent of days/365*
- *Equity indexes:*
    - *365 days per year and continuous compounding*
    - *Raise Euler's number "e" to an exponent of "r" times days/365*

LOS 40.a: Describe and compare how equity, interest rate, fixed-income, and currency forward and futures contracts are priced and valued.

LOS 40.b: Calculate and interpret the no-arbitrage value of equity, interest rate, fixed-income, and currency forward and futures contracts.

CFA® Program Curriculum, Volume 5, pages 295 and 297

We now turn our attention to determining the price of different types of forward contracts and their valuation after inception.

Equity Forward Contracts With Discrete Dividends

Recall that the no-arbitrage forward price in our earlier example was calculated for an asset with no periodic payments. A stock, a stock portfolio, or an equity index may have expected dividend payments over the life of the contract. In order to price such a contract, we must either adjust the spot price for the present value of the expected dividends (PVD) over the life of the contract or adjust the forward price for the future value of the dividends (FVD) over the life of the contract. The **no-arbitrage price of an equity forward contract** in either case is:

$$\text{FP}(\text{on an equity security}) = (S_0 - \text{PVD}) \times (1 + R_f)^T$$

$$\text{FP}(\text{on an equity security}) = \left[S_0 \times (1 + R_f)^T\right] - \text{FVD}$$

For equity contracts, use a 365-day basis for calculating *T*. For example, if it is a 60-day contract, T = 60 / 365.

Example: Calculating the price of a forward contract on a stock

Calculate the no-arbitrage forward price for a 100-day forward on a stock that is currently priced at $30.00 and is expected to pay a dividend of $0.40 in 15 days, $0.40 in 85 days, and $0.50 in 175 days. The annual risk-free rate is 5%, and the yield curve is flat.

Answer:

Ignore the dividend in 175 days because it occurs after the maturity of the forward contract.

$$\text{PVD} = \frac{\$0.40}{1.05^{15/365}} + \frac{\$0.40}{1.05^{85/365}} = \$0.7946$$

$$\text{FP} = (\$30.00 - \$0.7946) \times 1.05^{100/365} = \$29.60$$

The time line of cash flows is shown in the following figure.

Pricing a 100-Day Forward Contract on Dividend-Paying Stock

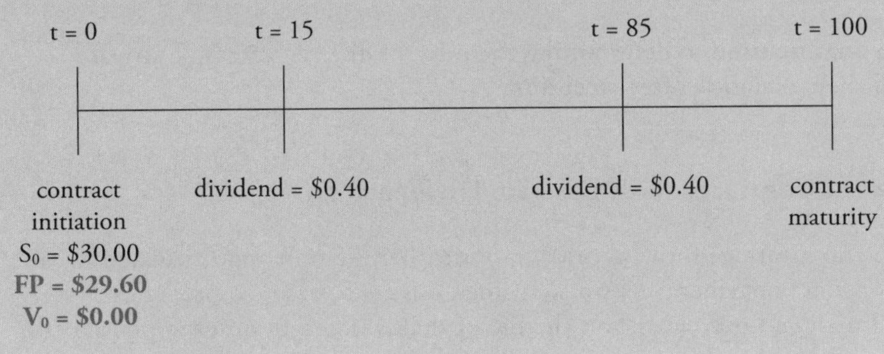

To calculate the **value of the long position in a forward contract on a dividend-paying stock**, we make the adjustment for the present value of the remaining expected discrete dividends at time *t* (PVDt) to get:

$$V_t\,(\text{long position}) = [S_t - \text{PVD}_t] - \left[\frac{\text{FP}}{(1+R_f)^{(T-t)}}\right]$$

Professor's Note: This formula still looks like the standard spot price minus present value of forward price. However, now the "spot price" has been adjusted by subtracting out the present value of the dividends because the long position in the forward contract does not receive the dividends paid on the underlying stock. So, now think adjusted spot price less present value of forward price.

Example: Calculating the value of an equity forward contract on a stock

After 60 days, the value of the stock in the previous example is \$36.00. Calculate the value of the equity forward contract on the stock to the long position, assuming the risk-free rate is still 5% and the yield curve is flat.

Answer:

There's only one dividend remaining (in 25 days) before the contract matures (in 40 days) as shown below, so:

$$PVD_{60} = \frac{\$0.40}{1.05^{25/365}} = \$0.3987$$

$$V_{60}(\text{long position}) = \$36.00 - \$0.3987 - \left[\frac{\$29.60}{1.05^{40/365}}\right] = \$6.16$$

Valuing a 100-Day Forward Contract After 60 Days

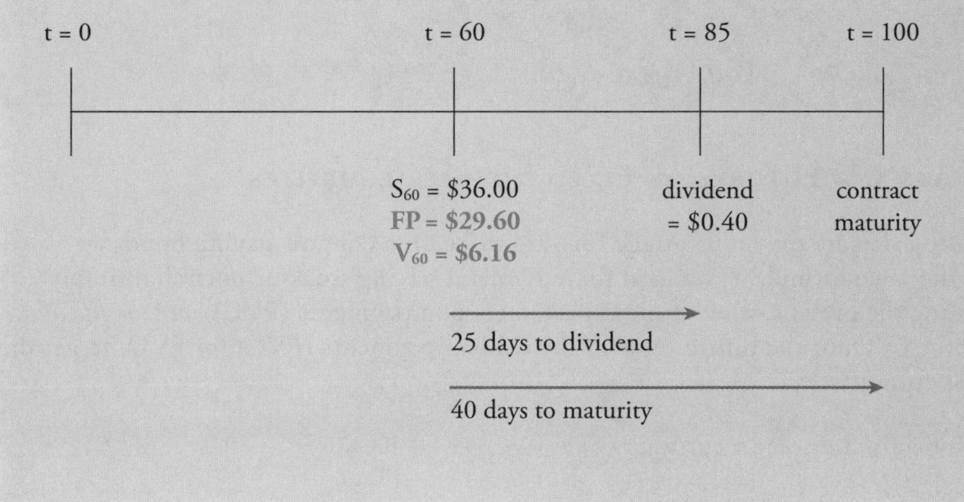

Equity Forward Contracts With Continuous Dividends

To calculate the price of an **equity index forward contract**, rather than take the present value of each dividend on (possibly) hundreds of stocks, we can make the calculation as if the dividends are paid continuously (rather than at discrete times) at the dividend yield rate on the index. Using continuous time discounting, we can calculate the no-arbitrage forward price as:

$$FP(\text{on an equity index}) = S_0 \times e^{(R_f^c - \delta^c) \times T} = \left(S_0 \times e^{-\delta^c \times T}\right) \times e^{R_f^c \times T}$$

where:
R_f^c = *continuously compounded risk-free rate*
δ^c = *continuously compounded dividend yield*

Professor's Note: The relationship between the periodically compounded risk-free rate R_f and the continuously compounded rate R_f^c is $R_f^c = ln(1 + R_f)$. For example, 5% compounded annually is equal to ln(1.05) = 0.04879 = 4.879% compounded continuously. The 2-year 5% future value factor can then be calculated as either $1.05^2 = 1.1025$ or $e^{0.04879 \times 2} = 1.1025$.

Example: Calculating the price of a forward contract on an equity index

The value of the S&P 500 Index is 1,140. The continuously compounded risk-free rate is 4.6% and the continuous dividend yield is 2.1%. Calculate the no-arbitrage price of a 140-day forward contract on the index.

Answer:

$$FP = 1{,}140 \times e^{(0.046-0.021)\times(140/365)} = 1{,}151$$

On a TI BA II PLUS calculator, use the following keystrokes:

0.046[−]0.021[=][×]140[÷]365[=][2nd][LN][×]1140[=]

Forwards and Futures on Fixed Income Securities

In order to calculate the no-arbitrage **forward price on a coupon-paying bond**, we can use the same formula as we used for a dividend-paying stock or portfolio, simply substituting the present value of the expected coupon payments (PVC) *over the life of the contract* for PVD, or the future value of the coupon payments (FVC) for FVD, to get the following formulas:

$$FP(\text{on a fixed income security}) = (S_0 - PVC) \times (1 + R_f)^T$$

or

$$= S_0 \times (1 + R_f)^T - FVC$$

The value of the forward contract prior to expiration is as follows:

$$V_t(\text{long position}) = [S_t - PVC_t] - \left[\frac{FP}{(1 + R_f)^{(T-t)}}\right]$$

In our examples, we assume that the spot price on the underlying coupon-paying bond includes accrued interest. For fixed income contracts, use a 365-day basis to calculate *T* if the contract maturity is given in days.

Example: Calculating the price of a forward on a fixed income security

Calculate the price of a 250-day forward contract on a 7% U.S. Treasury bond with a spot price of $1,050 (including accrued interest) that has just paid a coupon and will make another coupon payment in 182 days. The annual risk-free rate is 6%.

Answer:

Remember that U.S. Treasury bonds make semiannual coupon payments, so:

$$C = \frac{\$1{,}000 \times 0.07}{2} = \$35.00$$

$$PVC = \frac{\$35.00}{1.06^{182/365}} = \$34.00$$

The forward price of the contract is therefore:

$$FP(\text{on a fixed income security}) = (\$1{,}050 - \$34.00) \times 1.06^{250/365} = \$1{,}057.37$$

Example: Calculating the value of a forward on a fixed income security

After 100 days, the value of the bond in the previous example is $1,090. Calculate the value of the forward contract on the bond to the long position, assuming the risk-free rate is 6.0%.

Answer:

There is only one coupon remaining (in 82 days) before the contract matures (in 150 days), so:

$$PVC = \frac{\$35.00}{1.06^{82/365}} = \$34.54$$

$$V_{100}(\text{long position}) = \$1{,}090 - \$34.54 - \left(\frac{\$1{,}057.37}{1.06^{150/365}}\right) = \$23.11$$

Bond futures contracts often allow the short an option to deliver any of several bonds, which will satisfy the delivery terms of the contract. This is called a delivery option and is valuable to the short. Each bond is given a conversion factor that is used to adjust the long's payment at delivery so the more valuable bonds receive a larger payment. These factors are multipliers for the futures price at settlement. The long pays the futures price at expiration multiplied by the conversion factor (CF).

Bond prices in some countries are quoted as **clean prices**. At settlement, the buyer actually pays the clean price plus an **accrued interest** or the full price.

$$\text{accrued interest} = \left(\frac{\text{days since last coupon payment}}{\text{days between coupon payments}}\right) \times \text{coupon amount}$$

full price = clean price + accrued interest = clean price + AI_0

The futures price can then be calculated as:

$$FP = \left[(\text{full price})(1+R_f)^T - AI_T - FVC\right]$$

where:
AI_T = the accrued interest at maturity of the futures contract

The quoted futures price adjusts this price based on the conversion factor (CF) as follows:

$$QFP = FP / CF = \left[(\text{full price})(1+R_f)^T - AI_T - FVC\right]\left(\frac{1}{CF}\right)$$

Example: Calculating the price of a Treasury bond futures contract

Suppose that you need to calculate the quoted futures price of a 1.2 year Treasury bond futures contract. The cheapest-to-deliver bond is a 7% T-bond with exactly 10 years remaining to maturity and a quoted price of \$1,040 with a conversion factor of 1.13. There is currently no accrued interest because the bond has just paid a coupon. The annual riskfree rate is 5%. The accrued interest on the bond at maturity of the futures contract will be \$14.

Answer:

The full price of the bond = \$1,040 quoted price + \$0 accrued interest = \$1,040. The semiannual coupon on a single, \$1,000 face-value 7% bond is \$35. A bondholder will receive one payment 0.5 years from now (when there are 0.7 years left to maturity of the futures contract) and one payment 1 year from now (when there are 0.2 years until maturity). The future value of these coupons at the end of 1.2 years (the expiration date) is:

$$FVC = \left(\$35 \times 1.05^{0.7}\right) + \left(\$35 \times 1.05^{0.2}\right) = \$71.56$$

The quoted futures price is then:

$$QFP = \left[(\$1{,}040 \times 1.05^{1.2}) - \$14 - \$71.56\right]\left(\frac{1}{1.13}\right) = \$900.13$$

Warm-Up: LIBOR-Based Loans and Forward Rate Agreements

Eurodollar deposit is the term for deposits in large banks outside the United States denominated in U.S. dollars. The lending rate on dollar-denominated loans between banks is called the **London Interbank Offered Rate (LIBOR)**. It is quoted as an annualized rate based on a 360-day year. In contrast to T-bill discount yields, LIBOR is an add-on rate, like a yield quote on a short-term certificate of deposit. LIBOR is used as a reference rate for floating rate U.S. dollar-denominated loans worldwide.

Example: LIBOR-based loans

Compute the amount that must be repaid on a $1 million loan for 30 days if 30-day LIBOR is quoted at 6%.

Answer:

The add-on interest is calculated as $1 million × 0.06 × (30 / 360) = $5,000. The borrower would repay $1,000,000 + $5,000 = $1,005,000 at the end of 30 days.

LIBOR is published daily by the British Banker's Association and is compiled from quotes from a number of large banks; some are large multinational banks based in other countries that have London offices. There is also an equivalent euro lending rate called **Euribor**, or Europe Interbank Offered Rate. Euribor, established in Frankfurt, is published by the European Central Bank.

The long position in a **forward rate agreement** (FRA) is the party that would borrow the money (long the loan with the contract price being the interest rate on the loan). If the floating rate at contract expiration (LIBOR for U.S. dollar deposits and Euribor for euro deposits) is above the rate specified in the forward agreement, the long position in the contract can be viewed as the right to borrow at below market rates and the long will receive a payment. If the floating rate at the expiration date is below the rate specified in the forward agreement, the short will receive a cash payment from the long. (The right to lend at *above* market rates would have a positive value.)

Professor's Note: We say "can be viewed as" because an FRA is settled in cash, so there is no requirement to lend or borrow the amount stated in the contract. For this reason, the creditworthiness of the long position is not a factor in the determination of the interest rate on the FRA. However, to understand the pricing and calculation of value for an FRA, viewing the contract as a commitment to lend or borrow at a certain interest rate at a future date is helpful.

The notation for FRAs is unique. There are two numbers associated with an FRA: the number of months until the contract expires and the number of months until the underlying loan is settled. The difference between these two is the maturity of the underlying loan. For example, a 2 × 3 FRA is a contract that expires in two months (60 days), and the underlying loan is settled in three months (90 days). The underlying rate is 1-month (30-day) LIBOR on a 30-day loan in 60 days. See Figure 3.

Figure 3: Illustration of a 2 × 3 FRA

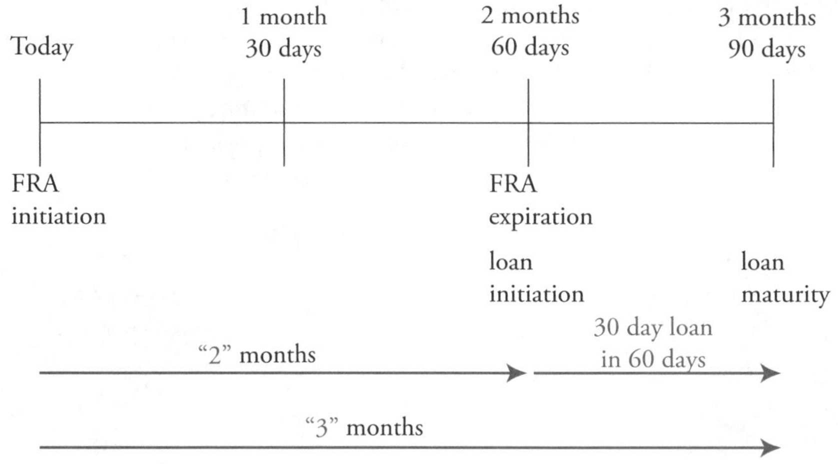

Pricing FRAs

There are three important things to remember about FRAs when we're pricing and valuing them:

1. LIBOR rates in the Eurodollar market are add-on rates and are always quoted on a 30/360 day basis in annual terms. For example, if the LIBOR quote on a 30-day loan is 6%, the actual unannualized monthly rate is 6% × (30/360) = 0.5%.

2. The long position in an FRA, in effect, is long the rate and wins when the rate increases.

3. Although the interest on the underlying loan won't be paid until the end of the loan (e.g., in three months in Figure 3), the payoff on the FRA occurs at the expiration of the FRA (e.g., in two months). Therefore, the payoff on the FRA is the present value of the interest savings on the loan (e.g., discounted one month in Figure 3).

The forward "price" in an FRA is actually a forward interest rate. The calculation of a forward interest rate is presented in Level I as the computation of forward rates from spot rates. We will illustrate this calculation with an example.

Example: Calculating the price of an FRA

Calculate the price of a 1 × 4 FRA (i.e., a 90-day loan, 30 days from now). The current 30-day LIBOR is 4% and the 120-day LIBOR is 5%.

Answer:

The actual (unannualized) rate on the 30-day loan is:

$$R30 = 0.04 \times \frac{30}{360} = 0.00333$$

The actual (unannualized) rate on the 120-day loan is:

$$R120 = 0.05 \times \frac{120}{360} = 0.01667$$

We wish to calculate the actual rate on a 90-day loan from day 30 to day 120:

$$\text{price of } 1 \times 4 \text{ FRA} = \frac{1+R120}{1+R30} - 1 = \frac{1.01667}{1.00333} - 1 = 0.0133$$

We can annualize this rate as:

$$0.0133 \times \frac{360}{90} = 0.0532 = 5.32\%$$

This is the no-arbitrage forward rate—the forward rate that will make the values of the long and the short positions in the FRA both zero at the initiation of the contract.

The time line is shown in the following figure.

Pricing a 1 × 4 FRA

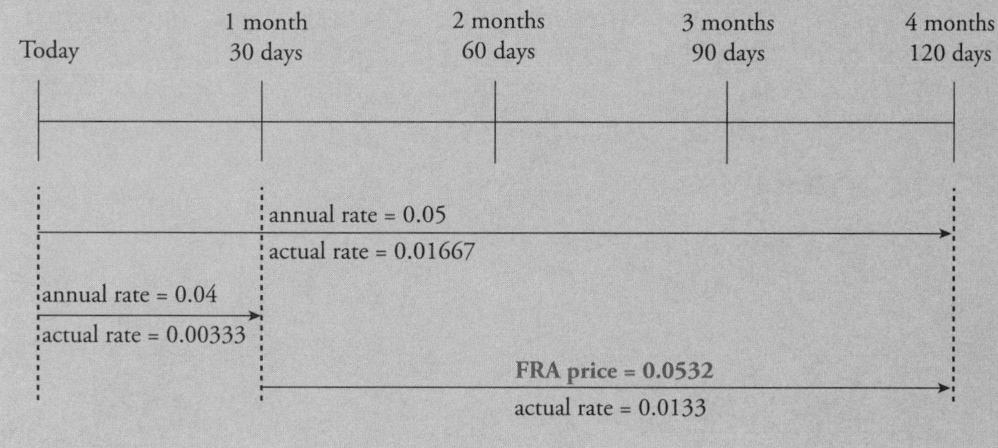

Valuing an FRA at Maturity

To understand the calculation of the value of the FRA *after the initiation of the contract*, recall that in the previous example the long in the FRA has the "right" to borrow money 30 days from inception for a period of 90 days at the forward rate. If interest rates increase (specifically the 90-day forward contract rate), the long will profit as the contract has fixed a borrowing rate below the now-current market rate. These "savings" will come at the end of the loan term, so to value the FRA we need to take the present value of these savings. An example incorporating this fact will illustrate the cash settlement value of an FRA at expiration.

Example: Calculating value of an FRA at maturity (i.e., cash payment at settlement)

Continuing the prior example for a 1 × 4 FRA, assume a notional principal of $1 million and that, at contract expiration, the 90-day rate has increased to 6%, which is above the contract rate of 5.32%. Calculate the value of the FRA at maturity, which is equal to the cash payment at settlement.

Answer:

The interest savings at the end of the loan term (compared to the market rate of 6%) will be:

$$\left[\left(0.0600\times\frac{90}{360}\right)-\left(0.0532\times\frac{90}{360}\right)\right]\times \$1{,}000{,}000=\$1{,}700$$

The present value of this amount at the FRA settlement date (90 days prior to the end of the loan term) discounted at the current rate of 6% is:

$$\frac{\$1{,}700}{1+\left(0.06\times\frac{90}{360}\right)}=\$1{,}674.88$$

This will be the cash settlement payment from the short to the long at the expiration of the contract. Note that we have discounted the savings in interest at the end of the loan term by the *market* rate of 6% that prevails at the contract settlement date for a 90-day term, as shown in the following figure.

Valuing a 1 x 4 FRA at Maturity

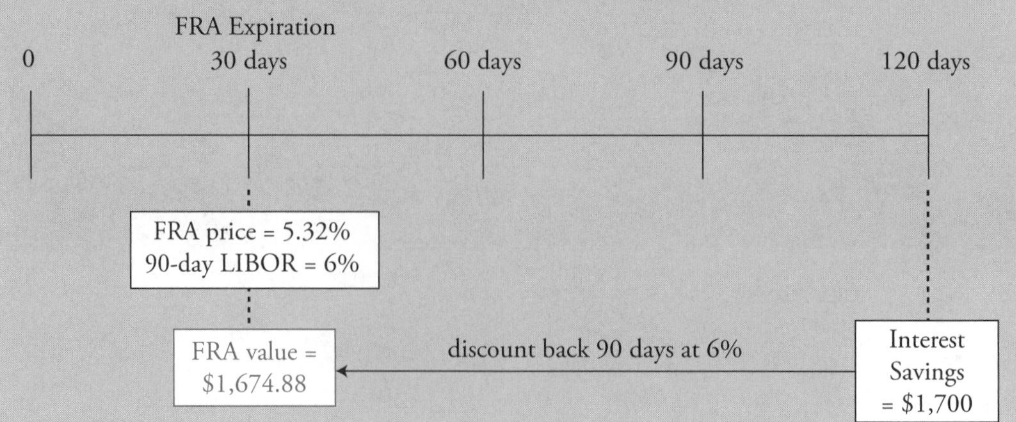

Valuing an FRA Before Maturity

To value an FRA before the settlement date, we need to know the number of days that have passed since the initiation of the contract. For example, let's suppose we want to value the same 1 × 4 FRA 10 days after initiation. Originally, it was a 1 × 4 FRA, which means the FRA now expires in 20 days. The calculation of the "savings" on the loan will be the same as in our previous example, except that we need to use the "new" FRA price that would be quoted on a contract covering the same period as the original "loan." In this case the "new" FRA price is the now-current market forward rate for a 90-day loan made at the settlement date (20 days in the future). Also, we need to discount the interest savings implicit in the FRA back an extra 20 days, or 110 days, instead of 90 days as we did for the value at the settlement date.

Example: Calculating value of an FRA before settlement

Value a 5.32% 1 × 4 FRA with a principal amount of $1 million 10 days after initiation if 110-day LIBOR is 5.9% and 20-day LIBOR is 5.7%.

Answer:

Step 1: Find the "new" FRA price on a 90-day loan 20 days from today. This is the current 90-day forward rate at the settlement date, 20 days from now.

$$\left[\frac{1+\left(0.059\times\frac{110}{360}\right)}{1+\left(0.057\times\frac{20}{360}\right)}-1\right]\times\frac{360}{90}=0.0592568$$

Step 2: Calculate the interest difference on a $1 million, 90-day loan made 20 days from now at the forward rate calculated previously compared to the FRA rate of 5.32%.

$$\left[\left(0.0592568\times\frac{90}{360}\right)-\left(0.0532\times\frac{90}{360}\right)\right]\times\$1{,}000{,}000=\$1{,}514.20$$

Step 3: Discount this amount at the current 110-day rate.

$$\frac{\$1{,}514.20}{1+\left(0.059\times\frac{110}{360}\right)}=\$1{,}487.39$$

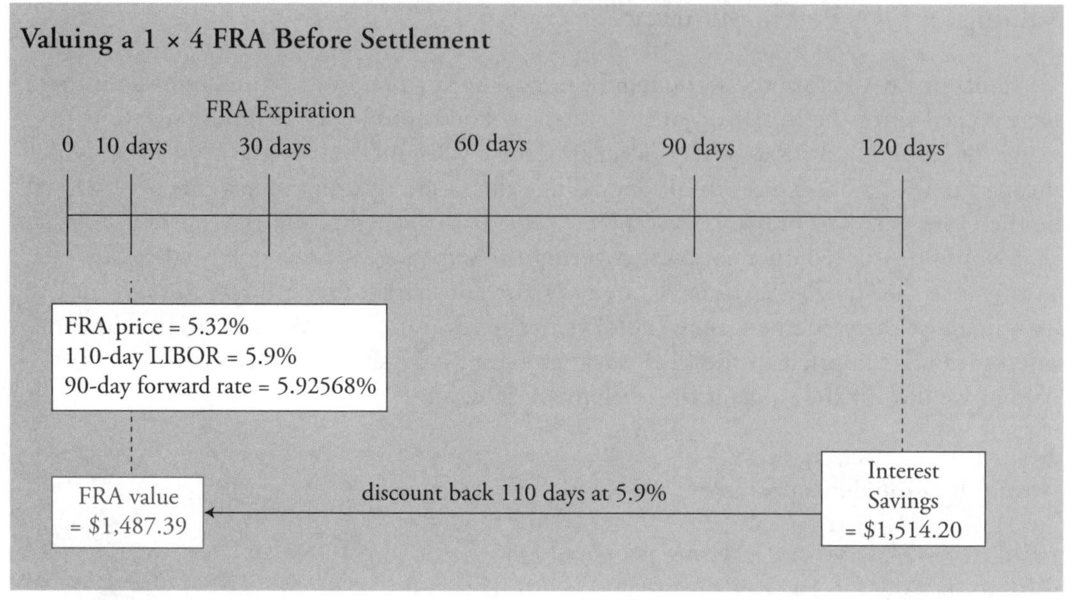

Professor's Note: I have tried to explain these calculations in such a way that you can value an FRA at any date from initiation to settlement using basic tools that you already know. Once you understand where the value of an FRA comes from (the interest savings on a loan to be made at the settlement date) and when this value is to be received (at the end of the loan), you can calculate the present value of these savings even under somewhat stressful test conditions. Just remember that if the rate in the future is less than the FRA rate, the long is "obligated to borrow" at above-market rates and will have to make a payment to the short. If the rate is greater than the FRA rate, the long will receive a payment from the short.

Study Session 14

Pricing Currency Forward Contracts

The **price and value of a currency forward contract** is refreshingly straightforward after that last bit of mental exercise. The calculation of the currency forward rate is just an application of covered interest parity from the topic review of foreign exchange parity relations in Study Session 4.

Recall that the interest rate parity result is based on an assumption that you should make the same amount when you lend at the riskless rate in your home country as you would if you bought *one unit* of the foreign currency at the current spot rate, S_0, invested it at the foreign risk-free rate, and entered into a forward contract to exchange the proceeds of the investment at maturity for the home currency at the forward rate of F_T (both the forward and the spot rates are quoted as quantity of price currency one unit of the base currency).

Covered interest rate parity gives us the no-arbitrage forward price of a unit of foreign currency in terms of the home currency for a currency forward contract of length *T* in years:

$$F_T\left(\text{currency forward contract}\right) = S_0 \times \frac{\left(1+R_{PC}\right)^T}{\left(1+R_{BC}\right)^T}$$

where:
F and S are quoted in price currency per unit of base currency
R_{PC} = price currency interest rate
R_{BC} = base currency interest rate

For foreign currency contracts, use a 365-day basis to calculate *T* if the maturity is given in days.

Professor's Note: The key is to remember our numerator/denominator rule: if the spot and forward quotes are in Currency A (i.e., the price currency, or PC) per unit of Currency B (i.e., the base currency, or BC), the Currency A interest rate should be on top and the Currency B interest rate should be on the bottom. For example, if S and F are in euros per Swiss franc, put the Euro interest rate on the top and the Swiss interest rate on the bottom.

If you recall the formula for this from the Economics portion of the curriculum, you will see two subtle differences. In derivatives we use periodically compounded rates (and not LIBOR-type rates). Also, we don't concern ourselves with bid-offer prices here. These differences reflect the preferences of the authors of the two different readings in the original CFA Institute curriculum.

Example: Calculating the price of a currency forward contract

The risk-free rates are 6% in the United States and 8% in Mexico. The current spot exchange rate is $0.0845 per Mexican peso (MXN). Calculate the forward exchange rate for a 180-day forward contract.

Answer:

$$F_T\left(\text{currency forward contract}\right) = \$0.0845 \times \frac{1.06^{180/365}}{1.08^{180/365}} = \$0.0837$$

Valuing Currency Forward Contracts After Initiation

After inception, currency forward contracts can be valued as:

$$V_t = \frac{[FP_t - FP] \times (\text{contract size})}{(1 + r_{PC})^{(T-t)}}$$

where:
V_t = value (in price currency units) to the party long the base currency
FP = forward price at inception of the contract maturing at time T (in PC/BC)
FP_t = forward price at time t (t < T) of contract maturing at T
r_{PC} = interest rate of price currency

Example:

David Hastings entered into a four-month forward contract to buy €10 million at a price of \$1.112 per euro. One month later, the three-month forward price is \$1.109 per euro. The USD interest rate is 0.30% and the euro interest rate is 0.40%. Calculate the value of Hastings's forward position.

Answer:

The value to the long party is given by:

$$V_t = \frac{[FP_t - FP] \times (\text{contract size})}{(1 + r_{PC})^{(T-t)}} = \frac{[1.109 - 1.112] \times 10{,}000{,}000}{(1.003)^{(0.25)}} = -29{,}978 \text{ USD}$$

Study Session 14

Futures Contracts

Futures contracts are very much like the forward contracts except that they trade on organized exchanges. Each exchange has a clearinghouse. The clearinghouse guarantees that traders in the futures market will honor their obligations. The clearinghouse does this by splitting each trade once it is made and acting as the opposite side of each position. To safeguard the clearinghouse, the exchange requires both sides of the trade to post margin and settle their accounts on a daily basis. Thus, the margin in the futures markets is a performance guarantee.

Marking to market is the process of adjusting the margin balance in a futures account each day for the change in the value of the contract from the previous trading day, based on the settlement price.

The pricing relationship discussed earlier also generally applies to futures contracts as well (see for example, our earlier discussion on treasury bond futures contract). Like forward contracts, futures contracts have no value at contract initiation. Unlike forward contracts, futures contracts do not accumulate value changes over the term of the contract. Since futures accounts are marked to market daily, the value after the margin deposit has been adjusted for the day's gains and losses in contract value is always zero.

The futures price at any point in time is the price that makes the value of a new contract equal to zero. The value of a futures contract strays from zero only during the trading periods between the times at which the account is marked to market:

value of futures contract = current futures price – previous mark-to-market price

If the futures price increases, the value of the long position increases. The value is set back to zero by the mark-to-market at the end of the mark-to-market period.

LOS 40.c: Describe and compare how interest rate, currency, and equity swaps are priced and valued.

LOS 40.d: Calculate and interpret the no-arbitrage value of interest rate, currency, and equity swaps.

CFA® Program Curriculum, Volume 5, page 331

The distinction between the price and the value of a swap is the same one we made for forward contracts. Remember that the price of a forward contract is the forward rate that yields a zero value for the contract at initiation. After contract initiation, as rates or prices change, the contract will likely have value to either the long or the short.

Consider an interest rate swap. One party agrees to pay floating (borrow at the floating rate) and receive fixed (lend at a fixed rate). At initiation of the swap, the fixed rate is selected so that the present value of the floating-rate payments is equal to the present value of the fixed-rate payments, which means the swap value is zero to both parties. This fixed rate is called the **swap rate** or the **swap fixed rate**. Determining the swap rate is equivalent to "pricing" the swap.

As short-term rates (and expected future short-term rates) change over the term of the swap, the value of the swap to one of the parties will be positive. The swap position is an asset to that party.

Computing the Swap Fixed Rate

The swap fixed rate is derived from the LIBOR curve corresponding to the swap tenor. Consider a two-year, semiannual interest rate swap. The swap fixed rate underlying this swap will be determined based on the LIBOR rates corresponding to the four settlement dates of this swap.

Using those four LIBOR rates, we calculate the discount factors (Zs) for each.

$$Z = \frac{1}{\left[1 + \left(\text{LIBOR} \times \frac{\text{days}}{360}\right)\right]}$$

The periodic swap fixed rate SFR(periodic) can then be calculated as:

$$SFR\left(\text{periodic}\right) = \frac{1 - \text{last discount factor}}{\text{sum of discount factors}}$$

swap fixed rate (annual) = SFR (periodic) × number of settlement periods per year

Example: Calculating the fixed rate on a swap with quarterly payments

Annualized LIBOR spot rates today are:

$R_{90\text{-day}} = 0.030$

$R_{180\text{-day}} = 0.035$

$R_{270\text{-day}} = 0.040$

$R_{360\text{-day}} = 0.045$

You're analyzing a 1-year swap with quarterly payments and a notional principal amount of $5,000,000. Calculate:

- The fixed rate in percentage terms.
- The quarterly fixed payments in $.

Answer:

First calculate the discount factors. Don't forget to convert from annualized rates to per-period rates.

$$Z_{90\text{-day}} = \frac{1}{1+\left(0.030\times\frac{90}{360}\right)} = 0.99256$$

$$Z_{180\text{-day}} = \frac{1}{1+\left(0.035\times\frac{180}{360}\right)} = 0.98280$$

$$Z_{270\text{-day}} = \frac{1}{1+\left(0.040\times\frac{270}{360}\right)} = 0.97087$$

$$Z_{360\text{-day}} = \frac{1}{1+\left(0.045\times\frac{360}{360}\right)} = 0.95694$$

Professor's Note: It's likely that on the exam you will be given a table of discount factors to use in pricing a swap, as in the next example. We've provided the calculations here so you know where the discount factors come from.

The quarterly fixed rate on the swap is:

$$\frac{1-0.95694}{0.99256+0.98280+0.97087+0.95694} = 0.011 = 1.1\%$$

The quarterly fixed-rate payments, assuming a notional principal of $5,000,000, are:

$$\$5{,}000{,}000 \times 0.011 = \$55{,}000$$

The fixed rate on the swap in annual terms is:

$$1.1\% \times \frac{360}{90} = 4.4\%$$

We have priced a swap in which one side pays quarterly LIBOR and the other side pays 4.4% fixed annually (1.1% quarterly).

Calculating the Market Value of an Interest Rate Swap

For the purpose of the exam, we are only responsible for valuation of an interest rate swap *on* settlement dates (after settlement has occurred), and not *between* settlement dates.

After the initiation of an interest rate swap, the swap will take on a positive or negative value as interest rates change. The party that is the fixed-rate payer benefits if rates increase because they are paying the older (and lower) fixed rate and receiving the newer (and higher) floating rate. Similarly, the fixed-rate receiver benefits if rates decrease because they are receiving the older (and higher) fixed rate while paying a newer (and lower) floating rate.

$$\text{value to the payer} = \Sigma Z \times (SFR_{New} - SFR_{Old}) \times \frac{\text{days}}{360} \times \text{notional principal}$$

where:
ΣZ = the sum of discount factors associated with the remaining settlement periods

Example: Valuing a swap on payment date

Let's continue our previous example of a one-year, quarterly settlement, $5 million notional swap with a swap fixed rate at initiation of 4.4%. Suppose that after 180 days, the LIBOR term structure is flat at 3.5% over the next year. Calculate the value of the swap to the fixed-rate receiver.

Answer:

Because the LIBOR term structure is flat at 3.5%, the new swap fixed rate must be 3.5%. At t=180, there are two more settlement dates remaining: 90 and 180 days in the future.

$$Z_{90\text{-day}} = \frac{1}{1+\left(0.035\times\frac{90}{360}\right)} = 0.9913$$

$$Z_{180\text{-day}} = \frac{1}{1+\left(0.035\times\frac{180}{360}\right)} = 0.9828$$

$$\Sigma Z = 0.9913 + 0.9828 = 1.9741$$

value of swap to the payer

$$= 1.9741\times(0.035-0.044)\times\frac{90}{360}\times\$5{,}000{,}000 = -\$22{,}209$$

value to the receiver = +$22,209

Currency Swaps

Determining the Fixed Rate and Foreign Notional Principal

Consider two currencies, the U.S. dollar ($) and the British pound (£), where the exchange rate is currently $2 per £ or £0.5 per $. Using the method introduced earlier to price an interest rate swap, we can solve for the fixed rate that will make the present value of the fixed-rate $ payments equal to $1.00, and the fixed rate that will make the present value of the fixed-rate foreign payments equal to £1.00 in Great Britain. The interest rates in a currency swap are simply the swap rates calculated from each country's yield curve or the floating (short-term) rates in the relevant country's currency. Don't forget: With currency swaps, there are two yield curves and two swap rates, one for each currency.

The principal amounts of the fixed-rate obligations must be adjusted for the current exchange rate. We need $2.00 to equal £1.00, so these are the notional amounts, exchanged at the inception of the swap and returned at the termination of the swap. For example, if the notional principal amount of the $ side of the swap is $25 million, the £ notional principal amount will be £12.5 million.

Example: Calculating the fixed rate and notional principal on a currency swap

In a previous example, we determined that the fixed rate on a 1-year quarterly $5,000,000 interest rate swap, given the following set of spot LIBOR rates, was 1.1% quarterly, or 4.4% on an annual basis.

$$R^{\$}_{\text{90-day}} = 0.030$$
$$R^{\$}_{\text{180-day}} = 0.035$$
$$R^{\$}_{\text{270-day}} = 0.040$$
$$R^{\$}_{\text{360-day}} = 0.045$$

The comparable set of £ rates are:

$$R^{£}_{\text{90-day}} = 0.04$$
$$R^{£}_{\text{180-day}} = 0.05$$
$$R^{£}_{\text{270-day}} = 0.06$$
$$R^{£}_{\text{360-day}} = 0.07$$

The current exchange rate is £0.50 per $.

Determine the fixed rate on a 1-year £ interest rate swap. Then determine the notional £ principal amount and the quarterly cash flows on a pay $ fixed, receive £ fixed currency swap.

Answer:

First calculate the £ discount factors. Don't forget to convert from annualized rates to per-period rates.

$$Z_{\text{90-day}}^{£} = \frac{1}{1+\left(0.04\times\frac{90}{360}\right)} = 0.99010$$

$$Z_{\text{180-day}}^{£} = \frac{1}{1+\left(0.05\times\frac{180}{360}\right)} = 0.97561$$

$$Z_{\text{270-day}}^{£} = \frac{1}{1+\left(0.06\times\frac{270}{360}\right)} = 0.95694$$

$$Z_{\text{360-day}}^{£} = \frac{1}{1+\left(0.07\times\frac{360}{360}\right)} = 0.93458$$

The quarterly fixed rate on the £ swap is:

$$\frac{1-0.93458}{0.99010+0.97561+0.95694+0.93458} = 0.017 = 1.7\%$$

The fixed rate on the £ swap in annual terms is:

$$1.7\% \times \frac{360}{90} = 6.8\%$$

The notional £ principal amount of the swap would be:

$5,000,000 × 0.50 = £2,500,000

At the initiation of the swap, we would exchange £2,500,000 for $5,000,000. We would pay 1.1% quarterly on the $5,000,000 notional principal ($55,000) and receive 1.7% on £2,500,000 quarterly (£42,500). At the end of one year, we would exchange the original principal amounts.

The value of a currency swap is calculated the same way as an interest rate swap. The value to any party is the present value of the cash flows they expect to receive minus the present value of the cash flows they are obligated to pay.

Example: Calculating the value of a currency swap after initiation

Use the data on the \$ and £ interest rate swaps in the previous examples to answer this question. After 300 days, the 60-day \$ interest rate is 5.4%, the 60-day £ interest rate is 6.6%, and the exchange rate is £0.52 per \$. Calculate the value of a \$5,000,000 swap in which the counterparty receives \$ fixed and pays £ fixed.

Answer:

Recall that the \$ fixed rate was calculated as 4.4% (or 1.1% per quarter) and the £ fixed rate was calculated as 6.8% (or 1.7% per quarter). After 300 days, the only cash flows remaining are the last interest payments and the principal payments in 60 days. We want to find the present value of those cash flows, so we need the 60-day discount factors based on the current 60-day rates:

$$Z_{60\text{-day}}^{\$} = \frac{1}{1+\left(0.054 \times \frac{60}{360}\right)} = 0.99108$$

$$Z_{60\text{-day}}^{£} = \frac{1}{1+\left(0.066 \times \frac{60}{360}\right)} = 0.98912$$

First calculate the value after 300 days of the \$ fixed payments. It is equivalent to the value of a \$5,000,000 bond that matures in 60 days and makes a coupon payment in 60 days of \$55,000 (\$5,000,000 × 0.011). The value in \$ of the \$ fixed side is the present value of \$5,055,000 discounted using the 60-day \$ discount factor of 0.99108:

value of \$ fixed side (in \$) = 0.99108 × \$5,055,000 = \$5,009,909

Next, calculate the value after 300 days of the £ fixed payments. This is equivalent to the value of a 6.8% fixed rate, £2,500,000 bond that matures in 60 days and pays a coupon payment of £42,500 (£2,500,000 × 0.017) in 60 days. The value in £ of the £ fixed side is the present value of £2,542,500 discounted using the 60-day £ discount factor of 0.98912:

value of £ fixed side (in £) = 0.98912 × £2,542,500 = £2,514,838

The last step is to convert that amount into \$ at the *current spot exchange rate* of £0.52 per \$ to find the value of the £ fixed side in \$:

value of £ fixed side (in \$) = £2,514,838 / 0.52 = \$4,836,227

Finally, the value of the receive \$ fixed, pay £ fixed side of the swap is equal to the value of the \$ fixed side minus the £ fixed side, or \$5,009,909 – \$4,836,227 = \$173,682.

Equity Swaps

To price an N-period pay-fixed equity swap, we can use the same formula as for a plain vanilla swap:

$$\text{SFR}(\text{periodic}) = \frac{1 - \text{last discount factor}}{\text{sum of discount factors}}$$

To value this swap after time has passed, determine the value of the equity or index portfolio and the value of the fixed-rate payments.

Example: Valuing a pay fixed, receive equity returns swap

A $10 million principal value equity swap has a fixed quarterly rate of 0.01513 and the other side pays the quarterly return on an index. The index is currently trading at 985. After 30 days have passed, the index stands at 996 and the term structure is the same as our earlier example using LIBOR annualized rates of 6%, 6.5%, 7%, and 7.5% for terms of 60, 150, 240, and 330 days. The discount factors are 0.99010, 0.97363, 0.95541, and 0.93567. The value of the pay-fixed side of the swap from that earlier example was $0.993993 per $ of notional principal. Calculate the value of the swap to the fixed-rate payer on day 30.

Answer:

We can calculate the value of the fixed-payer side of the swap by multiplying the value per $ of notional principal by the $10 million notional principal:

$$\text{value of fixed-pay side} = 0.993993 \times \$10{,}000{,}000 = \$9{,}939{,}930$$

The value of $10,000,000 invested in the index after 30 days is:

$$\$10{,}000{,}000 \times \frac{996}{985} = \$10{,}111{,}675$$

The fixed-rate liability has decreased from its original value of $10,000,000. From the standpoint of the fixed-rate payer, the value of the swap after 30 days is:

$$\$10{,}111{,}675 - \$9{,}939{,}930 = \$171{,}745$$

A swap of returns on two different stocks can be viewed as buying one stock (receiving the returns) and shorting an equal value of a different stock (paying the returns). There is no "pricing" at swap initiation, and we can value the swap at any point in time by taking the difference in returns (since the last payment date) times the notional principal.

Example: Valuing a "one-equity-return-for-another" swap

An investor is the Stock A returns payer (and Stock B returns receiver) in a $1million quarterly-pay swap. After one month, Stock A is up 1.3% and Stock B is down 0.8%. Calculate the value of the swap to the investor.

Answer:

The investor pays the Stock A returns and receives Stock B returns. However, the Stock B returns are negative, so he pays those as well:

$$\text{value of swap} = (-0.013 - 0.008) \times \$1{,}000{,}000 = -\$21{,}000$$

Key Concepts

LOS 40.a, b

$$V_0(\text{of long position at initiation}) = S_0 - \left[\frac{FP}{(1+R_f)^T}\right]$$

$$V_t(\text{of long position during life of contract}) = S_t - \left[\frac{FP}{(1+R_f)^{T-t}}\right]$$

$$V_T(\text{of long postion at maturity}) = S_T - FP$$

$$V_T(\text{of short position at maturity}) = FP - S_T$$

The calculation of the forward price for an equity forward contract is different because the periodic dividend payments affect the no-arbitrage price calculation. The forward price is reduced by the future value of the expected dividend payments; alternatively, the spot price is reduced by the present value of the dividends.

$$FP(\text{on an equity security}) = (S_0 - PVD) \times (1+R_f)^T = \left[S_0 \times (1+R_f)^T\right] - FVD$$

The value of an equity forward contract to the long is the spot equity price minus the present value of the forward price minus the present value of any dividends expected over the term of the contract:

$$V_t(\text{long position}) = [S_t - PVD_t] - \left[\frac{FP}{(1+R_f)^{(T-t)}}\right]$$

We typically use the continuous time versions to calculate the price and value of a forward contract on an equity index using a continuously compounded dividend yield.

$$FP(\text{on an equity index}) = S_0 \times e^{(R_f^c - \delta^c) \times T} = \left(S_0 \times e^{-\delta^c \times T}\right) \times e^{R_f^c \times T}$$

For forwards on coupon-paying bonds, the price is calculated as the spot price minus the present value of the coupons times the quantity one plus the risk-free rate:

$$FP(\text{on a fixed income security}) = (S_0 - PVC) \times (1+R_f)^T = S_0 \times (1+R_f)^T - FVC$$

The value of a forward on a coupon-paying bond *t* years after inception is the spot bond price minus the present value of the forward price minus the present value of any coupon payments expected over the term of the contract:

$$V_t(\text{long position}) = [S_t - PVC_t] - \left[\frac{FP}{(1+R_f)^{(T-t)}}\right]$$

In a futures contract, the short may have delivery options (to decide which bond to deliver). In such a case, the quoted futures price is adjusted using the conversion factor for the cheapest-to-deliver bond:

$$QFP = FP / CF = \left[(\text{full price})(1+R_f)^T - AI_T - FVC\right]\left(\frac{1}{CF}\right)$$

where
the full price = clean price + accrued interest at t=0
AI_T = accrued interest at futures contract maturity.

The "price" of an FRA is the implied forward rate for the period beginning when the FRA expires to the maturity of the underlying "loan."

The value of an FRA at maturity is the interest savings to be realized at maturity of the underlying "loan" discounted back to the date of the expiration of the FRA at the current LIBOR. The value of an FRA before maturity is the interest savings estimated by the implied forward rate discounted back to the valuation date at the current LIBOR.

For a currency forward, the price is the exchange rate implied by covered interest rate parity. The value at settlement is the gain or loss to the long from making a currency exchange in the amounts required by the contract at the contract exchange rate, rather than at the prevailing market rate:

$$F_T(\text{currency forward contract}) = S_0 \times \frac{(1+R_{DC})^T}{(1+R_{FC})^T}$$

where:
F and S are quoted in domestic currency per unit of foreign currency

Before settlement, the value of a currency forward is the present value of any gain or loss to the long from making a currency exchange in the amounts required by the contract at the contract exchange rate, compared to an exchange at the prevailing forward exchange rate at the settlement date:

$$V_t = \frac{[FP_t - FP] \times (\text{contract size})}{(1+r_{PC})^{(T-t)}}$$

where:
V_t = value (in price currency units) to the party long the base currency
FP = forward price at inception of the contract maturing at time T (PC/BC)
FP_t = forward price at time t (t < T) of the contract maturing at T
r_{PC} = interest rate of price currency

The continuous time price formula for a currency forward contract is:

$$F_T(\text{currency forward contract}) = S_0 \times e^{\left(R^c_{DC} - R^c_{FC}\right) \times T}$$

LOS 40.c, d

The fixed periodic-rate on an *n*-period swap at initiation (as a percentage of the principal value) can be calculated as:

$$\text{SFR}(\text{periodic}) = \frac{1 - \text{last discount factor}}{\text{sum of discount factors}}$$

where:

$$\text{discount factor} = Z = \frac{1}{\left[1 + \left(\text{LIBOR} \times \frac{\text{days}}{360}\right)\right]}$$

The value of a swap *on* a payment date has a simple relationship to the difference between the new swap fixed rate and the original swap fixed rate:

$$\text{value to the payer} = \Sigma Z \times (\text{SFR}_{\text{New}} - \text{SFR}_{\text{Old}}) \times \frac{\text{days}}{360} \times \text{notional principal}$$

where:
ΣZ = sum of discount factors associated with the *remaining* settlement periods

The fixed rates in a fixed-for-fixed currency swap are determined using the yield curves for the relevant currencies. The notional principal amounts in the two currencies are of equal value, based on the the exchange rate at inception of the swap.

The fixed-rate side of an equity swap is priced and valued just like an interest rate swap. The equity side can be valued by multiplying the notional amount of the contract by 1 + the percentage equity appreciation since the last payment date. Use the difference in values to value the swap.

Concept Checkers

1. A stock is currently priced at $30 and is expected to pay a dividend of $0.30 20 days and 65 days from now. The contract price for a 60-day forward contract when the interest rate is 5% is *closest* to:
   A. $29.46.
   B. $29.70.
   C. $29.94.

2. After 37 days, the stock in Question 1 is priced at $21, and the risk-free rate is still 5%. The value of the forward contract on the stock to the short position is:
   A. –$8.85.
   B. +$8.85.
   C. +$9.00.

3. The contract rate (annualized) for a 3 × 5 FRA if the current 60-day rate is 4%, the current 90-day rate is 5%, and the current 150-day rate is 6%, is *closest* to:
   A. 6.0%.
   B. 6.9%.
   C. 7.4%.

4. A 6% Treasury bond is trading at $1,044 (including accrued interest) per $1,000 of face value. It will make a coupon payment 98 days from now. The yield curve is flat at 5% over the next 150 days. The forward price per $1,000 of face value for a 120-day forward contract, is *closest* to:
   A. $1,014.52.
   B. $1,030.79.
   C. $1,037.13.

5. The forward price of a 200-day stock index futures contract when the spot index is 540, the continuous dividend yield is 1.8%, and the continuously compounded risk-free rate is 7% (with a flat yield curve) is *closest* to:
   A. 545.72.
   B. 555.61.
   C. 568.08.

6. An analyst who mistakenly ignores the dividends when valuing a short position in a forward contract on a stock that pays dividends will *most likely*:
   A. overvalue the position by the present value of the dividends.
   B. undervalue the position by the present value of the dividends.
   C. overvalue the position by the future value of the dividends.

7. The current U.S. dollar ($) to Canadian dollar (C$) exchange rate is 0.7. In a $1 million fixed-for-floating currency swap, the party that is entering the swap to hedge an existing exposure to a C$-denominated fixed-rate liability will:
   A. receive $1 million at the termination of the swap.
   B. pay a fixed rate based on the yield curve in the United States.
   C. receive a fixed rate based on the yield curve in Canada.

8. Annualized LIBOR spot rates and the present value factors today are:

	Rate	Present value factor
90-day LIBOR	4.2%	0.98961
180-day LIBOR	4.8%	0.97656
270-day LIBOR	5.0%	0.96386
360-day LIBOR	5.2%	0.95057
Total		3.88060

Based on a notional principal of $40,000,000, the annualized swap rate is *closest* to:
A. 1.27%.
B. 2.54%.
C. 5.08%.

Use the following information to answer Questions 9 and 10.

Two parties enter into a 2-year fixed-for-floating interest rate swap with semiannual payments. The floating-rate payments are based on LIBOR. The 180-, 360-, 540-, and 720-day annualized LIBOR rates and present value factors are:

	Rate	Present value factor
180-day LIBOR	5.0%	0.9756
360-day LIBOR	6.0%	0.9434
540-day LIBOR	6.5%	0.9112
720-day LIBOR	7.0%	0.8772

9. The swap rate is *closest* to:
A. 6.62%.
B. 6.87%.
C. 7.03%.

10. After 180 days, the swap is marked-to-market when the 180-, 360-, and 540-day annualized LIBOR rates are 4.5%, 5%, and 6%, respectively. The present value factors, respectively, are 0.9780, 0.9524, and 0.9174. What is the market value of the swap per $1 notional principal, and which of the two counterparties (the fixed-rate payer or the fixed-rate receiver) would make the payment to mark the swap to market?

	Market value	Payment made by
A.	$0.01166	Fixed-rate payer
B.	$0.04290	Fixed-rate payer
C.	$0.01166	Fixed-rate receiver

11. A bank entered into a $5,000,000, 1-year equity swap with quarterly payments 300 days ago. The bank agreed to pay an annual fixed rate of 4% and receive the return on an international equity index. The index was trading at 3,000 at the end of the third quarter, 30 days ago. The current 60-day LIBOR rate is 3.6%, the discount factor is 0.9940, and the index is now at 3,150. The value of the swap to the bank is *closest* to:
A. –$257,795.
B. –$114,676.
C. $230,300.

Challenge Problems

12. A portfolio manager owns Macrogrow, Inc., which is currently trading at $35 per share. She plans to sell the stock in 120 days, but is concerned about a possible price decline. She decides to take a short position in a 120-day forward contract on the stock. The stock will pay a $0.50 per share dividend in 35 days and $0.50 again in 125 days. The risk-free rate is 4%. The value of the trader's position in the forward contract in 45 days, assuming in 45 days the stock price is $27.50 and the risk-free rate has not changed, is *closest* to:
    A. $7.17.
    B. $7.50.
    C. $7.92.

13. The CFO of Yellow River Company received a report from the economics department that states that short-term rates are expected to increase 50 basis points in the next 90 days. As a floating rate borrower (typically against 90-day LIBOR), the CFO recognizes that he must hedge against an increase in future borrowing costs over the next 90 days because of a potential increase in short-term interest rates. He considers many options, but decides on entering into a long forward rate agreement (FRA). The 30-day LIBOR is 4.5%, 90-day LIBOR is 4.7%, and 180-day LIBOR is 4.9%. To *best* hedge this risk, Yellow River should enter into a:
    A. 3 × 3 FRA at a rate of 4.48%.
    B. 3 × 6 FRA at a rate of 4.48%.
    C. 3 × 6 FRA at a rate of 5.02%.

14. Consider a U.K.-based company that exports goods to the EU. The U.K. company expects to receive payment on a shipment of goods in 60 days. Because the payment will be in euros, the U.K. company wants to hedge against a decline in the value of the euro against the pound over the next 60 days. The U.K. risk-free rate is 3%, and the EU risk-free rate is 4%. No change is expected in these rates over the next 60 days. The current spot rate is 0.9230 £ per €. To hedge the currency risk, the U.K. company should take a short position in a euro contract at a forward price of:
    A. 0.9205.
    B. 0.9215.
    C. 0.9244.

15. A bank entered into a 1-year currency swap with quarterly payments 200 days ago by agreeing to swap $1,000,000 for €800,000. The bank agreed to pay an annual fixed rate of 5% on the €800,000 and receive a fixed rate of 4.2% on the $1,000,000. Current LIBOR and Euribor rates and present value factors are shown in the following table.

	Rate	*Present Value Factor*
70-day LIBOR	4.0%	0.9923
90-day LIBOR	4.4%	0.9891
160-day LIBOR	4.8%	0.9791
180-day LIBOR	5.2%	0.9747
70-day Euribor	5.2%	0.9900
90-day Euribor	5.6%	0.9862
160-day Euribor	6.1%	0.9736
180-day Euribor	6.3%	0.9695

The current spot exchange rate is €0.75 per $1.00. The value of the swap to the bank today is *closest* to:

A. –$64,888.
B. –$42,049.
C. $42,049.

To access other content related to this topic review that may be included in the Schweser package you purchased, log in to your Schweser.com online dashboard. Schweser's OnDemand Video Lectures deliver streaming instruction covering every LOS in this topic review, while SchweserPro™ QBank provides additional quiz questions to help you practice and recall what you've learned.

Answers – Concept Checkers

1. **C** The dividend in 65 days occurs after the contract has matured, so it's not relevant to computing the forward price.

$$PVD = \frac{\$0.30}{1.05^{20/365}} = \$0.2992$$

$$FP = (\$30.00 - \$0.2992) \times 1.05^{60/365} = \$29.94$$

2. **B** $V(\text{long position}) = \$21.00 - \left[\frac{\$29.94}{1.05^{23/365}}\right] = -\$8.85$

$V(\text{short position}) = +\$8.85$

3. **C** The actual (unannualized) rate on the 90-day loan is:

$$R90 = 0.05 \times \frac{90}{360} = 0.0125$$

The actual rate on the 150-day loan is:

$$R150 = 0.06 \times \frac{150}{360} = 0.025$$

The price of the 3 × 5 FRA (the 60-day forward rate in 90 days) is:

$$\left(\frac{1.025}{1.0125} - 1\right) \times \frac{360}{60} = 0.074 = 7.4\%$$

4. **B** Remember that U.S. Treasury bonds make semiannual coupon payments, so:

$$C = \frac{\$1,000 \times 0.06}{2} = \$30.00$$

$$PVC = \frac{\$30.00}{1.05^{98/365}} = \$29.61$$

The forward price of the contract is therefore:

FP (on a fixed income security) = $(\$1,044 - \$29.61) \times (1.05)^{120/365} = \$1,030.79$

5. **B** Use the dividend rate as a continuously compounded rate to get:

$FP = 540 \times e^{(0.07 - 0.018) \times (200 / 365)} = 555.61$

6. **B** The value of the long position in a forward contract on a stock at time *t* is:

$$V_t(\text{long position}) = [S_t - PVD_t] - \left[\frac{FP}{(1+R_f)^{(T-t)}}\right]$$

If the dividends are ignored, the *long* position will be overvalued by the present value of the dividends; that means the *short* position (which is what the question asks for) will be undervalued by the same amount.

7. C A receive-fixed C$ position will hedge the liability risk. That party would receive $1 million at swap inception (in exchange for $\frac{1{,}000{,}000}{0.7}$ = C$1,428,571) and pay it back at termination. The fixed-rate received will be calculated using the yield curve in Canada at the initiation of the swap. Because this is a fixed-for-floating currency swap, the receive-fixed position will pay a floating rate based on the U.S. yield curve.

8. C The quarterly fixed rate on the swap is:

$$\frac{1-0.95057}{3.88060} = 0.0127 = 1.27\%$$

The fixed rate on the swap in annual terms is:

$$1.27\% \times \frac{360}{90} = 5.08\%$$

9. A Calculate the swap rate:

$$\text{semi-annual swap rate} = \frac{1-0.8772}{0.9756+0.9434+0.9112+0.8772} = 0.0331$$

$$\text{swap rate} = 0.0331 \times \frac{360}{180} = 0.0662 = 6.62\%$$

10. A
$$\text{value of fixed-rate side (per \$ of notional principal)} = [\$0.0331 \times (0.9780+0.9524+0.9174)] + (\$1.00 \times 0.9174) = \$1.01166$$

The market value of the floating-rate side is $1.0000 because we're at a payment date. The market value of the swap per $ of notional principal to the receive-fixed (and pay-floating) side is $1.01166 – $1.0000 = $0.01166. As the swap is marked to market, the pay-fixed swap holder makes a payment of $0.01166 to the receive-fixed holder for each $1 of notional principal.

11. C The quarterly 4% fixed-rate payment in 60 days will be in the amount of:

$5,000,000 × (4%/4) = $50,000

So the total cash flow at that time is $50,000 + $5,000,000 = $5,050,000.

$$\text{value of fixed-rate side} = 0.9940 \times \$5{,}050{,}000 = \$5{,}019{,}700$$

$$\text{value of index return side} = \$5{,}000{,}000 \times \frac{3{,}150}{3{,}000} = \$5{,}250{,}000$$

$$\text{value of swap to bank} = \$5{,}250{,}000 - \$5{,}019{,}700 = \$230{,}300$$

Answers – Challenge Problems

12. A The dividend in 125 days is irrelevant because it occurs after the forward contract matures.

$$PVD = \frac{\$0.50}{1.04^{35/365}} = \$0.4981$$

$$FP = (\$35 - \$0.4981) \times 1.04^{120/365} = \$34.95$$

$$V_{45}(\text{short position}) = -\left(\$27.50 - \frac{\$34.95}{1.04^{75/365}}\right) = \$7.17$$

13. C A 3 × 6 FRA expires in 90 days and is based on 90-day LIBOR, so it is the appropriate hedge for 90-day LIBOR 90 days from today. The rate is calculated as:

$$R90 = 0.047 \times \frac{90}{360} = 0.0118$$

$$R180 = 0.049 \times \frac{180}{360} = 0.0245$$

$$\text{price of } 3 \times 6 \text{ FRA} = \left(\frac{1.0245}{1.0118} - 1\right) \times \frac{360}{90} = 0.0502 = 5.02\%$$

14. B The U.K. company will be receiving euros in 60 days, so it should short the 60-day forward on the euro as a hedge. The no-arbitrage forward price is:

$$F_T = £0.923 \times \frac{1.03^{60/365}}{1.04^{60/365}} = 0.9215$$

15. A coupon on \$ fixed side = \$1,000,000 × (0.042 / 4) = \$10,500

value of the \$ fixed side = (0.9923 × \$10,500) + (0.9791 × \$1,010,500) = \$999,800

coupon on € fixed side = €800,000 × (0.05 / 4) = €10,000

value of € fixed side (in €) = (0.9900 × €10,000) + (0.9736 × €810,000) = €798,516

$$\text{value of € fixed side (in \$)} = \frac{798{,}516}{0.75} = \$1{,}064{,}688$$

value of swap to bank = \$999,800 – \$1,064,688 = –\$64,888

The following is a review of the Derivatives Instruments: Valuation and Strategies principles designed to address the learning outcome statements set forth by CFA Institute. Cross-Reference to CFA Institute Assigned Reading #41.

Valuation of Contingent Claims

Study Session 14

Exam Focus

This topic review covers the valuation of options. Candidates need to be able to calculate value of an option using the binomial tree framework and should also understand the inputs into the Black Scholes model and how they influence the value of an option. While this topic review is somewhat quantitative, candidates need to understand the material conceptually as well. This reading has a lot of testable material.

LOS 41.a: Describe and interpret the binomial option valuation model and its component terms.

LOS 41.b: Calculate the no-arbitrage values of European and American options using a two-period binomial model.

LOS 41.e: Describe how the value of a European option can be analyzed as the present value of the option's expected payoff at expiration.

CFA® Program Curriculum, Volume 5, pages 362, 364, and 384

Binomial Model

A **binomial model** is based on the idea that, over the next period, the value of an asset will change to one of two possible values (binomial). To construct a binomial model, we need to know the beginning asset value, the size of the two possible changes, and the probability of each of these changes occurring.

One-Period Binomial Model

Consider a share of stock currently priced at $30. Suppose also that the size of the possible price changes, and the probability of these changes occurring are as follows:

S_0 = current stock price = $30
U = up move factor = (1 + % up) = S^+/S = 1.333
D = down move factor = (1 – % down) = S^-/S = 0.75
S^+ = stock price if an up move occurs = $S_0 \times U = 30 \times 1.333$ = $40
S^- = stock price if a down move occurs = $S_0 \times D = 30 \times 0.75$ = $22.50
π_U = probability of an up move
π_D = probability of a down move = $(1 - \pi_U)$

A one-period binomial tree for this stock is shown in Figure 1. The beginning stock value of $30 is to the left, and to the right are the two possible paths the stock can take, based on that starting point and the size of an up- or down-move. If the stock price increases by a factor of 1.333 (a return of 33.3%), it ends up at $40.00; if it falls by a factor of 0.75 (a return of –25%), it ends up at $22.50.

Figure 1: One-Period Binomial Tree

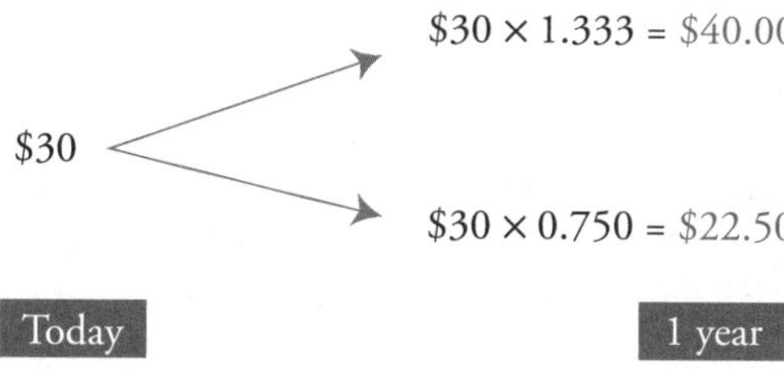

The probabilities of an up-move and a down-move are calculated based on the size of the moves, as well as the risk-free rate, as:

$$\pi_U = \frac{1 + R_f - D}{U - D}$$

where:
R_f = periodically compounded annual risk-free rate

Professor's Note: These up- and down-move probabilities are not the ***actual*** *probabilities of up- or down-moves. They are the risk-neutral probabilities that are consistent with investor risk-neutrality. The distinction between actual probabilities and risk-neutral probabilities is not relevant for the exam.*

We can calculate the value of an option on the stock by:

- Calculating the payoff of the option at maturity in both the up-move and down-move states.
- Calculating the expected value of the option in one year as the probability-weighted average of the payoffs in each state.
- Discounting the expected value back to today at the risk-free rate.

Example: Calculating call option value with a one-period binomial tree

Calculate the value today of a one-year call option on a stock that has an exercise price of $30. Assume that the periodically compounded (as opposed to continuously compounded) risk-free rate is 7%, the current value of the stock is $30, the up-move factor is 1.333, and the down move factor is 0.75.

Answer:

First, we have to calculate the probabilities:

$$\pi_U = \frac{1+R_f - D}{U - D} = \frac{1+0.07-0.75}{1.33-0.75} = 0.55$$

$\pi_D = 1 - 0.55 = 0.45$

Next, determine the option payoffs in each state. If the stock moves up to \$40, the call option with an exercise price of \$30 will pay off \$10. If the stock moves down to \$22.50, the call option will be worthless. The option payoffs are illustrated in the following figure.

Let the stock values for the up-move and down-move be S^+ and S^- and for the call values, C^+ and C^-.

With X = \$30

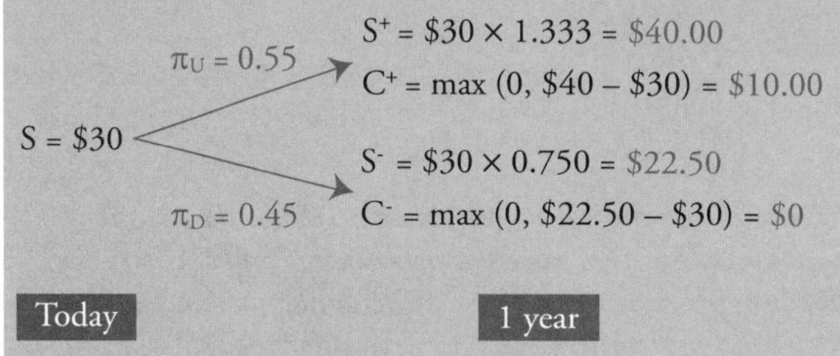

$\pi_U = 0.55$

$S^+ = \$30 \times 1.333 = \$40.00$

$C^+ = \max(0, \$40 - \$30) = \$10.00$

S = \$30

$S^- = \$30 \times 0.750 = \$22.50$

$C^- = \max(0, \$22.50 - \$30) = \$0$

$\pi_D = 0.45$

Today | 1 year

The expected value of the option in one period is:

E(call option value in 1 year) = (\$10 × 0.55) + (\$0 × 0.45) = \$5.50

The value of the option today, after discounting at the risk-free rate of 7%, is:

$$C = \frac{\$5.50}{1.07} = \$5.14$$

We can use the same framework to value a one-period put option on the stock.

Example: Valuing a one-period put option on a stock

Use the information in the previous example to calculate the value of a put option on the stock that has an exercise price of \$30.

Answer:

If the stock moves up to \$40, a put option with an exercise price of \$30 will be worthless. If the stock moves down to \$22.50, the put option will be worth \$7.50.

The probabilities are 0.55 and 0.45 for an up- and down-move, respectively. The expected value of the put option in one period is thus:

$$\text{E(put option value in 1 year)} = (\$0 \times 0.55) + (\$7.50 \times 0.45) = \$3.375$$

The value of the option today, after discounting at the risk-free rate of 7%, is:

$$P = \frac{\$3.375}{1.07} = \$3.154$$

Put-Call Parity

Put option value can also be computed using put-call parity, which recognizes that the value of a fiduciary call (long call, plus an investment in a zero-coupon bond with a face value equal to the strike price) is equal to the value of a protective put (long stock and long put):

$$S_0 + P_0 = C_0 + PV(X)$$

Note that both options are on the same underlying stock have the same exercise price, and the same maturity.

In our previous example, PV(X) = 30 / 1.07 = \$28.04. We can verify the put call parity as:

$$S_0 + P_0 = \$30 + \$3.15 = \$33.15.$$

$$C_0 + PV(X) = \$5.14 + 28.04 = \$33.19 \text{ (rounding error accounts for the difference).}$$

Put call parity can be used to create a synthetic instrument that replicates the desired instrument.

For example, a synthetic call can be created by creating a portfolio that combines a long position in the stock, a long position in a put and a short position in a zero coupon bond with a face value equal to the strike price (i.e., borrowing the present value of the exercise price at the risk-free rate).

$$C_0 = S_0 + P_0 - PV(X)$$

Example: Using put-call parity

A 1-year call option on the common stock of Cross Reef Inc., with an exercise price of \$60 is trading for \$8. The current stock price is \$62. The risk-free rate is 4%. Calculate the price of the put option implied by put-call parity.

Answer:

According to put-call parity, to prevent arbitrage, the price of the put option must be:

$$P_0 = C_0 - S_0 + \left[\frac{X}{(1+R_f)^T}\right]$$

$$= \$8 - \$62 + \frac{\$60}{1.04}$$

$$= \$3.69$$

Two-Period Binomial Model

Valuing an option using a two-period binomial model requires more steps, but uses the same method:

- Calculate the stock values at the end of two periods (there are three possible outcomes, because an up-then-down move gets you to the same place as a down-then-up move).
- Calculate the three possible option payoffs at the end of two periods.
- Calculate the expected option payoff at the end of two periods (t = 2) using the up- and down-move probabilities.
- Discount the expected option payoff (t = 2) back one period at the risk-free rate to find the option values at the end of the first period (t = 1).
- Calculate the expected option value at the end of one period (t = 1) using up- and down-move probabilities.
- Discount the expected option value at the end of one period (t = 1) back one period at the risk-free rate to find the option value today (t=0).

Let's look at an example to illustrate the steps involved.

Example: Valuing a call option on a stock with a two-period model

Suppose you own a stock currently priced at \$50 and that a two-period European call option on the stock is available with a strike price of \$45. The up-move factor is 1.25 and the down-move factor is 0.80. The risk-free rate per period is 7%. Compute the value of the call option using a two-period binomial model.

Answer:

First, compute the probability of an up-move and a down-move, and then compute the theoretical value of the stock at the end of each period:

$$\pi_U = \frac{1+R_f-D}{U-D} = \frac{1+0.07-0.80}{1.25-0.80} = 0.60$$

$$\pi_D = 1 - 0.60 = 0.40$$

The two-period binomial tree for the stock is shown in the following figure.

Two-Period Binomial Tree for Stock Price

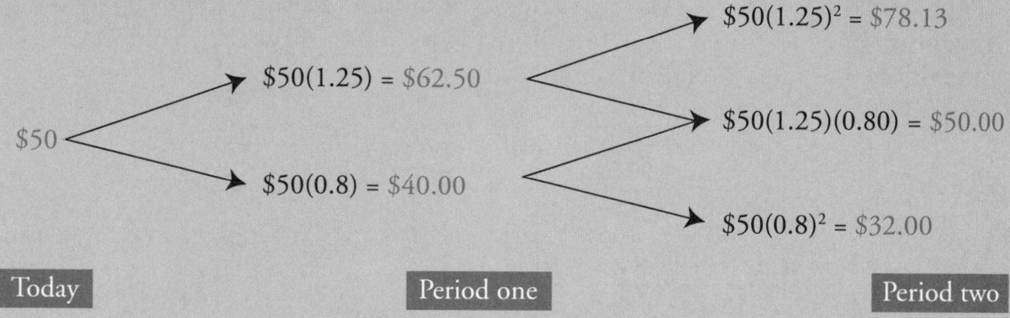

We know the value of the option at expiration in each state is equal to the stock price minus the exercise price (or zero, if that difference is negative):

$$C^{++} = \max(0, \$78.13 - \$45.00) = \$33.13$$

$$C^{-+} = \max(0, \$50.00 - \$45.00) = \$5.00$$

$$C^{+-} = \max(0, \$50.00 - \$45.00) = \$5.00$$

$$C^{--} = \max(0, \$32.00 - \$45.00) = \$0$$

We will approach this problem by using the single-period binomial model for each period. Using this method, we can compute the value of the call option in the up-state in period one as follows:

$$C^{+} = \frac{(\pi_U \times C^{++}) + (\pi_D \times C^{+-})}{1+R_f} = \frac{E(\text{call option value})}{1+R_f}$$

$$= \frac{(0.6 \times \$33.13) + (0.4 \times \$5.00)}{1.07}$$

$$= \frac{\$21.88}{1.07} = \$20.45$$

The value of the call in the down-state at t=1 is computed as:

$$C^- = \frac{(\pi_U \times C^{-+}) + (\pi_D \times C^{--})}{1+R_f} = \frac{E(\text{call option value})}{1+R_f}$$

$$= \frac{(0.6 \times \$5.00) + (0.4 \times \$0.00)}{1.07}$$

$$= \frac{\$3.00}{1.07} = \$2.80$$

Now we know the value of the option in both the up-state (C^+) and the down-state (C^-) one period from now. To get the value of the option today, we simply apply our methodology one more time. Therefore, bringing (C^+) and (C^-) back one more period to the present, the value of the call option today is:

$$C = \frac{(\pi_U \times C^{+}) + (\pi_D \times C^{-})}{1+R_f} = \frac{E(\text{call option value})}{1+R_f}$$

$$= \frac{(0.6 \times \$20.45) + (0.4 \times \$2.80)}{1.07}$$

$$= \frac{\$13.39}{1.07} = \$12.51$$

The binomial tree for the call option is shown below.

Two-Period Binomial Tree for Option Price

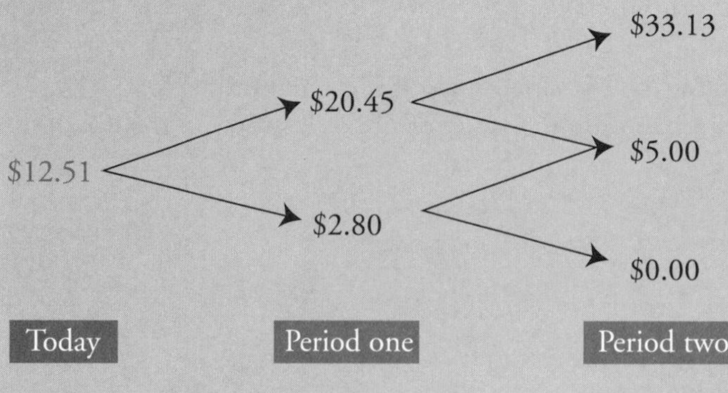

American-Style Options

Our discussion so far has been limited to European-style options (i.e., options that can only be exercised at maturity). American-style options allow for exercise any point until maturity of the option. While the early exercise feature is not valuable for call options on non-dividend paying stocks, deep-in-the-money put options could benefit from early exercise. When an investor exercises an option early, she captures only the intrinsic value of the option and forgoes the time value. While the intrinsic value can be invested at risk-free rate, the interest so earned is less than the time value in most cases. For a deep-in-the money put option, the upside is limited (because the stock price cannot fall below zero). In such cases, the interest on intrinsic value can exceed the option's time value.

Example: Early exercise of a put option

Consider a stock currently trading at $50 and the periodically compounded interest rate is 3%. Suppose that U = 1.3 and D = 0.80. Calculate the value of a two-period European-style put option on the stock that has an exercise price of $50. Also, determine if early exercise would make economic sense.

Answer:

The tree below shows put option value at each of the nodes in the binomial tree.

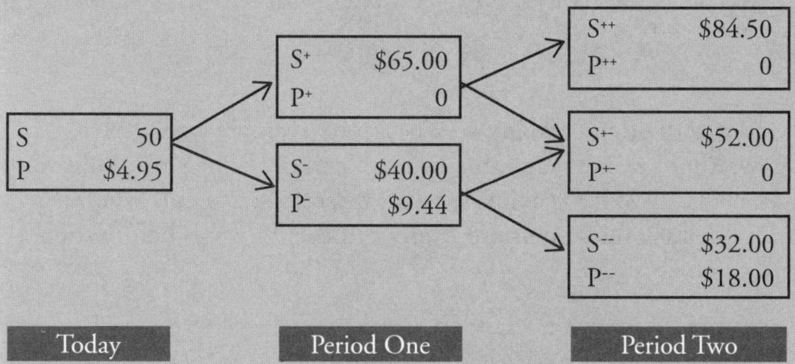

The value of the option for the down node at t=1 is calculated as:

$$P^{-} = \frac{(\pi_U \times P^{+-} + \pi_D \times P^{--})}{(1+R_f)} = \frac{(0.46 \times 0 + 0.54 \times 18)}{(1.03)} = \$9.44$$

The value of the option at time=0 is calculated as:

$$P = \frac{(\pi_U \times P^{+} + \pi_D \times P^{-})}{(1+R_f)} = \frac{(0.46 \times 0 + 0.54 \times 9.44)}{(1.03)} = \$4.95$$

For the down move at t = 1, the exercise value of the put option is $10, calculated as Max(0, X-S) or Max(0, 50-40). Clearly, for this node, early exercise results in higher value ($10 as opposed to $9.44).

Had the option in the previous example been an American-style put option, the value would be $5.24 as shown in Figure 2.

Figure 2: Valuing an American-Style Put Option

The value of the put option at time 0 can be calculated as the present value of the expected value of the option at time t=1.

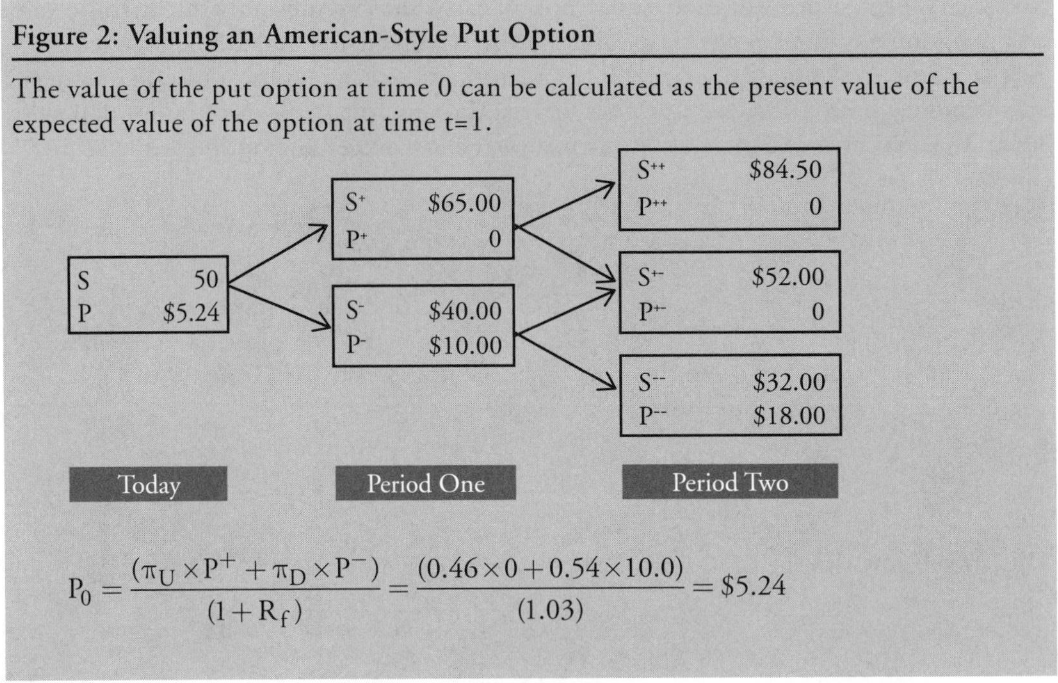

$$P_0 = \frac{(\pi_U \times P^+ + \pi_D \times P^-)}{(1+R_f)} = \frac{(0.46 \times 0 + 0.54 \times 10.0)}{(1.03)} = \$5.24$$

American-style call options on dividend-paying stocks can be evaluated similarly: determine at each node whether the exercise value is greater than the intrinsic value and, if so, use that higher value. For dividend-paying stocks, the stock price falls when the stock goes ex-dividend, and it may make sense to exercise the call option before such a decline in price.

Study Session 14

LOS 41.c: Identify an arbitrage opportunity involving options and describe the related arbitrage.

CFA® Program Curriculum, Volume 5, page 367

Arbitrage With a One-Period Binomial Model

Let's revisit our original example of a single period binomial model. Recall that the call option has a strike price equal to the stock's current price of $30, U = 1.333, D = 0.75, and the risk-free rate is 7%. We calculated that the probability of an up-move is 55% and that of a down-move 45%.

If the market price of the one-period $30 call option were to be different from the $5.14 value calculated before, there would be an arbitrage opportunity. This arbitrage will involve the call option and shares of the stock. If the option is overpriced in the market, we would sell the option and buy a fractional share of the stock for each option we sold. If the call option is underpriced in the market, we could purchase the option and short a fractional share of stock for each option purchased.

The fractional share of stock needed in the arbitrage trade (commonly referred to as the **hedge ratio** or delta), is calculated in the one-period model as:

$$h = \frac{C^{+} - C^{-}}{S^{+} - S^{-}}$$

Example: Calculating arbitrage profit

Suppose that the call option in the previous example is actually selling for \$6.50. Illustrate how this opportunity can be exploited to earn an arbitrage profit. Assume we trade 100 call options.

Answer:

Because the option is overpriced, we will sell 100 call options and purchase a number of shares of stock determined by the hedge ratio:

$$h = \frac{\$10 - \$0}{\$40 - \$22.50} = 0.5714 \text{ shares per option.}$$

Total number of shares to purchase = 100 × 0.5714 = 57.14

A portfolio that is long 57.14 shares of stock at \$30 per share and short 100 calls at \$6.50 per call has a net cost of:

net portfolio cost = (57.14 × \$30) – (100 × \$6.50) = \$1,064

We will borrow \$1,064 at 7%, and then will have to repay \$1,064 × (1.07) = \$1,138.48 at the end of one year. (In an arbitrage transaction, we assume that we begin with \$0.)

The values of this portfolio at maturity if the stock moves up to \$40 or down to \$22.50 are identical:

portfolio value after up-move = (57.14 × \$40) – (100 × \$10) = \$1,286

portfolio value after down-move = (57.14 × \$22.50) – (100 × \$0) = \$1,286

Profit on the portfolio at the end of one year in either state after repayment of loan = \$1,286 – \$1,138.48 = \$147.52.

The present value of the arbitrage profit is \$147.52 / 1.07 = \$137.87.

The above calculations can be represented by the following:

$$-hS_0 + C_0 = \frac{(-hS^{-} + C^{-})}{(1 + R_f)}$$

Therefore, $C_0 = hS_0 + \frac{(-hS^{-} + C^{-})}{(1 + R_f)}$

Or equivalently,

$$C_0 = hS_0 + \frac{(-hS^+ + C^+)}{(1+R_f)}$$

We can value the call option using the first relationship as:

$$C_0 = (0.5714 \times \$30) + \frac{(-0.5714 \times \$22.50) + \$0}{(1.07)}$$

$= \$5.12$ *(the small difference is due to rounding)*

Similarly, a put option can be valued as:

$$P_0 = hS_0 + \frac{(-hS^- + P^-)}{(1+R_f)} = hS_0 + \frac{(-hS^+ + P^+)}{(1+R_f)}$$

LOS 41.d: Calculate and interpret the value of an interest rate option using a two-period binomial model.

CFA® Program Curriculum, Volume 5, page 385

Warm-Up: Binomial Interest Rate Trees

We can use an estimate of the volatility of an interest rate to create a set of possible rate paths for interest rates in the future called a **binomial interest rate tree**. The diagram in Figure 3 depicts a two-period binomial interest rate tree.

Figure 3: Two-Period Binomial Interest Rate Tree

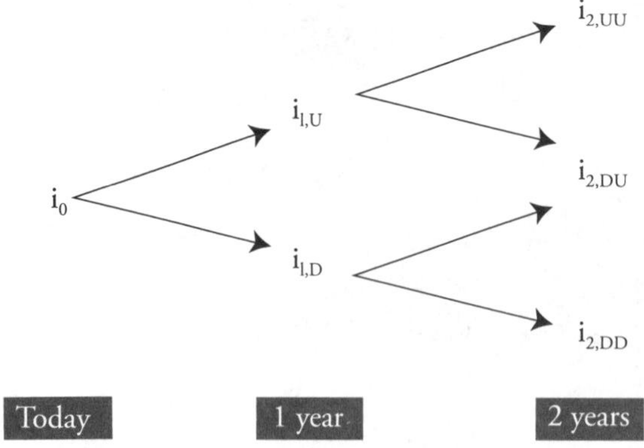

The interest rate at each node is a one-period forward rate. Beyond the root of the tree, there is more than one one-period forward rate for each nodal period (i.e., at year 1, we have two 1-year forward rates, $i_{1,U}$ and $i_{1,D}$). The interest rates are selected so that the (risk-neutral) probabilities of up- and down-moves are both equal to 0.5.

Professor's Note: You will not have to construct a tree for the exam—just be able to use the given tree to value an interest rate option.

Interest Rate Options

An interest rate call option has a positive payoff when the reference rate is greater than the exercise rate:

call payoff = notional principal × [Max (0, reference rate – exercise rate)]

Interest rate call options increase in value when rates increase.

An interest rate put option has a positive payoff when the reference rate is less than the exercise rate:

put payoff = notional principal × [Max (0, exercise rate – reference rate)]

Interest rate put option values increase in value when rates decrease. Valuing interest rate options using the binomial tree is similar to valuing stock options; the value at each node is the present value of the expected value of the option. While LIBOR-based contracts pay interest in arrears, to keep things simple, we assume that options cash settle at maturity.

Example: Interest rate call option valuation

Given the two-period interest rate tree below, what is the value of a two-period European interest rate call option with an exercise rate of 5.50% and a notional principal of $1 million? (Assume that options cash settle at time T = 2.)

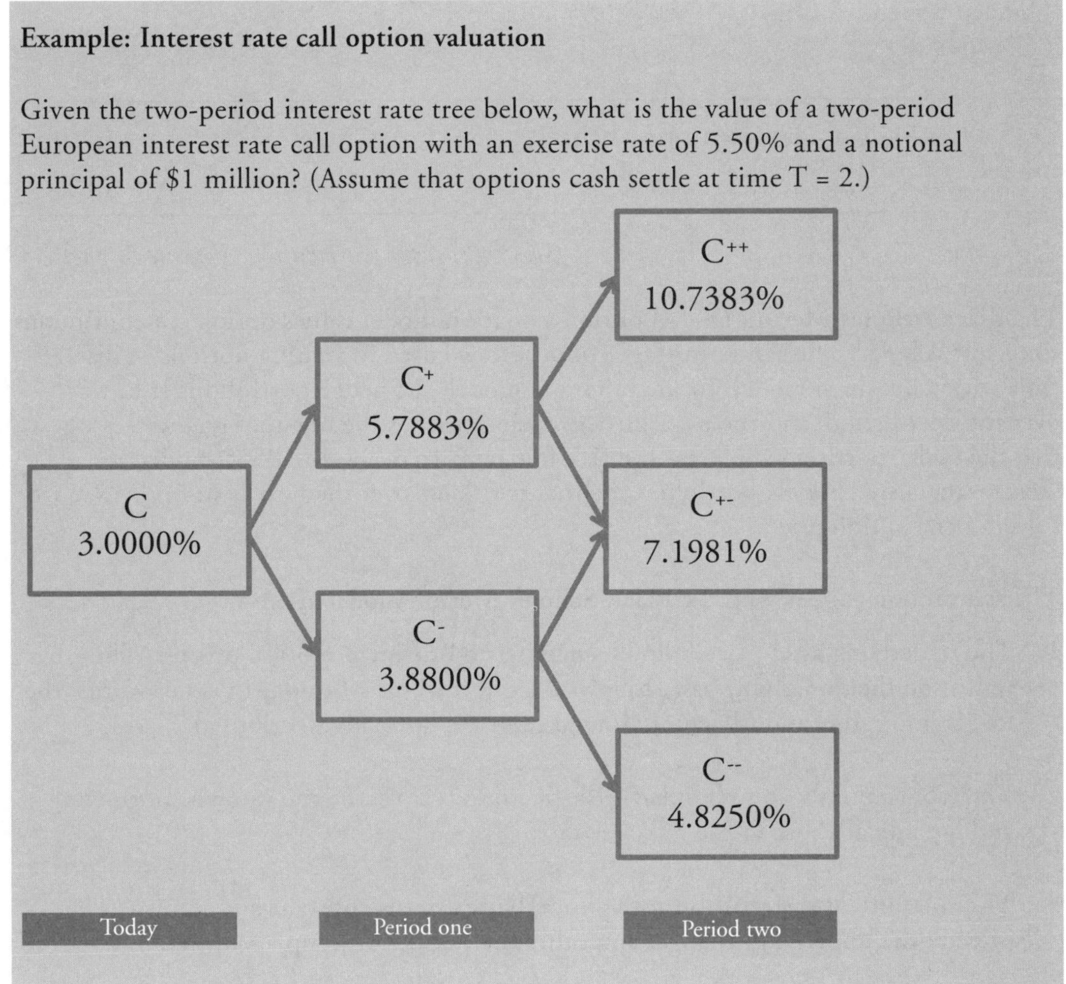

Answer:

Given the exercise rate of 5.50%, the call option has a positive payoff for nodes C^{++} and C^{+-}.

The value of the option at node C^{++} can be calculated as:

[Max (0, 0.107383 – 0.055)] × $1,000,000 = $52,383

Similarly, the value at node C^{+-} can be calculated as:

[Max (0, 0.071981 – 0.055)] × $1,000,000 = $16,981

Value at node C^{+} = [(0.5 × 52,383) + (0.5 × 16,981)] / (1.057883) = $32,784

(note that the discount rate is not constant)

Value at node C^{-} = [(0.5 × 16,981) + 0] / (1.0388) = $8,173

Value at node C = [(0.5 × 32,784) + (0.5 × 8,173)] / (1.03) = $19,882

LOS 41.f: Identify assumptions of the Black-Scholes-Merton option valuation model.

CFA® Program Curriculum, Volume 5, page 388

The **Black-Scholes-Merton** (BSM) option valuation **model** values options in continuous time, but is based on the no-arbitrage condition we used in valuing options in discrete time with a binomial model. In the binomial model, the hedge portfolio is riskless over the next period, and the no-arbitrage option price is the one that guarantees that the hedge portfolio will yield the risk-free rate. To derive the BSM model, an "instantaneously" riskless portfolio (one that is riskless over the next instant) is used to solve for the option price.

The assumptions underlying the Black-Scholes-Merton model are:

1. The underlying asset price follows a geometric Brownian motion process. The return on the underlying asset follows a lognormal distribution. In other words, the logarithmic continuously compounded return is normally distributed.

2. The (continuously compounded) risk-free rate is constant and known. Borrowing and lending are both at the risk-free rate.

3. The volatility of the returns on the underlying asset is constant and known. The price of the underlying changes smoothly (i.e., does not jump abruptly).

4. Markets are "frictionless." There are no taxes, no transactions costs, and no restrictions on short sales or the use of short-sale proceeds. Continuous trading is possible, and there are no arbitrage opportunities in the marketplace.

5. The (continuously compounded) yield on the underlying asset is constant.

6. The options are European options (i.e., they can only be exercised at expiration).

LOS 41.g: Interpret the components of the Black-Scholes-Merton model as applied to call options in terms of leveraged position in the underlying.

CFA® Program Curriculum, Volume 5, page 391

The formula for valuing a European option using the BSM model is:

$$C_0 = S_0N(d_1) - e^{-rT}XN(d_2)$$

and

$$P_0 = e^{-rT}XN(-d_2) - S_0N(-d_1)$$

where:

$$d_1 = \frac{\ln(S/X) + (r + \sigma^2/2)T}{\sigma\sqrt{T}}$$

$$d_2 = d_1 - \sigma\sqrt{T}$$

C_0 and P_0 = values of call and put option
T = time to option expiration
r = continuously compounded risk-free rate
S_0 = current asset price
X = exercise price
σ = annual volatility of asset returns
$N(*)$ = cumulative standard normal probability
$N(-x)$ = $1 - N(x)$

While the BSM model formula looks complicated, its interpretations are not:

1. The BSM value can be thought of as the present value of the expected option payoff at expiration. For a call, that means $C_0 = PV\{S_0e^{rT}N(d_1) - XN(d_2)\}$. Similarly, for a put option, $P_0 = PV\{XN(-d_2) - S_0e^{rT}N(-d_1)\}$.

2. Calls can be thought of as a leveraged stock investment where $N(d_1)$ units of stock are purchased using $e^{-rT}XN(d_2)$ of borrowed funds. (A short position in bonds can also be interpreted as borrowing funds.) A portfolio that replicates a put option consists of a long position in $N(-d_2)$ bonds and a short position in $N(-d_1)$ stocks.

3. $N(d_2)$ is interpreted as the risk-neutral probability that a call option will expire in the money. Similarly, $N(-d_2)$ or $1 - N(d_2)$ is the risk-neutral probability that a put option will expire in the money.

Example: BSM model

Stock of XZ Inc., is currently trading at \$50. Suppose that the return volatility is 25% and the continuously compounded risk-free rate is 3%. Calls and puts with a strike price of \$45 and expiring in 6 months (T=0.5) are trading at \$7.00 and \$1.00 respectively. If $N(d_1) = 0.779$ and $N(d_2) = 0.723$, calculate the value of replicating portfolios and any arbitrage profits on both options.

Answer:

The replicating portfolio for the call can be constructed as long 0.779 shares (0.779 × \$50 = \$38.95), and borrow $45 \times e^{-0.03(0.5)} \times (0.723)$ = \$32.05.

net cost = \$38.95 – \$32.05 = \$6.90

Because the market price of the call is \$7.00, the profitable arbitrage transaction entails writing a call at \$7.00 and buying the replicating portfolio for \$6.90 to yield an arbitrage profit of \$0.10 per call.

For the put option valuation, note that $N(-d_1) = 1 - N(d_1) = 1 - 0.779 = 0.221$ and $N(-d_2) = 1 - 0.723 = 0.277$.

The replicating portfolio for the put option can be constructed as a long bond position of $45 \times e^{-0.03(0.5)} \times (0.277)$ = \$12.28 and a short position in 0.221 shares resulting in short proceeds of \$50 × 0.221 or \$11.05.

net cost = \$12.28 – \$11.05 = \$1.23

Because the market price of the put option is \$1.00, arbitrage profits can be earned by selling the replicating portfolio and buying puts, for an arbitrage profit of \$0.23 per put.

LOS 41.h: Describe how the Black–Scholes–Merton model is used to value European options on equities and currencies.

CFA® Program Curriculum, Volume 5, page 395

Options on Dividend Paying Stocks

So far we have assumed that the underlying stock does not pay dividends. If it does, we can adjust the model using a lowercase delta (δ) to represent the dividend yield, as follows:

$$C_0 = S_0e^{-\delta T}N(d_1) - e^{-rT}XN(d_2)$$

$$P_0 = e^{-rT}XN(-d_2) - S_0e^{-\delta T}N(-d_1)$$

where:
δ = continuously compounded dividend yield

$$d_1 = \frac{\ln(S/X) + (r - \delta + \sigma^2/2)T}{\sigma\sqrt{T}}$$

$$d_2 = d_1 - \sigma\sqrt{T}$$

Note that $S_0e^{-\delta T}$ is the stock price, reduced by the present value of any dividends expected to be paid during the option's life.

The put-call parity relation must also be modified if the stock pays dividends:

$$P_0 + S_0e^{-\delta T} = C_0 + e^{-rT}X$$

Options on Currencies

We can also use the Black-Scholes-Merton model to value foreign exchange options. Here, the underlying is the spot exchange rate instead of a stock price.

The value of an option on a currency can be thought of as being made up of two components, a bond component and a foreign exchange component. The value can be calculated as:

$$C_0 = S_0e^{-r(B)T}N(d_1) - e^{-r(P)T}XN(d_2)$$

and

$$P_0 = e^{-r(P)T}XN(-d_2) - S_0e^{-r(B)T}N(-d_1)$$

where:
$r(P)$ = continuously compounded price currency interest rate
$r(B)$ = continuously compounded base currency interest rate

For currencies, the carry benefit is not a dividend but rather interest earned on a deposit of the foreign currency. The spot exchange rate, S_0, is discounted at the base or foreign currency interest rate, and the bond component, $e^{-r(P)T}X$, is the exercise exchange rate discounted at the price or domestic currency interest rate.

LOS 41.i: Describe how the Black model is used to value European options on futures.

CFA® Program Curriculum, Volume 5, page 398

The Black Model

If we ignore the mark-to-market feature of the futures contract, The Black model can be used to price European options on forwards and futures:

$$C_0 = e^{-R_f^c \times T}\left[F_T \times N(d_1) - X \times N(d_2)\right]$$

$$d_1 = \frac{\ln\left(F_T / X\right) + \left(\frac{\sigma^2}{2}\right)T}{\sigma\sqrt{T}}$$

$$d_2 = d_1 - \sigma\sqrt{T}$$

where:
σ = standard deviation of returns on the futures contract
F_T = futures price

Note that the Black model is just the BSM model with $e^{-R_f^c \times T}F_T$ substituted for S_0.

Analogous to the interpretations of the BSM model, an option on futures can be thought of as follows:

- The value of a call option on futures is equal to the value of a portfolio with a long futures position (the PV of the futures price multiplied by $N(d_1)$) and a short bond position (the PV of the exercise price multiplied by $N(d_2)$).
- The value of a put option is equal to the value of a portfolio with a long bond and a short futures position.
- The value of a call can also be thought of as the present value of the difference between the futures price (adjusted by $N(d_1)$) and the exercise price (adjusted by $N(d_2)$).

LOS 41.j: Describe how the Black model is used to value European interest rate options and European swaptions.

CFA® Program Curriculum, Volume 5, page 400

Interest Rate Options

Interest rate options are options on forward rates (or options on FRAs). A call option on an FRA gains when rates rise, and a put option on an FRA gains when rates fall. Interest rates are fixed in advance (i.e., at the beginning of the loan term) and settled in arrears (i.e., paid at maturity of the loan). While FRAs generally use a 30/360 convention, options on FRAs use an actual/365 convention.

Consider an interest rate call option on an (M×N) FRA expiring in M months that has a strike rate of X. The underlying is an (N-M) month forward rate. A call option on this FRA can be valued as:

$$C_0 = (AP)e^{-r(\text{actual}/365)}\left[FRA_{(M\times N)}N(d_1) - XN(d_2)\right] \times NP$$

where:

AP = accrual period = $\left[\dfrac{\text{actual}}{365}\right]$

NP = notional principal on the FRA

Equivalencies in Interest Rate Derivative Contracts

Combinations of interest rate options can be used to replicate other contracts, for example:

1. A long interest rate call and a short interest rate put (with exercise rate = current FRA rate) can be used to replicate a long FRA (i.e., a forward contract to receive a floating rate and pay a fixed rate).

2. Similarly, if the exercise rate = the current FRA rate, a short interest rate call and long interest rate put can be combined to replicate a short FRA position (i.e., a pay-floating, receive-fixed forward contract).

3. A series of interest rate call options with different maturities and the same exercise price can be combined to form an interest rate cap. (Each of the call options in an interest rate cap is known as a caplet.) A floating rate loan can be hedged using a long interest rate cap.

4. Similarly, an interest rate floor is a portfolio of interest rate put options, and each of these puts is known as a floorlet. Floors can be used to hedge a long position in a floating rate bond.

5. If the exercise rate on a cap and floor is same, a long cap and short floor can be used to replicate a payer swap.

6. Similarly, a short cap and long floor can replicate a receiver swap.

7. If the exercise rate on a floor and a cap are set equal to a market swap fixed rate, the value of the cap will be equal to the value of the floor.

Swaptions

A **swaption** is an option that gives the holder the right to enter into an interest rate swap. A **payer swaption** is the right to enter into a specific swap at some date in the future at a predetermined rate as the fixed-rate payer. As interest rates increase, the right to take the pay-fixed side of a swap (a payer swaption) becomes more valuable. The holder of a payer swaption would exercise it and enter into the swap if the market rate is greater than the exercise rate at expiration.

A **receiver swaption** is the right to enter into a specific swap at some date in the future as the fixed-rate receiver (i.e., the floating-rate payer) at the rate specified in the swaption. As interest rates decrease, the right to enter the receive-fixed side of a swap (a receiver swaption) becomes more valuable. The holder of a receiver swaption would exercise if market rates are less than the exercise rate at expiration.

A swaption is equivalent to a an option on a series of cash flows (annuity), one for each settlement date of the underlying swap, equal to the difference between the exercise rate on the swaption and the market swap fixed rate.

If PVA represents the present value of such an annuity, the value of a payer swaption using the Black model can be calculated as:

$$\text{PAY} = (\text{AP})\ \text{PVA}\ [\text{SFR}\ N(d_1) - X\ N(d_2)]\ \text{NP}$$

where:
PAY = value of the payer swaption
AP = 1/# of settlement periods per year in the underlying swap
SFR = current market swap fixed rate
X = exercise rate specified in the payer swaption
NP = notional principal of the underlying swap

$$d_1 = \frac{\ln(\text{SFR}/X) + (\sigma^2/2)T}{\sigma\sqrt{T}}$$

$$d_2 = d_1 - \sigma\sqrt{T}$$

The value of a payer swaption is essentially the present value of the expected option payoff:

$$\text{PAY} = \text{PV}\ (\text{E(payoff)})$$

Similarly, the value of a receiver swaption (which we'll call "REC") can be calculated as:

$$\text{REC} = (\text{AP})\ \text{PVA}\ [X\ N(-d_2) - \text{SFR}\ N(-d_1)]\ \text{NP}$$

Equivalencies

A receiver swap can be replicated using a long receiver swaption and a short payer swaption with the same exercise rates. Conversely, a payer swap can be replicated using a long payer swaption and short receiver swaption with the same exercise rates. If the exercise rate is set such that the values of the payer and receiver swaptions are equal, then the exercise rate must be equal to the market swap fixed rate.

A long callable bond can be replicated using a long option-free bond plus a short receiver swaption.

LOS 41.k: Interpret each of the option Greeks.

CFA® Program Curriculum, Volume 5, page 406

There are five inputs to the BSM model: asset price, exercise price, asset price volatility, time to expiration, and the risk-free rate. The relationship between each input (except the exercise price) and the option price is captured by sensitivity factors known as "the **Greeks.**"

Delta describes the relationship between changes in asset prices and changes in option prices. Delta is also the hedge ratio. Call option deltas are positive because as the underlying asset price increases, call option value also increases. Conversely, the delta of a put option is negative because the put value falls as the asset price increases. See Figure 4.

Figure 4: Call and Put Delta: The Relationship Between Option Price and Underlying Asset Price

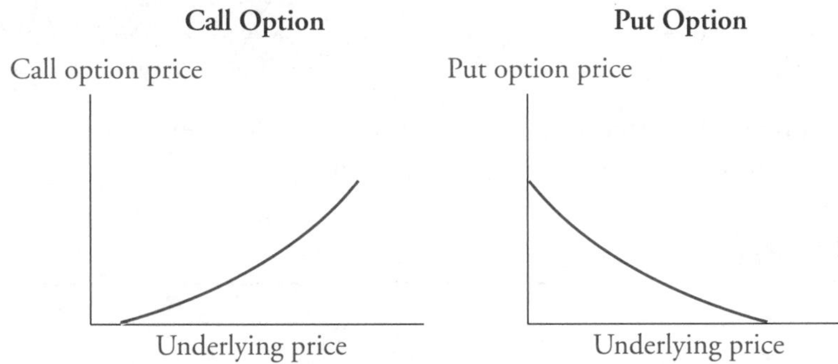

Deltas for call and put options on dividend paying stocks are given by:

$$\text{delta}_C = e^{-\delta T}N(d_1)$$

$$\text{delta}_P = -e^{-\delta T}N(-d_1)$$

where:
δ = continuously compounded dividend yield

However, because we're now using a linear relationship to estimate a non-linear change, the following relationships are only approximations:

$$\Delta C \approx e^{-\delta T} N(d_1) \times \Delta S$$

$$\Delta P \approx -e^{-\delta T} N(-d_1) \times \Delta S$$

where:
ΔC and ΔP = change in call and put price

The approximations are close for small changes in stock price, but the approximation becomes less accurate as the ΔS becomes larger.

Example: Calculating change in option price

$e^{-\delta T} N(d_1)$ from the BSM model is 0.58. Calculate the approximate change in the price of a call option on the stock if the stock price increases by $0.75.

Answer:

$$\Delta C \approx 0.58 \times \$0.75 = \$0.435$$

Interpreting Delta

The payoff diagrams for a European call option before- and at-expiration are shown in Figure 5. The "at expiration" line represents the call option's intrinsic value, which is equal to:

- Zero when the call option is out-of-the-money.
- The stock price minus the exercise price when the option is in-the-money.

Before expiration, the option also has time value, so the prior-to-expiration curve lies above the at-expiration diagram by the amount of the time value.

Figure 5: European Call Option Payoff Diagrams

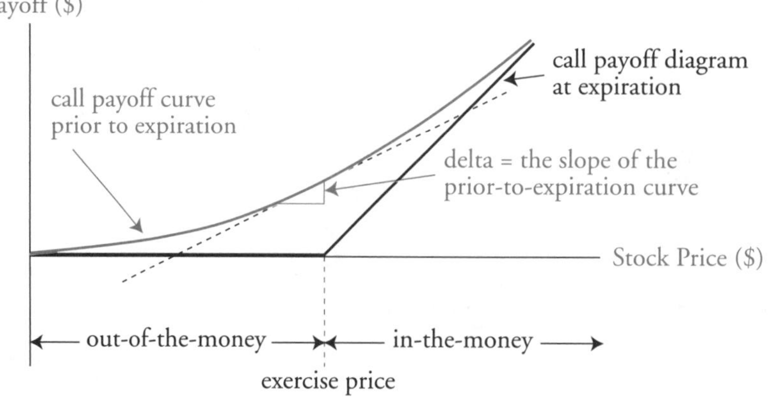

The slope of the "prior-to-expiration" curve is the change in call price per unit change in stock price. Sound familiar? It should—that's also the definition of delta. That means *delta is the slope of the prior-to-expiration curve*. The delta of the put option is also the slope of the *prior-to-expiration* put curve.

Take a closer look at Figure 5. When the call option is deep out-of-the-money, the slope of the at-expiration curve is close to zero, which means the call delta will be close to zero. For deep out-of-the-money call options (when the stock price is low), the option price does not change much for a given change in the underlying stock. When the call option is in-the-money (when the stock price is high), the slope of the at-expiration curve is close to 45 degrees, which means the call delta is close to one. In this case, the call option price will change almost one-for-one for a given change in the underlying stock price.

The bottom line is that *a call option's delta will increase from 0 to* $e^{-\delta T}$ *as stock price increases*. For a non-dividend paying stock, the delta will increase from 0 to 1 as the stock price increases.

For a put option, the put delta is close to zero when the put is out-of-the-money (when the stock price is high). When the put option is in-the-money (the stock price is close to zero), the put delta is close to $-e^{-\delta T}$.

The bottom line is that *a put option's delta will increase from* $-e^{-\delta T}$ *to 0 as stock price increases.* For a non-dividend paying stock, the put delta increases from –1 to 0 as the stock price increases.

Now, let's consider what happens to delta as the option approaches maturity, assuming that the underlying stock price doesn't change. The effects on call and put options are different and will depend on whether the options are in- or out-of-the-money.

Remember that a call option delta is between 0 and $e^{-\delta T}$. Assuming that the underlying stock price doesn't change, if the call option is:

- **Out-of-the-money** (the stock price is less than exercise price), the call delta **moves closer to 0** as time passes.
- **In-the-money** (the stock price is greater than exercise price), the call delta **moves closer to** $e^{-\delta T}$ as time passes.

Remember that a put option delta is between $-e^{-\delta T}$ and 0. If the put option is:

- **Out-of-the-money** (the stock price is greater than exercise price), the put delta **moves closer to 0** as time passes.
- **In-the-money** (the stock price is less than exercise price), the put delta **moves closer to** $-e^{-\delta T}$ as time passes.

Gamma measures the *rate of change in delta* as the underlying stock price changes. Gamma captures the curvature of the option value versus stock price relationship. Long positions in calls and puts have positive gammas. For example, a gamma of 0.04 implies that a $1.00 increase in the price of the underlying stock will cause a call option's *delta* to increase by 0.04, making the call option more sensitive to changes in the stock price.

Gamma is highest for at-the-money options. Deep in-the-money or deep out-of-money options have low gamma. Gamma changes with stock price and with time to expiration. To lower (increase) the overall gamma of a portfolio, one should short (go long) options.

Recall that delta provides an approximation for change in option value in response to change in the price of underlying. Including gamma in our equation would improve the precision with which change in option value would be estimated (similar to how convexity improves the estimate of change in a bond's price in response to a change in interest rate).

$$\Delta C \approx \text{call delta} \times \Delta S + \tfrac{1}{2}\,\text{gamma} \times \Delta S^2$$

$$\Delta P \approx \text{put delta} \times \Delta S + \tfrac{1}{2}\,\text{gamma} \times \Delta S^2$$

Call and put options on the same underlying asset with the same exercise price and time to expiration will have equal gammas.

Vega measures the sensitivity of the option price to changes in the volatility of returns on the underlying asset, as shown in Figure 6. Both call and put options are more valuable, all else equal, the higher the volatility, so vega is positive for both calls and puts. Volatility is a very important input to any option valuation model (and thus vega is an important sensitivity measure) because option values can be very sensitive to changes in volatility. Note that vega gets larger as the option gets closer to being at-the-money.

Figure 6: Call and Put Vega: The Relationship Between Option Price and Volatility

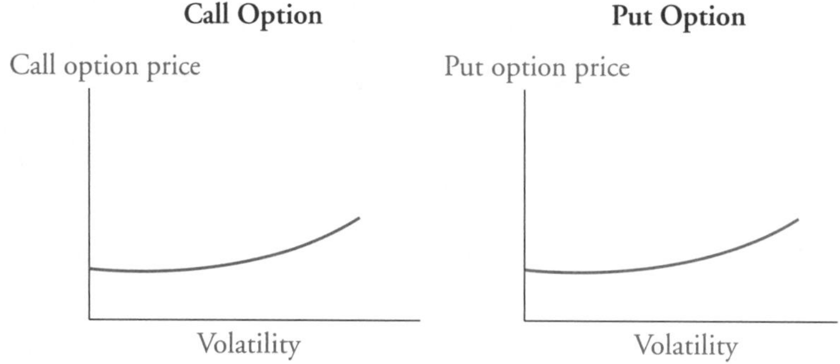

Rho measures the sensitivity of the option price to changes in the risk-free rate, as shown in Figure 7. The price of a European call or put option does not change much if we use different inputs for the risk-free rate, so rho is not a very important sensitivity measure. Call options increase in value as the risk-free rate increases (the rho of a call option is positive). You can see this by looking at the BSM model. As the risk-free rate increases, the second term decreases, and the value of the call option increases.

$$C_0 = \left[S_0 \times N(d_1)\right] - \left[X \times e^{-R_f^c \times T} \times N(d_2)\right]$$

Put options decrease in value as the risk-free rate increases (the rho of a put option is negative).

Figure 7: Call and Put Rho: The Relationship Between Option Price and the Risk-Free Rate

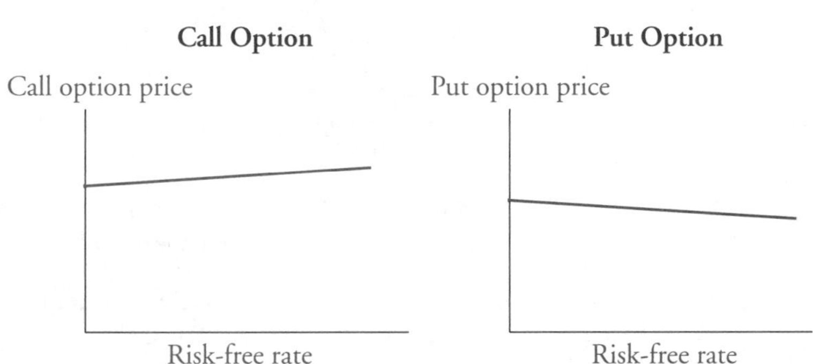

Theta measures the sensitivity of the option price to the passage of time, as shown in Figure 8. As time passes and a call option approaches maturity, its speculative value declines, all else equal. This is called time decay. This is also true for *most* put options (though *deep in-the-money* put options close to maturity may actually *increase* in value as time passes). Notice that because it is a measure of time decay, *theta is less than zero*: as time passes and the option approaches the maturity date, the option value decreases (holding other factors constant).

Figure 8: Call and Put Theta: The Relationship Between Option Price and the Time to Expiration

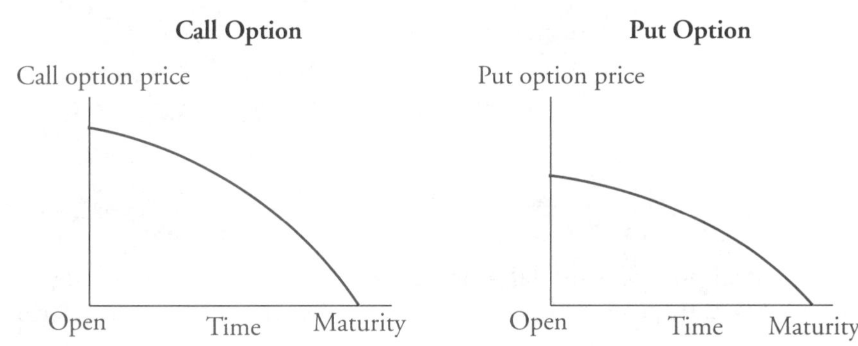

Professor's Note: The statement that theta is less than zero is counterintuitive to many Level II candidates because there are two ways to state the relationship between time and option value:

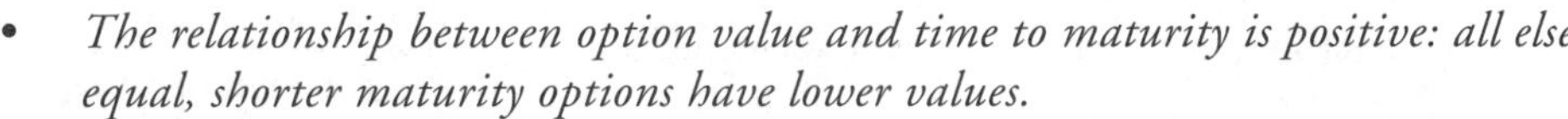

- *The relationship between option value and time to maturity is positive: all else equal, shorter maturity options have lower values.*
- *The relationship between option value and the passage of time is negative: all else equal, as time passes and the option approaches maturity, the value of the option decays.*

The key to understanding why theta is less than zero is to recognize that it is capturing the intuition of the second statement.

Figure 9: Direction of European Option Prices for a Change in the Five Black-Scholes-Merton Model Inputs

Sensitivity Factor (Greek)	*Input*	*Calls*	*Puts*
Delta	Asset price (S)	Positively related Delta > 0	Negatively related Delta < 0
Gamma	Delta	Positive Gamma > 0	Positive Gamma > 0
Vega	Volatility (σ)	Positively related Vega > 0	Positively related Vega > 0
Rho	Risk-free rate (r)	Positively related Rho > 0	Negatively related Rho < 0
Theta	Time to expiration (T)	Time value ⟶ \$0 as call ⟶ maturity Theta < 0	Time value ⟶\$0 as put ⟶ maturity Theta < 0*
	Exercise price (X)	Negatively related	Positively related

* There is an exception to the general rule that European put option thetas are negative. The put value may increase as the option approaches maturity if the option is deep in-the-money and close to maturity.

LOS 41.l: Describe how a delta hedge is executed.

CFA® Program Curriculum, Volume 5, page 406

Dynamic Hedging

The goal of a **delta-neutral portfolio** (or **delta-neutral hedge**) is to combine a long position in a stock with a *short* position in a call option so that the value of the portfolio does not change as the stock price changes. The number of calls to sell is equal to:

$$\text{number of } \textit{short} \text{ call options needed to delta hedge} = \frac{\text{number of shares hedged}}{\text{delta of call option}}$$

Delta-neutral portfolios can also be constructed using put options. In such a case, a long stock position is combined with a *long* position in puts. (Remember that put deltas are negative).

$$\text{number of long put options needed to delta hedge} = -\frac{\text{number of shares}}{\text{delta of the put option}}$$

Delta neutral portfolios are best illustrated with an example.

Example: Hedging with call options, part 1

Suppose you own 60,000 shares of Arthurall Company common stock that is currently selling for \$50. A call option on Arthurall with a strike price of \$50 is selling for \$4 and has a delta of 0.60. Determine the number of call options necessary to create a delta-neutral hedge.

Answer:

In order to determine the number of call options necessary to hedge against instantaneous movements in Arthurall's stock price, we calculate:

$$\text{number of options needed to delta hedge} = \frac{60{,}000}{0.60}$$

$$= 100{,}000 \text{ options, or } 1{,}000 \text{ option contracts}$$

Because we are long the stock, we need to short the options.

Example: Hedging with call options, part 2

Calculate the effect on portfolio value of a \$1 increase in the price of Arthurall stock.

Answer:

If the price of Arthurall stock increased instantly by \$1.00, the value of your call option position would decrease by \$0.60 because you have sold the call option contracts. Therefore, the net impact of the price change on the value of the hedged portfolio would be zero:

total change in value of stock position = 60,000 × \$1 = +\$60,000

total change in value of option position = 100,000 × –\$0.60 = –\$60,000

total change in portfolio value = \$60,000 – \$60,000 = \$0

A key consideration in delta-neutral hedging is that the delta hedged asset position is only risk free for a very small change in the value of the underlying stock. The delta-neutral portfolio must be continually rebalanced to maintain the hedge; for this reason, it is called a dynamic hedge. As the underlying stock price changes, so does the delta of the call option, and thus too the number of calls that need to be sold to maintain a hedged position. Hence, continuously maintaining a delta-neutral position involves significant transaction costs.

LOS 41.m: Describe the role of gamma risk in options trading.

CFA® Program Curriculum, Volume 5, page 409

If the assumptions of the BSM hold, changes in stock price will be continuous rather than abrupt, and hence there will be no gamma risk. In this context, gamma can be viewed as a measure of how poorly a dynamic hedge will perform when it is not rebalanced in response to a change in the asset price. **Gamma risk** is therefore the risk that stock price might abruptly "jump," leaving an otherwise delta-hedged portfolio unhedged.

Consider a delta hedge involving a long position in stock and short position in calls. If the stock price falls abruptly, the loss in the long stock position will not equal the gain in the short call position. This is the gamma risk of the hedge.

Given that a stock's delta is always 1, its gamma is 0. A delta-hedged portfolio with a long position in stocks and a short position in calls will have negative gamma exposure.

LOS 41.n: Define implied volatility and explain how it is used in options trading.

CFA® Program Curriculum, Volume 5, page 415

Future volatility is one of the inputs in the BSM model. Estimates based on historical volatility are often used because future volatility is not directly observable.

Implied volatility is the standard deviation of continuously compounded asset returns that is "implied" by the market price of the option. Of the five inputs into the BSM model, four are observable: stock price, exercise price, risk-free rate, and time to maturity. If we plug these four inputs into the BSM model, we can solve for the value of volatility that makes the BSM model value equal the market price.

Volatility enters the BSM pricing equation in a complex way, and there is no closed-form solution for the volatility that will produce a value equal to market price. Rather, implied volatility must be found by iteration (trial and error).

Traders often use implied volatilities to gauge market perceptions. For example, implied volatilities in options with different exercise prices on the same underlying may reflect different implied volatilities (a violation of BSM assumption of constant volatility).

Traders can also use implied volatility as a mechanism to quote option prices. In this way, options with different exercise prices and maturity dates can be quoted using the same unit of measurement.

Example: Implied volatility

Calls on Blue stock are currently trading at an implied volatility of 22%. A trader estimates that the future volatility will actually be closer to 25%. To capitalize on her beliefs, the trader should:

A. change her model.

B. buy calls on Blue stock.

C. write calls on Blue stock.

Answer:

B. Based on the trader's beliefs, call options on Blue stock are underpriced in the market. Accordingly, she should buy the calls.

Key Concepts

LOS 41.a

To value an option using a two-period binomial model:

- Calculate the stock values at the end of two periods (there are three possible outcomes because an up-down move gets you to the same place as a down-up move).
- Calculate option payoffs at the end of two periods.
- Calculate expected values at the end of two periods using the up- and down-move probabilities. Discount these back one period at the risk-free rate to find the option values at the end of the first period.
- Calculate expected value at the end of period one using the up- and down-move probabilities. Discount this back one period to find the option value today.

To price an option on a bond using a binomial tree, (1) price the bond at each node using projected interest rates, (2) calculate the intrinsic value of the option at each node at maturity of the option, and (3) calculate the value of the option today.

LOS 41.b

The value of a European call option using the binomial option valuation model is the present value of the expected value of the option in the 2 states.

$$C_0 = \frac{(\pi_U \times C^+ + \pi_D \times C^-)}{(1+R_f)}$$

The value of an American-style call option on a non-dividend paying stock is the same as the value of an equivalent European-style call option. American-style put options may be more valuable than equivalent European-style put options due to the ability to exercise early and earn interest on the intrinsic value.

LOS 41.c

Synthetic call and put options can be created using a replicating portfolio. A replication portfolio for a call option consists of a leveraged position in *h* shares where *h* is the hedge ratio or delta of the option. A replication portfolio for a put option consists of a long position in a risk-free bond and a short position in *h* shares. If the value of the option exceeds the value of the replicating portfolio, an arbitrage profit can be earned by writing the option and purchasing the replicating portfolio.

LOS 41.d

The value of an interest rate option is computed similarly to the value of options on stocks: as the present value of the expected future payoff. Unlike binomial stock price trees, binomial interest rate trees have equal (risk-neutral) probabilities of the up and down states occurring.

LOS 41.e

Option values can be calculated as present value of expected payoffs on the option, discounted at the risk-free rate. The probabilities used to calculate the expected value are risk-neutral probabilities.

LOS 41.f

The assumptions underlying the BSM model are:

- The price of the underlying asset changes smoothly (i.e., does not jump) and follows a lognormal distribution.
- The (continuous) risk-free rate is constant and known.
- The volatility of the underlying asset is constant and known.
- Markets are "frictionless."
- The underlying asset generates no cash flows.
- The options are European.

LOS 41.g

Calls can be thought of as leveraged stock investment where $N(d_1)$ units of stock is purchased using $e^{-rT}XN(d_2)$ of borrowed funds. A portfolio that replicates a put option can be constructed by combining a long position in $N(-d_2)$ bonds and a short position in $N(-d_1)$ stocks.

LOS 41.h

European options on dividend-paying stock can be valued by adjusting the model to incorporate the yield on the stock: the current stock price is adjusted by subtracting the present value of dividends expected up until option expiration. Options on currencies incorporate a yield on the foreign currency based on the interest rate in that currency.

LOS 41.i

The Black model is simply the BSM model with $e^{-R_f^c \times T}F_T$ substituted for S_0.

LOS 41.j

The Black model can be used to value interest rate options by substituting the current forward rate in place of the stock price and the exercise rate in place of exercise price. The value is adjusted for accrual period (i.e., the period covered by the underlying rate).

A swaption is an option that gives the holder the right to enter into an interest rate swap. A payer (receiver) swaption is the right to enter into a swap as the fixed-rate payer (receiver). A payer (receiver) swaption gains value when interest rates increase (decrease).

LOS 41.k

Direction of BSM option value changes for an increase in the five model inputs:

Sensitivity Factor (Greek)	*Input*	*Calls*	*Puts*
Delta	Asset price (S)	Positively related Delta > 0	Negatively related Delta < 0
Gamma	Delta	Positively related Gamma > 0	Positively related Gamma > 0
Vega	Volatility (σ)	Positively related Vega > 0	Positively related Vega > 0
Rho	Risk-free rate (r)	Positively related Rho > 0	Negatively related Rho < 0
Theta	Time to expiration (T)	Time value → \$0 as call → maturity Theta < 0	Time value usually → \$0 as put → maturity Theta < 0
	Exercise price (X)	Negatively related	Positively related

Delta is the change in the price of an option for a one-unit change in the price of the underlying security. $e^{-\delta T}N(d_1)$ from the BSM model is the delta of a call option, while $-e^{-\delta T}N(-d_1)$ is the put option delta.

As stock price increases, delta for a call option increases from 0 to $e^{-\delta T}$, while delta for a put option increases from $-e^{-\delta T}$ to 0.

LOS 41.l

The goal of a delta-neutral portfolio (or delta-neutral hedge) is to combine a long position in a stock with a short position in call options (or a long position in put options) so that the portfolio value does not change when the stock value changes. Given that delta changes when stock price changes, a delta hedged portfolio needs to be continuously rebalanced. Gamma measures how much delta changes as the asset price changes and, thus, offers a measure of how poorly a fixed hedge will perform as the price of the underlying asset changes.

LOS 41.m

When the price of the underlying stock abruptly jumps, a violation of BSM, the delta of the option would change (captured by the option gamma), leaving a previously delta hedged portfolio unhedged. This is the gamma risk of a delta hedged portfolio.

LOS 41.n

Implied volatility is the volatility that, when used in the Black-Scholes formula, produces the current market price of the option. If an option is overvalued, implied volatility is too high.

Concept Checkers

1. Compare the call and put prices on a stock that doesn't pay a dividend (NODIV) with comparable call and put prices on another stock (DIV) that is the same in all respects except it pays a dividend. Which of the following statements is *most accurate*? Price of:
   A. DIV call will be less than price of NODIV call.
   B. NODIV call will equal price of NODIV put.
   C. NODIV put will be greater than price of DIV put.

2. In a one-period binomial model, the hedge ratio is 0.35. To construct a riskless arbitrage involving 1,000 call options if the option is "overpriced," what is the appropriate portfolio?

	Calls	Stock
A.	Buy 1,000 options	Short 350 shares
B.	Buy 1,000 options	Short 2,857 shares
C.	Sell 1,000 options	Buy 350 shares

3. Which of the following statements is *least accurate*? The value of a:
   A. call option will decrease as the risk-free rate increases.
   B. put option will decrease as the exercise price decreases.
   C. call option will decrease as the underlying stock price decreases.

4. Which of the following inputs into the Black-Scholes-Merton model is *least likely* to have opposite effects on put and call prices?
   A. Volatility.
   B. Strike price.
   C. Risk-free rate.

5. Which of the following statements is *most accurate*? Implied volatility:
   A. requires market prices.
   B. requires a series of past returns.
   C. is equal for otherwise identical options with different maturities.

6. The delta of a put is –0.43. If the price of the underlying stock increases from \$40 to \$44, the price of the put option:
   A. increases by approximately 4.3%.
   B. decreases by approximately 4.3%.
   C. decreases by approximately \$1.72.

7. A synthetic European put option is created by:
   A. buying the discount bond, buying the call option, and short-selling the stock.
   B. buying the call option, short-selling the discount bond, and short-selling the stock.
   C. short-selling the stock, buying the discount bond, and selling the call option.

Challenge Problems

8. Which of the following is not an assumption underlying the Black-Scholes-Merton options pricing model?
   A. The underlying asset does not generate cash flows.
   B. Continuously compounded returns are lognormally distributed.
   C. The option can only be exercised at maturity.

Use the following information to answer Questions 9 and 10.

Stock ABC trades for $60 and has 1-year call and put options written on it with an exercise price of $60. ABC pays no dividends. The annual standard deviation estimate is 10%, and the continuously compounded risk-free rate is 5%. The value of the call is $4.09.

Chefron, Inc., common stock trades for $60 and has a 1-year call option written on it with an exercise price of $60. The annual standard deviation estimate is 10%, the continuous dividend yield is 1.4%, and the continuously compounded risk-free rate is 5%.

9. The value of the put on ABC stock is *closest* to:
   A. $1.16.
   B. $3.28.
   C. $4.09.

10. The value of the call on Chefron stock is *closest* to:
    A. $3.51.
    B. $4.16.
    C. $5.61.

11. Zepo Inc. stock price is currently $80. The stock price will move up by 15% or down by 13% each period. The value of a two-period call option with an exercise price of $62 if the risk-free rate is 4% per period is *closest* to:
    A. $19.17.
    B. $22.99.
    C. $27.11.

12. The current stock price of Heart, Inc., is $80. Call and put options with exercise prices of $50 and 15 days to maturity are currently trading. Which of these scenarios is *most likely* to occur if the stock price falls by $1?

	Call value	Put value
A.	Decrease by $0.94	Increase by $0.08
B.	Decrease by $0.76	Increase by $0.96
C.	Decrease by $0.07	Increase by $0.89

13. A put option with an exercise price of $45 is trading for $3.50. The current stock price is $45. What is the *most likely* effect on the option's delta and gamma if the stock price increases to $50?
    A. Both delta and gamma will increase.
    B. Both delta and gamma will decrease.
    C. One will increase and the other will decrease.

14. From the Black-Scholes-Merton model, $N(d_1) = 0.42$ for a 3-month call option on Panorama Electronics common stock. If the stock price falls by $1.00, the price of the call option will:
    A. decrease by less than the increase in the price of the put option.
    B. increase by more than the decrease in the price of the put option.
    C. decrease by the same amount as the increase in the price of the put option.

15. An analyst has calculated the value of a 2-year European call option to be $0.80. The strike price of the option is 100.00, and the underlying asset is a 7% annual coupon bond with three years to maturity. The two-period binomial tree for the European option is shown in the following figure.

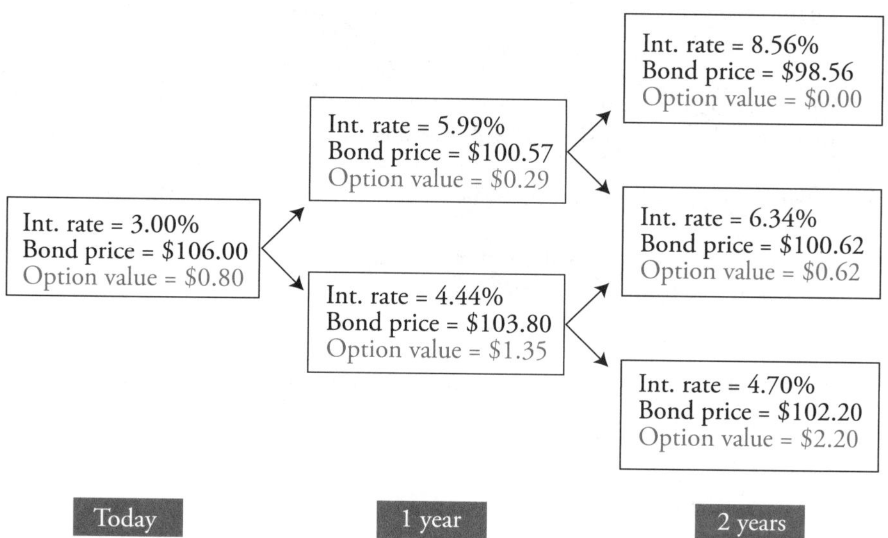

The value of the comparable 2-year American call option (exercisable after 1 year) with a strike price of 100.00 is *closest* to:

A. $1.56.
B. $2.12.
C. $3.80.

To access other content related to this topic review that may be included in the Schweser package you purchased, log in to your Schweser.com online dashboard. Schweser's OnDemand Video Lectures deliver streaming instruction covering every LOS in this topic review, while SchweserPro™ QBank provides additional quiz questions to help you practice and recall what you've learned.

Answers – Concept Checkers

1. **A** The dividend affects option values because if you own the option, you do not have access to the dividend. Hence, if the firm pays a dividend during the life of the option, this must be considered in the valuation formula. Dividends decrease the value of call options, all else equal, and they increase the value of put options.

2. **C** The hedge ratio in a one-period model is equivalent to a delta, the ratio of the call price change to the stock price change. We will sell the 1,000 calls because they are overpriced. Buying 350 shares of stock will produce a riskless hedge. The payoff at expiration will return more than the riskless rate on the net cost of the hedge portfolio. Borrowing to finance the hedge portfolio and earning a higher rate than the borrowing rate produces arbitrage profits.

3. **A** The value of a call and the risk-free rate are positively related, so as the risk-free rate increases, the value of the call will increase.

4. **A** Volatility increases will increase the values of both puts and calls.

5. **A** Implied volatility is the volatility that produces market option prices from the BSM model. Its use for pricing options is limited because it is based on market prices. Past returns are used to calculate historical volatility.

6. **C** The put option will decrease in value as the underlying stock price increases:

   $-0.43 \times \$4 = -\$1.72$.

7. **A** A synthetic European put option is formed by:
   - Buying a European call option.
   - Short-selling the stock.
   - Buying (i.e., investing) the present value of the exercise price worth of a pure-discount riskless bond.

Answers – Challenge Problems

8. **B** To derive the BSM model, we need to assume no arbitrage is possible and that:
   - Asset prices (not returns) follow a lognormal distribution.
   - The (continuous) risk-free rate is constant.
   - The volatility of the underlying asset is constant.
   - Markets are "frictionless."
   - The asset has no cash flows.
   - The options are European (i.e., they can only be exercised at maturity).

9. **A** According to put/call parity, the put's value is:

$$P_0 = C_0 - S_0 + \left(X \times e^{-R_c^f \times T}\right) = \$4.09 - \$60.00 + \left[\$60.00 \times e^{-(0.05 \times 1.0)}\right] = \$1.16$$

10. **A** ABC and Chefron stock are identical in all respects except Chefron pays a dividend. Therefore, the call option on Chefron stock must be worth less than the call on ABC (i.e., less than \$4.09). \$3.51 is the only possible answer.

11. **B** **Stock Tree**

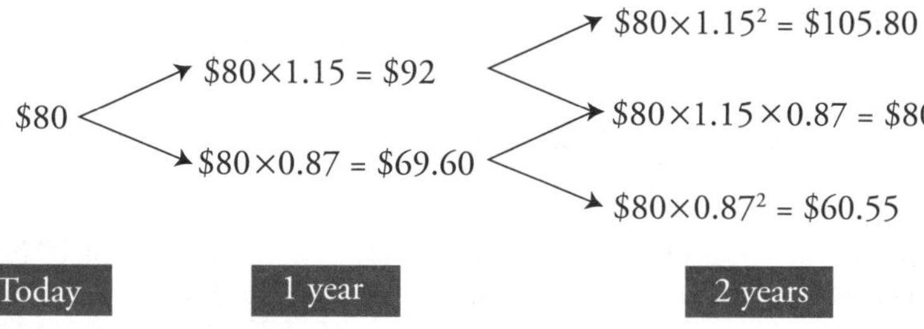

Option Tree

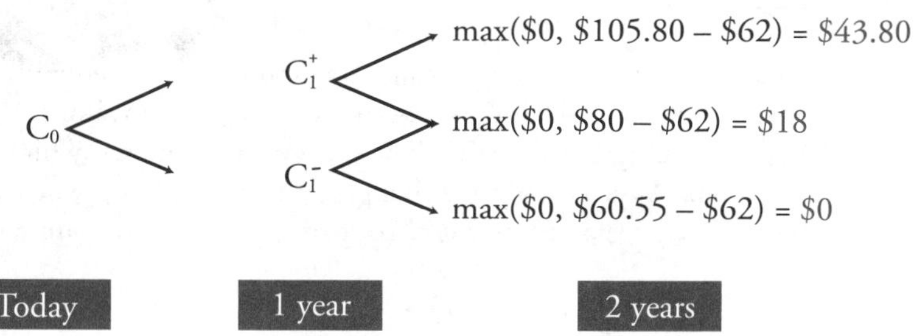

$$U = 1.15$$

$$D = 0.87$$

$$\pi_U = \frac{1.04 - 0.87}{1.15 - 0.87} = 0.61$$

$$\pi_D = 1 - 0.61 = 0.39$$

$$C_2^{++} = \$43.80$$

$$C_2^{+-} = C_2^{-+} = \$18.00$$

$$C_2^{--} = \$0$$

$$C_1^{+} = \frac{(0.61 \times \$43.80) + (0.39 \times \$18.00)}{1.04} = \$32.44$$

$$C_1^{-} = \frac{(0.61 \times \$18.00) + (0.39 \times \$0)}{1.04} = \$10.56$$

$$C_0 = \frac{(0.61 \times \$32.44) + (0.39 \times \$10.56)}{1.04} = \$22.99$$

12. A The call option is deep in-the-money and must have a delta close to one. The put option is deep out-of-the-money and will have a delta close to zero. Therefore, the value of the in-the-money call will decrease by close to \$1 (e.g., \$0.94), and the value of the out-of-the-money put will increase by a much smaller amount (e.g., \$0.08). The call price will fall by more than the put price will increase.

13. C The put option is currently at-the-money because its exercise price is equal to the stock price of \$45. As stock price increases, the put option's delta (which is less than zero) will increase toward zero, becoming less negative. The put option's gamma, which measures the rate of change in delta as the stock price changes, is at a maximum when the option is at-the-money. Therefore, as the option moves out-of-the-money, its gamma will fall.

14. A If $\Delta S = -\$1.00$, $\Delta C \approx 0.42 \times (-1.00) = -\$0.42$, and $\Delta P \approx (0.42 - 1) \times (-1.00) = \$0.58$, the call will decrease by less (\$0.42) than the increase in the price of the put (\$0.58).

15. B In the upper node at the end of the first year, the European option is worth \$0.29, but the American option can be exercised and a profit of \$0.57 realized (the difference between the bond price of \$100.57 and the exercise price of \$100).

In the lower node at the end of the first year, the European option is worth \$1.35, but the American option can be exercised and a profit of \$3.80 realized (the difference between the bond price of \$103.80 and the exercise price of \$100).

The value of the American option today is therefore:

$$\text{American option price} = \frac{(\$0.57 \times 0.5) + (\$3.80 \times 0.5)}{1.03} = \$2.12$$

The following is a review of the Derivatives Instruments: Valuation and Strategies principles designed to address the learning outcome statements set forth by CFA Institute. Cross-Reference to CFA Institute Assigned Reading #42.

Derivatives Strategies

Study Session 14

Exam Focus

This topic review focuses on uses of derivatives in portfolio management, including hedging, changing risk profiles, and trading based on opinion on market conditions. Make sure to understand the risk and return profiles of each strategy. Also be able to compute key metrics such as maximum profit, maximum loss, and breakeven price for each strategy.

LOS 42.a: Describe how interest rate, currency, and equity swaps, futures, and forwards can be used to modify portfolio risk and return.

CFA® Program Curriculum, Volume 5, page 434

Swaps can be used by a portfolio manager to modify the risk and return of a portfolio.

Interest Rate Swaps

Interest rate swaps can be used to modify the **duration** (i.e., interest rate risk) of a fixed-income portfolio. Recall that the value of an interest rate swap is equal to the difference in the value of two bonds.

value of a payer swap = value of a floating rate note – value of fixed rate bond

Therefore, the duration of a payer swap can be calculated as the difference in duration of the two bonds.

duration of a payer swap
= duration of floating rate note – duration of fixed rate bond

And similarly:

duration of a receiver swap
= duration of fixed rate bond – duration of floating rate note

Given that the duration of a fixed rate bond is greater than the duration of a floating rate note, the duration of a payer swap is negative. Similarly, the duration of a receiver swap is positive. A portfolio manager can increase (decrease) the duration of her portfolio by entering into a receiver (payer) swap.

Interest Rate Futures

Futures contracts are exchange traded and hence not subject to the counterparty risk that is present in OTC contracts such as swaps or forward contracts. Bond futures (also known as interest rate futures) can also be used to modify the duration of a portfolio. A portfolio manager seeking to increase the duration of the portfolio, say in anticipation of declining interest rates, can do so by going long in bond futures. Conversely, managers seeking to lower their portfolio's duration can do so by taking short positions in bond futures contracts.

Currency Swaps

Currency swaps can be used by parties that have a relative advantage in borrowing in their own capital markets as opposed to the capital markets of the currency in which they actually want to borrow. For example, a Japanese company may have favorable access to borrow yen but needs to borrow Swiss francs (perhaps for their Swiss subsidiary). Similarly, a Swiss company may have a need to borrow in yen. The Japanese company can engage in a yen-for-Swiss franc swap where the Japanese company borrows money in yen, turns it over to the Swiss counterparty and receives an equivalent amount in Swiss francs. In subsequent periods, the Japanese company makes interest payments in Swiss francs to the counterparty and receives yen interest, which it then pays to their lender. At maturity of the swap, both parties return the original exchanged principal amounts. In this way, both parties can take advantage of favorable borrowing terms in their respective markets, while effectively receiving loans in their desired foreign currency.

Currency Futures

Currency futures (or forward) contracts can be used to hedge an asset or liability in a foreign currency that is expected to be settled in the future. For example, an American company may have a euro liability due in six months and wants to hedge the risk of the euro appreciating (if the euro appreciates, the dollar cost to settle the liability will be higher for the American company). The American company can hedge this euro liability by purchasing euro futures contracts (i.e., going long euro vs. USD in the futures market) maturing in six months.

Equity Swaps

Equity swaps entail the exchange of returns on an equity index (or a single stock) for returns on another asset. Equity swaps can be used by equity portfolio managers seeking to temporarily reduce their exposure to stock market returns without liquidating their holdings. For example, a portfolio manager may be bearish about the prospects for equity markets over the next two years. The manager can enter into a two-year equity swap as a total return payer. This removes the exposure to equity from the portfolio over the specified time period (in exchange for receiving a fixed interest payment) without actually disrupting the portfolio (i.e., no transaction costs or taxes are incurred).

Stock Index Futures

Index futures can also be used to change the exposure of equities in a portfolio. For example, a manager seeking to temporarily rotate out of equities can do so by going short the appropriate number of index futures contracts. Conversely, a portfolio manager can rotate money out of bonds and into equities by taking a long position in appropriate number of equity index futures contracts.

Example: Changing equity exposure

A portfolio manager with an existing \$50 million long position in stocks wants to temporarily reallocate the portfolio to cash. The portfolio is highly correlated with the S&P 500 Index. S&P 500 Index futures are trading at 2000 and have a multiplier of 250.

Calculate the trade necessary for the manager to achieve his objective.

Answer:

Because the manager wants to remove an existing long exposure, he will go short futures contracts:

number of contracts short
= (portfolio value to be hedged) / (index value × multiplier)

= \$50 million / (2000 × 250)

= 100 contracts.

Accordingly, the manager should take a short position in 100 futures contracts on the S&P 500 Index.

LOS 42.b: Describe how to replicate an asset by using options and by using cash plus forwards or futures.

CFA® Program Curriculum, Volume 5, page 440

Synthetic Stock Using Options

A long position in a stock can be synthetically replicated over a specific horizon by using a portfolio of options. This portfolio consists of a long call and short put, both with a strike price equal to current market price of the stock. The long call provides exactly the same potential upside as a long position in stock does. Similarly, the short put provides exactly the same potential downside as a long position in stock. Hence, an at-the-money long call and short put replicate a stock, albeit only temporarily (i.e., until the maturity of the options).

A short position in a stock can be replicated by a portfolio consisting of at-the-money short calls, plus long put options.

Synthetic Puts and Calls

We can similarly create synthetic calls and puts. A long call can be replicated by a long stock position coupled with a long put. A synthetic put position can be created by a long call and a short position in stock.

Professor's Note: An easy way to remember the derivation of synthetic calls, puts and stock is to recall the put call parity relationship: $S_0 + P_0 = C_0 + PV(X)$. *(We can disregard the bond PV(X) when we are considering the impact of changes in the stock's price because the bond's value is unaffected).*

Example: Synthetic call

Suppose a stock is currently trading at $30. State the positions that are needed to create a synthetic call, and calculate the payoff to the call and synthetic call if the stock price had increased or decreased by $10 at expiry.

Answer:

A synthetic call can be created by combining a long stock and a long put. Both options should have a strike price equal to the stock's current price of $30.

If the stock price increased by $10, the call option payoff would be $10 while the put option would be worthless. The long stock position gains $10 while the long put gains $0, for a total gain of $10 for the synthetic call portfolio.

When the stock price falls by $10, the call option will expire worthless while the put option will have a payoff of $10. The synthetic portfolio has a loss of $10 on the long stock position and a gain of $10 on the long put. The net gain for the synthetic call portfolio is $0—the same as the gain for the call option.

Synthetic Assets With Forwards/Futures

A long position in futures on a stock, collateralized by the risk-free asset, can replicate a stock:

long futures + risk-free asset = long stock

We can re-arrange the previous formula to:

long stock + short futures = risk-free asset

In other words, we can hedge an existing long position in a stock by taking a short futures position. Because the resulting long-short portfolio is risk-free, the rate of return earned should be the risk-free rate.

Foreign Currency Options

Foreign currency options can be used to hedge an existing asset or liability denominated in a foreign currency. For example, an American company with euro debt that is maturing in six months might purchase a six-month call option on euros. If the euro appreciates relative to the dollar over the six month horizon, the gain on the call offsets the loss from the higher dollar cost to settle the liability. Note that call options on euro (vs. USD) are equivalent to puts on USD (vs. euros).

Options are superior to futures if one wants to hedge downside risk without giving away potential upside gains. If in the previous example (where the firm has euro-denominated debt) the euro depreciates rather than appreciating, the company can let the option expire and capture the gains from a lower dollar cost to settle the liability. The cost of removing only the downside risk is the premium paid on the option.

Example: Hedging Foreign Exchange Risk

Jim Sheinbucks is the CFO of Alpah Marrieta Mfg. (AMM). AMM is an industrial firm based in the United States. AMM has a GBP 5 million liability due in 3 months and has a CAD 3 million receivable due in 6 months.

Sheinbucks expects volatility in the GBP/USD rate and does not want it to negatively impact the company's profits for the current fiscal year. Sheinbucks does want to keep the potential upside should the USD appreciate relative to the GBP. Sheinbucks is also concerned that the USD may appreciate against CAD and wants to hedge that possibility at the lowest possible cost.

What trades should Sheinbucks undertake to manage his exposure?

Answer:

Because Sheinbucks wants to limit the downside of the GBP liability without giving up the upside, he should purchase a call option on the GBP (against USD). Alternatively, he can purchase a put on USD (against GBP). If the GBP appreciates against USD, the USD cost to settle the liability for AMM would increase. However, the call (or put) option would pay off, offsetting the loss.

A forward trade to sell CAD would be the best hedge against a decline in the value of CAD. A call option on USD (against CAD) could be purchased, but the option premium would be costly. Since Sheinbucks wants to keep the cost low, a forward contract would be a better choice.

LOS 42.c: Describe the investment objectives, structure, payoff, and risk(s) of a covered call position.

CFA® Program Curriculum, Volume 5, page 445

A **covered call** option strategy is a long position in a stock combined with a short call. A covered call strategy gives up the upside on the stock (when the stock price rises, the short call loses value—offsetting the gain on the long stock) but earns income via the premium on the call.

Investment objectives for covered calls include:

- **Income generation.** A long stock investor can accrue additional income by writing out-of-the-money call options. If the stock price does not exceed the exercise price by the maturity of the option, the option expires worthless and the investor earns the option premium as additional income. The drawback of this strategy is that the investor gives up the upside on the stock: if the stock price goes up beyond the exercise price, the call gets exercised and the gain on the long stock position cancels out against the losses on the short call.
- **Improving on the market.** An investor with a long stock position who wants to sell the stock can potentially get a better price by using a covered call with an in-the-money call option. The premium on the call option will be higher than its intrinsic value (i.e., the option has both time value and intrinsic value). Suppose that a stock is currently trading at $50 and calls with exercise price of $45 are trading for $8 (i.e., time value of $3 on top of the intrinsic value of $5). If the stock price remains stable, the option would be exercised, but the writer effectively sells the stock at a higher price. The difference is the time value. Hence, when the option gets exercised, the investor receives the exercise price of $45 plus the option premium of $8 for an effective selling price of $53.
- **Target price realization.** Suppose that the current stock price is $50 and the investor has a price target of $55 (at which point the stock would be sold). Accordingly, the investor writes a call option on the stock with an exercise price of $55 (i.e., the exercise price is set to equal the target price). Suppose that the option premium is $2.00. If the stock actually goes above the target price, the option will get exercised. However, the investor was able to sell at her target price *and* earn an extra return in

the form of an option premium. If the stock fails to rise above the target price, the investor gets to keep the premium and a new option will be written until the target price is realized or revised. The risk of this strategy (versus an outright sale of the stock) is that it retains the downside risk of the long stock position (and the stock could suffer steep losses). As always, the covered call position gives up the upside on the stock above the exercise price.

Profit or Loss at Expiration of a Covered Call

Notations:

S_0 and S_T = stock price at time 0 and T respectively
T = option maturity
X = exercise price
C_0 and P_0 = time 0 call and put option values respectively

The convention for quoting options is the month of expiration followed by the exercise price. For example 'Sep 25 call' indicates a call option that expires in September and has an exercise price of $25.

For a covered call, important relationships are:

investment at inception = $S_0 - C_0$
value at expiration = $S_T - \max(S_T - X, 0)$
profit at expiration = $\min(X, S_T) - (S_0 - C_0)$

maximum gain = $X - S_0 + C_0$
maximum loss = $S_0 - C_0$
breakeven point = $S_0 - C_0$

LOS 42.d: Describe the investment objectives, structure, payoff, and risk(s) of a protective put position.

CFA® Program Curriculum, Volume 5, page 445

Protective Put

A **protective put** position is composed of a long stock position and a long put position. The long put serves as an insurance policy to provide protection on the downside for the long stock position. The deductible on this insurance policy is (S_0 – X), and the policy premium is the put premium. The investor can reduce the premium on the insurance policy by increasing the deductible (i.e., choosing a lower exercise price).

Because the investor is long the put option, the investor does not give up the upside on the long stock position. The maximum loss is the deductible plus the premium cost.

For a protective put, important relationships are:

investment at inception = $S_0 + P_0$
value at expiration = max (S_T, X)
profit at expiration = max $(S_T, X) - (S_0 + P_0)$

maximum gain = $S_T - (S_0 + P_0)$ = theoretically unlimited
maximum loss = $(S_0 - X) + P_0$
breakeven point = $S_0 + P_0$

Risk

While protective puts provide protection against the downside risks in a long stock position, the put premium reduces the total portfolio return. If the risk of a portfolio is measured as the probability of failing to achieve portfolio objectives, the lower realized return actually increases the risk of the portfolio. Consistently insuring a portfolio using a protective put would significantly reduce portfolio returns. However, occasional use of protective puts (especially in times of anticipated market volatility that is not already reflected in option prices) may be advisable.

LOS 42.e: Calculate and interpret the value at expiration, profit, maximum profit, maximum loss, and breakeven underlying price at expiration for covered calls and protective puts.

CFA® Program Curriculum, Volume 5, page 448

Example: Covered Call and Protective Put Strategies

Bill Marve is using a covered call strategy on 100 shares of Xunoty, Inc. The stock is purchased at the current price of \$12. Marve has a target price of \$14. The following options are available to be purchased/written.

Calls		*Puts*	
Sep 12	\$2.24	Sep 12	\$1.76
Sep 14	\$0.88	Sep 14	\$3.92
Oct 10	\$3.59	Oct 10	\$0.59

Marve is also considering a protective put strategy for Xunoty and is wondering about the maximum loss, breakeven stock price, and profit at expiration of such a strategy.

1. Which option would Marve use to execute a target price realization strategy?
   A. Sep 12
   B. Sep 14
   C. Oct 10

2. If Marve uses a Sep 12 option for the covered call, what is the *maximum* loss and *maximum* gain?

	Maximum loss	Maximum gain
A.	\$ 9.76	\$2.24
B.	\$12.00	unlimited
C.	\$14.24	\$10.88

3. What is the breakeven point and the profit at expiration if the stock price at expiration is \$15, assuming that Marve uses the Sep 14 option for a covered call?

	Breakeven point	Profit at expiration
A.	\$12.00	\$2.24
B.	\$14.24	\$0
C.	\$11.12	\$2.88

4. If Marve uses the Sep 12 put option for the protective put insurance strategy, what is the policy deductible and policy premium?

	Deductible	Premium
A.	\$0	\$1.76
B.	\$12.00	\$0.92
C.	\$14.24	\$10.88

5. If Marve uses the Sep 12 put option for the protective put insurance strategy, what is the *maximum* loss that this position could suffer?
   A. \$0
   B. \$0.38
   C. \$1.76

6. If Marve uses the Oct 10 put option for the protective put insurance strategy, what is the breakeven stock price at expiration of the option?
   A. \$12
   B. \$12.59
   C. \$13.76

Answers:

1. B For a target price realization objective, the investor would write a call option with an exercise price equal to the target price on the stock (given as \$14). Hence, the option with an exercise price of \$14 should be chosen (i.e., Sep 14 option).

2. A maximum loss = $S_0 - C_0$ = \$12 – \$2.24 = \$9.76

   maximum gain = $X - S_0 + C_0$ = \$12 – \$12 + \$2.24 = \$2.24

   Note that the question is asking us to use Sep 12 option regardless of our answer to question 1.

3. C breakeven point = $S_0 - C_0$ = \$12 – \$0.88 = \$11.12

profit at expiration = Min (X, S_T) – ($S_0 - C_0$) = Min (14, 15) – (12 – 0.88)

= 14 – 11.12 = \$2.88

4. A policy deductible = $S_0 - X$ = \$12 – \$12 = \$0

premium = put cost = P_0 = \$1.76

5. C maximum loss = $S_0 - X + P_0$ = \$12 – \$12 + \$1.76 = \$1.76

6. B breakeven stock price = $S_0 + P_0$ = \$12 + \$0.59 = \$12.59

LOS 42.f: Contrast protective put and covered call positions to being long an asset and short a forward on the asset.

CFA® Program Curriculum, Volume 5, page 454

Recall that option **delta** measures the change in option price for a change in price of the underlying stock. The delta of a call (put) is positive (negative). For a non-dividend-paying stock, call deltas are between 0 and 1, and put deltas are between 0 and –1.

A long stock position has a delta of 1 by definition: the long position benefits dollar to dollar for an increase in the stock's price. Similarly, a short position in stock has a position delta of –1. A long forward position similarly has a delta of +1 and a short forward position has a delta of –1.

For a covered call strategy where the underlying call option has a delta of, say, 0.6, the delta of the strategy will be 0.4 as shown below:

covered call position = long stock + short call

Hence, covered call delta = delta of stock – delta of call option = 1.0 – 0.6 = 0.4.

Thus, this covered call position will increase in value by \$0.40 for every \$1 increase in stock price.

Similarly, the delta of a protective put position = delta of stock + delta of put option.

Example: Delta Strategies

Marve is contemplating using a covered call strategy, protective put strategy, or forwards position, in conjunction with a long position in 100 shares of Xunoty, Inc. The call option that Marve would use to construct the covered call position has a delta of 0.7. The put option that Marve would use to construct the protective put position has a delta of –0.8.

What forward position would give Marve the same position delta as the covered call? Protective put?

Answer:

covered call delta = delta of stock – delta of call option = 1.0 – 0.7 = 0.3

protective put delta = delta of stock + delta of put option = 1.0 – 0.8 = 0.2

To replicate the delta of the covered call, Marve would go short in a forward contract for 70 shares.

long stock delta + short forward delta = 1 – 0.7 = 0.3

To replicate the delta of the protective put, Marve should take the short position in a forward contract for 80 shares.

long stock delta + short forward delta = 1 – 0.8 = 0.2

Cash-Secured Puts

Cash-secured puts are created by writing a put option and depositing an amount equal to the put exercise price in a designated account. The writer of the put receives the option premium but takes the downside risk on the stock. The payoff on the short put is the same as the payoff on the covered call (as discussed earlier in put-call parity).

LOS 42.g: Describe the investment objective(s), structure, payoffs, and risks of the following option strategies: bull spread, bear spread, collar, and straddle.

LOS 42.h: Calculate and interpret the value at expiration, profit, maximum profit, maximum loss, and breakeven underlying price at expiration of the following option strategies: bull spread, bear spread, collar, and straddle.

CFA® Program Curriculum, Volume 5, page 459

A spread strategy in options entails a long position in one option and a short position in another. Spread strategies can be based on market sentiment (i.e., bull or bear) or based on upfront cash flow (i.e., debit or credit). A bull (bear) spread is based on the expectation of a higher (lower) price of the underlying stock at expiration of the options.

Bull spreads can be established with calls or puts where the exercise price of the long option is lower than the exercise price of the short option. Conversely, a **bear spread** has a higher exercise price for the long position and lower exercise price for the short position.

Bull Call Spread

A **bull call spread** provides *limited* upside if the underlying rises (hence the label "bull") with limited downside. It can be constructed by purchasing a call option with a low exercise price, X_L, and subsidizing that purchase price by selling a call with a higher exercise price, X_H. The call option premiums are C_{L0} and C_{H0}, respectively. At inception, the following relationships hold:

$$X_L < X_H$$

$$C_{L0} > C_{H0}$$

Consider a Xunoty Sep 12/14 bull call spread. This bull spread involves buying a Sep 12 call and writing a Sep 14 call. Recall that the option premiums were \$2.24 and \$0.88 for Sep 12 and Sep 14 calls respectively. Therefore, the net cost of the spread is \$2.24 – \$0.88 = \$1.36.

Suppose at expiration the stock price is \$15. The Sep 12 long call pays off \$3, and the Sep 14 short call results in a loss of \$1, for a net payoff of \$2; the difference in exercise prices of the two options. When the stock price closes at or above the higher exercise price, the payoff on the bull spread is the positive difference between the two exercise prices. The profit on the spread is the payoff at expiration minus the initial net cost. In our example, the profit is \$2.00 – \$1.36 or \$0.64.

$$\text{bull call spread profit} = \max(0, S_T - X_L) - \max(0, S_T - X_H) - C_{L0} + C_{H0}$$

$$\text{bull call spread maximum profit} = X_H - X_L - C_{L0} + C_{H0}$$

$$\text{bull call spread maximum loss} = C_{L0} - C_{H0}$$

$$\text{bull call spread breakeven price} = X_L + C_{L0} - C_{H0}$$

A bull call spread produces a gain if the stock price increases, but at a lower cost than the cost of the single lower exercise price call alone. The upper limit is capped, however, which is the price of lowering the cost.

Example: Bull call spread

An investor purchases a call for C_{L0} = \$2.10 with a strike price of X_L = \$45 and sells a call for C_{H0} = \$0.50 with a strike price of X_H = \$50.

1. Demonstrate the expression for the profit and compute the maximum profit and loss and the breakeven price.

2. Compute the bull call spread profits when the stock price is \$0, \$35, \$45, \$48, \$50, and \$55.

Answer:

1. $\text{profit} = \max(0, S_T - X_L) - \max(0, S_T - X_H) - C_{L0} + C_{H0}$

$= \max(0, S_T - 45) - \max(0, S_T - 50) - \$2.10 + \$0.50$

$= \max(0, S_T - 45) - \max(0, S_T - 50) - \$1.60$

$\text{maximum profit} = X_H - X_L - C_{L0} + C_{H0}$

$= \$50.00 - \$45.00 - \$2.10 + \$0.50 = \$3.40$

$\text{maximum loss} = C_{L0} - C_{H0} = \$2.10 - \$0.50 = \$1.60$

$\text{breakeven price} = X_L + C_{L0} - C_{H0}$

$= \$45.00 + \$2.10 - \$0.50 = \$46.60$

2. The following figure shows the calculations of the profit on the bull spread.

Stock Price S_T	*Bull Spread Strategy Profit* $= \max(0, S_T - X_L) - \max(0, S_T - X_H) - C_{L0} + C_{H0}$
\$0	max(0, \$0 – \$45) – max(0, \$0 – \$50) – \$2.10 + \$0.50 = –\$1.60
\$35	max(0, \$35 – \$45) – max(0, \$35 – \$50) – \$2.10 + \$0.50 = –\$1.60
\$45	max(0, \$45 – \$45) – max(0, \$45 – \$50) – \$2.10 + \$0.50 = –\$1.60
\$48	max(0, \$48 – \$45) – max(0, \$48 – \$50) – \$2.10 + \$0.50 = \$1.40
\$50	max(0, \$50 – \$45) – max(0, \$50 – \$50) – \$2.10 + \$0.50 = \$3.40
\$55	max(0, \$55 – \$45) – max(0, \$55 – \$50) – \$2.10 + \$0.50 = \$3.40

Bear Call Spread

A bear call spread provides a (limited) income if the underlying declines (hence the label "bear") with limited downside (if the underlying does not decline). It is constructed by selling a call with a low strike price and purchasing a call with a high strike price. If the stock's price falls, the writer keeps the premium from the written call, net of the long call premium. The purpose of the long call is to protect the writer from sharp increases in stock's price.

Bear Put Spread

A bear put spread entails buying a higher exercise price put and writing a lower exercise price put. A bear put spread provides (limited) upside if the value of the underlying falls.

$$\text{profit} = \max(0, X_H - S_T) - \max(0, X_L - S_T) - P_{H0} + P_{L0}$$

$$\text{maximum profit} = X_H - X_L - P_{H0} + P_{L0}$$

$$\text{maximum loss} = P_{H0} - P_{L0}$$

$$\text{breakeven price} = X_H + P_{L0} - P_{H0}$$

Example: Bear put spread

An investor purchases a put for P_{H0} = \$4.00 with a strike price of X_H = \$25.00 and sells a put for P_{L0} = \$1.80 with a strike price of X_L = \$20.00.

1. Demonstrate the expression for profit and compute the maximum profit and loss and the breakeven price.

2. Calculate the profits when the stock price is \$0, \$15, \$20, \$22, \$25, and \$30.

Answer:

1. $\text{profit} = \max(0, X_H - S_T) - \max(0, X_L - S_T) - P_{H0} + P_{L0}$

$= \max(0, 25 - S_T) - \max(0, 20 - S_T) - \$4.00 + \$1.80$

$= \max(0, 25 - S_T) - \max(0, 20 - S_T) - \$2.20$

$\text{maximum profit} = X_H - X_L - P_{H0} + P_{L0}$

$= \$25.00 - \$20.00 - \$4.00 + \$1.80 = \$2.80$

$\text{maximum loss} = P_{H0} - P_{L0}$

$= \$4.00 - \$1.80 = \$2.20$

$\text{breakeven price} = X_H + P_{L0} - P_{H0}$

$= \$25.00 + \$1.80 - \$4.00 = \$22.80$

2.

Bear Spread Profits

S_T	*Bear Spread Profit* $= \max(0, X_H - S_T) - \max(0, X_L - S_T) - P_{L0} + P_{H0}$
\$0	max(0, \$25 – \$0) – max(0, \$20 – 0) – \$4.00 + \$1.80 = \$2.80
\$15	max(0, \$25 – \$15) – max(0, \$20 – \$15) – \$4.00 + \$1.80 = \$2.80
\$20	max(0, \$25 – \$20) – max(0, \$20 – \$20) – \$4.00 + \$1.80 = \$2.80
\$22	max(0, \$25 – \$22) – max(0, \$20 – \$22) – \$4.00 + \$1.80 = \$0.80
\$25	max(0, \$25 – \$25) – max(0, \$20 – \$25) – \$4.00 + \$1.80 = –\$2.20
\$30	max(0, \$25 – \$30) – max(0, \$20 – \$30) – \$4.00 + \$1.80 = –\$2.20

Risks of Spreads

As can be seen from the maximum profit and maximum loss formulae for the various spreads, the upside and the downside of these strategies is limited. Spreads limit the downside risk but at a cost of also limiting the upside. This is similar to a collar strategy (discussed next).

Hence a spread strategy could be viewed as "chopping off the tails" of an asset's return distribution.

Collar

A **collar** combines the concepts of a protective put and a covered call. The objective of a collar is to decrease the volatility of investment returns. To set up a collar, the owner of the underlying stock buys a protective put and simultaneously sells a call to offset the put premium. If the premiums of the two are equal, it is called a **zero-cost collar.**

Generally for a collar, the put strike (X_L) < the call strike (X_H). A collar effectively puts a band around the possible returns of a long stock position. Any stock price movement above X_H is lost (due to the short call), and any movement below X_L is protected (due to the long put).

A collar structured such that $X_L = X_H = X$ ensures a locked-in profit or loss of $(X - S_0)$.

The profit on the collar is comprised of the return on the stock, plus payoff on the long put, plus payoff on the short call, minus the initial net cost of the options.

For a collar, important relationships are:

$$\text{profit} = (S_T - S_0) + \max(0, X_L - S_T) - \max(0, S_T - X_H) - (P_0 - C_0)$$

$$\text{maximum profit} = X_H - S_0 - (P_0 - C_0)$$

$$\text{maximum loss} = S_0 - X_L + (P_0 - C_0)$$

$$\text{breakeven price} = S_0 + (P_0 - C_0)$$

Risks of a Collar

A collar gives up the upside on a stock in exchange for downside protection. Similar to spreads, collars can be thought of as "chopping off the tails" of the return distribution.

Example: Zero-cost collar

An investor purchases a stock for \$29 and a put for P_0 = \$0.20 with a strike price of X_L = \$27.50. The investor sells a call for C_0 = \$0.20 with a strike price of X_H = \$30.

1. Demonstrate the expression for the profit and calculate the maximum profit and loss and the breakeven price.
2. Calculate the profits when the stock price is \$0.00, \$20.00, \$25.00, \$28.50, \$30.00, and \$100.00.

Answer:

1. This is a zero-cost collar because the premiums on the call and put are equal (i.e., $C_0 = P_0$).

$$\text{profit} = (S_T - S_0) + \max(0, X_L - S_T) - \max(0, S_T - X_H) - (P_0 - C_0)$$

$$= (S_T - \$29) + \max(0, \$27.50 - S_T) - \max(0, S_T - \$30.00) - 0$$

$$\text{maximum profit} = X_H - S_0 - (P_0 - C_0)$$

$$= \$30 - \$29 - 0 = \$1$$

$$\text{maximum loss} = S_0 - X_L + (P_0 - C_0)$$

$$= \$29.00 - \$27.50 + 0$$

$$= \$1.50$$

$$\text{breakeven price} = S_0 + (P_0 - C_0) = \$29 + 0 = \$29.$$

2. The table shows the calculations for profits on this zero-cost collar.

Profits on a Zero-Cost Collar

Stock Price S_T	*Zero-Cost Collar Profit* $= max(0, X_L - S_T) - max\ (0, S_T - X_H) + S_T - S_0$
\$0.00	max(0, \$27.50 – \$0) – max(0, \$0 – \$30.00) + \$0 – \$29.00 = –\$1.50
\$20.00	max(0, \$27.50 – \$20.00) – max(0, \$20.00 – \$30.00) + \$20.00 – \$29.00 = –\$1.50
\$25.00	max(0, \$27.50 – \$25.00) – max(0, \$25.00 – \$30.00) + \$25.00 – \$29.00 = –\$1.50
\$28.50	max(0, \$27.50 – \$28.50) – max(0, \$28.50 – \$30.00) + \$28.50 – \$29.00 = –\$0.50
\$30.00	max(0, \$27.50 – \$30.00) – max(0, \$30.00 – \$30.00) + \$30.00 – \$29.00 = \$1.00
\$100.00	max(0, \$27.50 – \$100.00) – max(0, \$100.00 – \$30.00) + \$100.00 – \$29.00 = \$1.00

Straddle

A long **straddle** consists of a long call and a long put with the same strike price and on the same underlying stock. An investor will use a straddle when she expects a large stock price move, but is unsure of the direction. A straddle is based on an expectation of higher future volatility: the investor will lose only if the stock price doesn't change much. Thus, a straddle can be thought of as a bet on higher future volatility. Recall that option value increases with volatility and hence long positions in both calls and puts increase in value if volatility increases after the position is established.

A straddle buyer pays two option premiums upfront and hopes that one of the two options pays off (more than the upfront cost). A long straddle investor is neutral on the direction of the market but expects a sharp increase in volatility. Conversely, a short straddle makes sense if the investor is neutral on market direction *and* does not expect sudden jumps in price.

For a straddle, important relationships are:

$$\text{profit} = \max(0, S_T - X) + \max(0, X - S_T) - (C_0 + P_0)$$

$$\text{maximum profit} = S_T - X - (C_0 + P_0) \text{ (unlimited upside as } S_T \text{ increases)}$$

$$\text{maximum loss} = C_0 + P_0$$

$$\text{breakeven price} = X - (C_0 + P_0) \text{ and } X + (C_0 + P_0)$$

Example: Straddle

An investor purchases a call on a stock, with an exercise price of \$45 and premium of \$3, and a put option with the same maturity/exercise price and premium of \$2.

1. Demonstrate the expressions for the profit and the maximum profit and compute the maximum loss and the breakeven price.

2. Compute the profits when the stock price is \$0, \$35, \$40, \$45, \$50, \$55, and \$100.

Answer:

1.

$$\text{Profit} = \max(0, S_T - X) + \max(0, X - S_T) - (C_0 + P_0)$$

$$= \max(0, S_T - \$45) + \max(0, \$45 - S_T) - \$3 - \$2$$

$$= \max(0, S_T - \$45) + \max(0, \$45 - S_T) - \$5$$

$$\text{Maximum profit} = S_T - X - (C_0 + P_0) = S_T - \$45 - \$5 = S_T - \$50$$

$$\text{Maximum loss} = C_0 + P_0 = \$5$$

$$\text{Breakeven price} = X - (C_0 + P_0) \text{ and } X + (C_0 + P_0)$$

$$= \$45 - \$5 \text{ and } \$45 + \$5$$

$$= \$40 \text{ and } \$50$$

2. The figure below shows the profit on Straddle at the different stock prices

Profits on a Long Straddle

S_T	*Straddle Profit* $= max(0, S_T - X) + max(0, X - S_T) - C_0 - P_0$
\$0	max(0, \$0 – \$45) + max(0, \$45 – \$0) – \$3 – \$2 = \$40
\$35	max(0, \$35 – \$45) + max(0, \$45 – \$35) – \$5 = \$5
\$40	max(0, \$40 – \$45) + max(0, \$45 – \$40) – \$5 = \$0
\$45	max(0, \$45 – \$45) + max(0, \$45 – \$45) – \$5 = –\$5
\$50	max(0, \$50 – \$45) + max(0, \$45 – \$50) – \$5 = \$0
\$55	max(0, \$55 – \$45) + max(0, \$45 – \$55) – \$5 = \$5
\$100	max(0, \$100 – \$45) + max(0, \$45 – \$100) – \$5 = \$50

LOS 42.i: Describe uses of calendar spreads.

CFA® Program Curriculum, Volume 5, page 466

Calendar Spread

Consider two call options on the same stock and with the same exercise price but with different maturities. A long **calendar spread** strategy is short the near-dated call and long the longer-dated call. A short calendar spread is short the longer-dated call and long the near-dated call.

Because the premium on a longer-dated option exceeds the premium on near-dated option, a long (short) calendar spread results in a negative (positive) initial cash flow. A calendar spread seeks to exploit differences in time decay between near-dated and longer-dated options. Calendar spreads can also be constructed using puts.

One use of a long calendar spread is when a trader believes that a stock's price will be flat in the near term but is poised to break out in the longer term. This expectation may be tied to anticipated positive news such as a new product release or the successful trial of a new drug. In such an instance, the trader believes that the short call will expire worthless, while the long call will be in-the-money after the news is released to the market.

LOS 42.j: Identify and evaluate appropriate derivatives strategies consistent with given investment objectives.

CFA® Program Curriculum, Volume 5, page 473

Investment Objectives

A trader will select an option strategy that is consistent with their investment objectives as well as their expectations of market direction and future volatility.

If the trader's view is for market prices to rise, the trader should consider whether this expectation is already priced into the premiums of the options concerned. As a generalization, long calls (puts) are appropriate for strong bullish (bearish) sentiment. Long calls and short puts (write calls and buy puts) would make sense for average bullish (bearish) sentiment. Writing puts (calls) is appropriate for weak bullish (bearish) sentiment.

If the trader has expectations of high (low) future volatility, a long (short) straddle would be an appropriate strategy. The volatility of a market is sometimes referred to as the market's "speed": an environment of high volatility is described as a "fast" market, while an environment of low volatility is described as a "slow" market.

Breakeven Price Analytics

For each of the strategies discussed, the corresponding breakeven price can be used to determine the volatility needed to earn neither a profit nor a loss. For the purpose of this discussion, annual volatility is measured over the number of trading days (approximately 252).

$$\sigma_{\text{annual}} = \%\Delta P \times \sqrt{\frac{252}{\text{trading days until maturity}}}$$

$$\text{where } \%\Delta P = \frac{|\text{breakeven price} - \text{current price}|}{\text{current price}}$$

The absolute value operator here ensures that the value for the change in price (and hence the standard deviation) is positive.

We can calculate the annualized %ΔP by multiplying it by (252 ÷ the number of trading days until maturity). (If we are instead given option expiration in *months*, use 12 divided by the number of months until expiration.)

Example: Annual volatility

The stock of Piperdine is trading at $50. A 90-day (64 trading days) call option with an exercise price of $50 is trading for $3. A 90-day put option with an exercise price of $50 is trading for $2.

What is the annual standard deviation needed on the stock to break even on a long straddle strategy?

Answer:

Breakeven price for long straddle = $X - (C_0 + P_0)$ and $X + (C_0 + P_0)$

= $50 – $5 and $50 + $5

Therefore, the stock has to move up or down by $5 for the straddle to break even. This represents a price change of %ΔP = $5 / $50 = 10%.

$$\sigma_{annual} = \%\Delta P \times \sqrt{\frac{252}{\text{trading days until maturity}}} = 10\%\sqrt{\frac{252}{64}} = 19.8\%$$

This 19.8% represents the annual standard deviation required to break even on the long straddle strategy.

Key Concepts

LOS 42.a
Combining a bond portfolio with a payer (receiver) swap reduces (increases) the duration of the bond portfolio and hence changes its interest rate risk. Bond futures can achieve the same objective. Equity swaps can be used to gain or reduce exposure to equities.

Currency swaps can be used to obtain favorable financing in otherwise expensive foreign currency capital markets.

Futures and forwards on currencies can be used to hedge a foreign currency denominated asset or liability.

LOS 42.b
A long futures contract on a stock when combined with a risk-free asset replicates a long position on the stock.

long futures + risk-free asset = long stock

A protective put has the same payoffs as a long call option (i.e., $S_0 + P_0 = C_0$) while a short put is same as a covered call (i.e., $S_0 - C_0 = -P_0$).

Call options on euro (vs. USD) are equivalent to puts on USD (vs. euros).

LOS 42.c, e
A covered call option strategy is a long position in a stock combined with a short call. Covered call strategies can be used for income generation, improving on the market, or target price realization.

The risk of a covered call is the opportunity cost of giving up the upside on the long stock position when the stock price rises beyond the exercise price of the short call.

$$\text{maximum gain} = X - S_0 + C_0$$

$$\text{maximum loss} = S_0 - C_0$$

$$\text{breakeven point} = S_0 - C_0$$

LOS 42.d, e
A protective put position is composed of a long stock position and a long put position. A protective put is like an insurance policy with the put premium representing the policy premium and the difference between the initial stock price and put exercise price representing the deductible.

Because long puts cost money, they end up being a drag on portfolio returns. Consistently insuring the portfolio using puts seriously jeopardizes the achievement of portfolio objectives.

$$\text{maximum gain} = S_T - (S_0 + P_0) = \text{theoretically unlimited}$$

$$\text{maximum loss} = (S_0 - X) + P_0$$

$$\text{breakeven point} = S_0 + P_0$$

LOS 42.f

Covered calls and protective puts are used to reduce the delta of a long stock position. Covered call delta = delta of stock – delta of call option, and protective put delta = delta of stock + delta of put option. A short forward contract also reduces the portfolio delta and can be used to replicate the deltas of covered call or protective put positions.

LOS 42.g,h

A bull spread can be established with calls or puts where the exercise price of the long option is lower than the exercise price of the short option. Conversely, a bear spread has a higher exercise price for the long option and lower exercise price for the short option.

Both spreads provide a *limited* upside with a limited downside.

For a bull call spread:

$$\text{maximum profit} = X_H - X_L - C_{L0} + C_{H0}$$

$$\text{maximum loss} = C_{L0} - C_{H0}$$

$$\text{breakeven price} = X_L + C_{L0} - C_{H0}$$

For a bear put spread:

$$\text{maximum profit} = X_H - X_L - P_{H0} + P_{L0}$$

$$\text{maximum loss} = P_{H0} - P_{L0}$$

$$\text{breakeven price} = X_H + P_{L0} - P_{H0}$$

A combination of a covered call and a protective put is a collar. Similar to spreads, collars limit downside risk but at a cost of limited upside.

$$\text{maximum profit} = X_H - S_0 - (P_0 - C_0)$$

$$\text{maximum loss} = S_0 - X_L + (P_0 - C_0)$$

$$\text{breakeven price} = S_0 + (P_0 - C_0)$$

A long straddle is constructed in expectation of higher future volatility and consists of a long call and a long put with the same strike price and on the same underlying stock.

maximum profit = $S_T - X - (C_0 + P_0)$ *(unlimited upside as S_T increases)*

$$\text{maximum loss} = C_0 + P_0$$

breakeven price = $X - (C_0 + P_0)$ and $X + (C_0 + P_0)$

LOS 42.i
A long calendar spread strategy is short the near-dated call and long the longer-dated call. A short calendar spread is short the longer-dated call and long the near-dated call.

Calendar spreads are used when volatility is expected to change (with a long position corresponding to maturity where volatility is expected to be higher).

LOS 42.j
Derivatives strategies need to be consistent with investment opinion about the direction of the market as well as expectations about future volatility. Strong bullish sentiment can be expressed by a long position in calls. Conversely, strong bearish sentiment can be expressed by a long position in puts. Average bullish (bearish) sentiment can be expressed by long calls and short puts (long puts, short calls). Weak bullish (bearish) sentiment can be expressed by writing puts (calls).

Concept Checkers

Use the following information to answer questions 1–10.

Bill Paxton, managing partner of Axis Asset Managers, manages a set of diverse client portfolios. This morning, Paxton is summarizing the discussion he had with Seeta Gandhi, the chief economist, regarding the outlook for markets over the coming year. Figure 1 shows the summary.

Figure 1: Market Outlook

1. Recently, the U.S. Treasury decided to increase auctions of longer-term bonds and lower the offerings of short-term bonds. This change is expected to steepen the yield curve. Because this shift in policy is only temporary, rates will revert back to current levels by the end of the year.
2. The change in Medicare reimbursement rates that was just announced should benefit Adalpia Pharmaceuticals. The market has not priced this information into Adalpia's stock yet. Also, Adalpia's stock should experience a boost after the announcement of third quarter earnings in six months.
3. Volatility in the equity market is poised to increase upon the announcement of election results in the country of Ilan, a key energy producer.

Paxton is also pondering increasing the use of derivatives for some of the client portfolios. He met with Bill Smith, CFA to review some of the strategies that Paxton could use. Smith provides Paxton with market price information as shown in Figure 2.

Figure 2: Information About ABC Stock and Options

Current stock price = $15

Option	*Call Price*	*Call Delta*	*Put Price*	*Put Delta*
Dec 15	$2.63	0.50	$1.10	–0.50
Dec 16	$1.90	0.61	$1.98	–0.42
Dec 17	$1.01	0.72	$2.67	–0.33

Paxton reviews the notes that Smith provided during their meeting and drafts a list of follow-up questions.

1. Based on the interest rate outlook as described in the first observation in Figure 1, which strategy is *most appropriate* to protect a portfolio of fixed income securities?
   A. Long position in T-bond futures maturing in one year.
   B. A one-year quarterly settlement receiver swap.
   C. A one-year quarterly settlement payer swap.

2. Based on the second point in Figure 1, which strategy would be most appropriate?
   A. Long calls and short puts on Adalpia stock.
   B. Short forward contracts on Adalpia stock.
   C. Long put and long calls on Adalpia stock.

3. Using the information in Figure 2, if Paxton wants to establish a covered call position using the Dec 16 option, the breakeven stock price will be *closest* to:
   A. $13.10.
   B. $14.40.
   C. $16.90.

4. Using the information in Figure 2, if Paxton wants to establish a protective put position using the Dec 16 option, the maximum loss is *closest* to:
   A. $0.60.
   B. $0.98.
   C. $1.98.

5. The risk of a protective put strategy is *most accurately* characterized by:
   A. an increase in return volatility.
   B. a decrease in stock price.
   C. a decrease in portfolio return.

6. Using the information in Figure 2, which position is *least likely* to replicate the delta of a covered call position on 100 shares of ABC stock using the Dec 15 option?
   A. A protective put using 100 shares and the Dec 15 option.
   B. A Dec 15/17 bull call spread.
   C. A short position in a forward contract on 50 ABC shares.

7. Which of the following positions is *least likely* to have a limited upside?
   A. A calendar spread.
   B. A bull call spread.
   C. A long straddle.

8. Based on information in the third observation of Figure 1, the *most appropriate* strategy is:
   A. a long straddle.
   B. a bull spread.
   C. a short straddle.

9. Based on information in Figure 2, the maximum profit for a bull spread using Dec 16 and Dec 17 calls is *closest* to:
   A. $0.11.
   B. Unlimited.
   C. $0.89.

10. A long calendar spread is *least likely* to have:
   A. an initial cash outflow.
   B. a short position in near-dated option.
   C. a short position in longer-dated option.

Answers – Concept Checkers

1. C The expectation is for long-term rates to rise, and the most appropriate strategy in that case is to reduce the duration of the portfolio. Of the choices provided, only a payer swap has a negative duration. We are also given that the relevant time horizon is one year and hence the swap maturity should be one year. A receiver swap and long position in bond futures would both *increase* the duration of the portfolio.

2. A Since the expectation is for an increase in the price of Adalpia stock, a long position in the stock (or a long call on the stock) would be desirable. A long call and short put can be used to synthetically create a long stock position. A long call and long put would also provide the upside (from the long call position) but is not ideal as the cost would be higher (a long put costs us a premium, while a short put offsets the cost of the long call).

3. A breakeven price on covered call = $S_0 - C_0$ = \$15 – \$1.90 = \$13.10.

4. B maximum loss on protective put = $S_0 - X + P_0$ = 15 – 16 + 1.98 = \$0.98.

5. C A protective put is analogous to an insurance policy and the put premium is similar to the policy premium. The premium cost acts as a drag on portfolio return. A protective put reduces downside risk and hence reduces return volatility. A protective put has no impact on stock price volatility.

6. B The question is asking for the *least* likely choice. From Figure 2, delta of Dec 15 call = delta of Dec 15 put = 0.50.

   position delta of covered call = delta of stock – delta of call option
   = 1.0 – 0.50 = 0.50

   position delta of protective put = delta of stock + delta of put option
   = 1.0 + (–0.50) = 0.50

   position delta of short forward on 50 (i.e., 50% of the shares)
   = delta of stock – (0.5 × delta of the forward) = 1.0 – 0.50 = 0.50

   Dec 15/17 bull call spread entails buying the Dec 15 call and writing the Dec 17 call.

   position delta of Dec 15/17 bull call spread
   = delta of Dec 15 call – delta of Dec 17 call = 0.50 – 0.72 = –0.22

   Out of the choices provided, only Dec 15/17 bull call spread does not have a delta of 0.50.

7. C The question is asking for the *least* likely choice. All spread strategies have limited upside. A long straddle has unlimited upside (because the long call in the straddle has unlimited upside).

8. A Based on the third observation in Figure 1, volatility is expected to increase. A long straddle would benefit the most from an increase in volatility (and a short straddle would lose most). The short option in a bull spread would limit the gain from an increase in volatility.

9. A maximum profit on bull call spread = $X_H - X_L - C_{L0} + C_{H0}$

$= 17 - 16 - 1.90 + 1.01$

$= \$0.11$

10. C The question is asking for the *least* likely choice. A long calendar spread strategy is short the near-dated call and long the longer-dated call on the same stock with the same exercise price. Because the longer-dated call has a higher time value than the near-dated call, a long calendar spread results in an initial cash outflow.

To access other content related to this topic review that may be included in the Schweser package you purchased, log in to your Schweser.com online dashboard. Schweser's OnDemand Video Lectures deliver streaming instruction covering every LOS in this topic review, while SchweserPro™ QBank provides additional quiz questions to help you practice and recall what you've learned.

Self-Test: Derivatives

You have now finished the Derivatives topic section. The following self-test will provide immediate feedback on how effective your study of this material has been. The test is best taken timed; allow 3 minutes per subquestion (18 minutes per item set). This self-test is more exam-like than typical Concept Checkers or QBank questions. A score less than 70% suggests that additional review of this topic is needed.

Use the following information to answer Questions 1 through 6.

Derrick Honny, CFA, has operated his own portfolio management business for many years. Several of his clients have fixed income positions, and one of Honny's analysts has advised him that the firm could improve the performance of these portfolios through swaps. Honny has begun investigating the properties of swaps. His plan is first to establish some minor positions to gain some experience before actively using swaps on behalf of his clients.

Honny knows that the most basic type of swap is the plain vanilla swap, where one counterparty pays LIBOR as the floating rate and the other counterparty pays a fixed rate determined by the swap market. He feels this would be a good place to begin and plans to enter into a 2-year, annual-pay plain vanilla swap where Honny pays LIBOR and receives the fixed swap rate from the other counterparty. To get an idea regarding the swap rate he can expect on the 2-year swap, he collects market data on LIBOR. Details are shown in Figure 1.

Figure 1: Market Data on Term Structure of Interest Rates

Year	*LIBOR*	*Discount Factor*
1	5.00%	0.9524
2	4.60%	0.9158

Honny knows that as interest rates change, the value of a swap position will change. Suppose that one year after inception, the LIBOR term structure is as given in Figure 2:

Figure 2: Term Structure of Interest Rates After One Year

Year	*LIBOR*	*Discount Factor*
0.5	4.80%	0.9766
1	4.88%	0.9535
1.5	4.90%	0.9315
2	5.02%	0.9088

One of Honny's clients, George Rosen, is aware of Honny's plans to use swaps and other derivatives in the management of Honny's clients' portfolios. Rosen has a position for which he thinks a swap strategy might be appropriate. Rosen asks Honny to arrange for him a payer swaption that matures in three years. Honny is uncertain of the level of Rosen's familiarity with swaps and swaptions, so Honny wants to make sure that the derivative is appropriate for the client. He asks Rosen exactly what he intends to accomplish by entering into the swaption. Honny also discusses the possible use of a covered call strategy for Rosen's portfolio. Rosen wonders about the motivations for such a strategy.

1. Which of the following would be the *least appropriate* position to replicate the exposure Honny will get from the 2-year, plain vanilla swap position that he plans to take?
   A. Long a series of interest rate puts and short a series of interest rate calls.
   B. Short a series of bond futures.
   C. Short a series of forward rate agreements.

2. Given the 1- and 2-year rates, the 2-year swap fixed rate would be *closest* to:
   A. 4.20%.
   B. 4.51%.
   C. 4.80%.

3. Which of the following is *most likely* to be a conclusion that Honny would reach if the payer swaption has the same exercise rate as the market swap fixed rate for the underlying swap?
   A. The payer swaption would be out of the money.
   B. The value of the payer swaption would be same as the value of an otherwise identical receiver swaption.
   C. The payer swaption would be worth more than an otherwise identical receiver swaption.

4. For this question only, assume that the swap fixed rate is 4.50% and the notional principal is $1 million. Based on the information in Figure 2, the value of the swap to Honny is *closest* to:
   A. –$3,623.
   B. –$3,800.
   C. –$6,790.

5. Which of the following is the *least appropriate* motivation for a covered call strategy?
   A. Income generation.
   B. Target price realization.
   C. Lowering the exit price.

6. The gamma position of a covered call strategy is *most likely* to be:
   A. positive.
   B. negative.
   C. zero.

Self-Test Answers: Derivatives

1. **B** Since Honny will pay the floating rate in the 2-year swap, he gains when the floating rate goes down and loses when it goes up (relative to expectations at inception). This exposure could be replicated with either a short position in a series of FRAs, or a series of short interest rate calls and long interest rate puts. Since short bond futures gain when floating rates increase and lose when floating rates decrease, such a position would give Honny an exposure opposite to the floating rate payer position in a fixed-for-floating interest rate swap.

2. **B** Given the discount factors, the swap-fixed rate can be calculated as:

$$\text{swap fixed rate} = \frac{1 - Z_{\text{2-year}}}{Z_{\text{1-year}} + Z_{\text{2-year}}} = \frac{1 - 0.9158}{0.9524 + 0.9158} = 0.0451$$

Since the rates are already in annual terms, no further adjustment is necessary.

3. **B** If the exercise rate of a receiver option and a payer swaption are equal to the at-market forward swap rate, then the receiver and payer swaptions will have the same value. When the exercise rate is equal to the market SFR, the payer option will be *at-the-money*.

4. **A** Value to the payer = $\Sigma DF \times (SFR_{New} - SFR_{Old}) \times \frac{\text{days}}{360} \times \text{notional principal}$

There is only one settlement date remaining (one year away). Hence the sum of discount factors = the discount factor for the last settlement (one year away) = 0.9535. Also, given the single settlement date, the new swap fixed rate has to be the LIBOR rate for that settlement date, or 4.88% (given in Figure 2).

value to the payer = 0.9535 × (0.0488 – 0.0450) × 360/360 × $1,000,000 = $3,623

The swap discussed is a receiver swap.

value to the receiver = –$3,623

5. **C** Motivations for using a covered call strategy include income generation, target price realization, and improving on the market. Lowering of the exit price is not a valid motivation for a covered call.

6. **B** A covered call strategy entails a long position combined with a short call. A long position in stock has zero gamma. Calls have positive gamma, and a short position in call would have a negative gamma. This negative gamma position from short call combined with zero gamma of long stock results in a net negative gamma position of a covered call portfolio.

Formulas

Study Sessions 12 and 13: Fixed Income

price of a T-period zero-coupon bond

$$P_T = \frac{1}{(1+S_T)^T}$$

forward price (at t = j) of a zero-coupon bond maturing at (j+k)

$$F_{(j,k)} = \frac{1}{[1+f(j,k)]^k}$$

forward pricing model

$$P_{(j+k)} = P_j F_{(j,k)}$$

Therefore:

$$F_{(j,k)} = \frac{P_{(j+k)}}{P_j}$$

forward rate model

$$[1 + S_{(j+k)}]^{(j+k)} = (1 + S_j)^j \, [1 + f(j,k)]^k$$

or

$$[1 + f(j,k)]^k = [1 + S_{(j+k)}]^{(j+k)} / (1 + S_j)^j$$

swap spread

$\text{swap spread}_t = \text{swap rate}_t - \text{Treasury yield}_t$

TED Spread

TED Spread = (3-month LIBOR rate) – (3-month T-bill rate)

LIBOR-OIS spread

LIBOR-OIS spread = LIBOR rate – "overnight indexed swap" rate

Portfolio value change due to level, steepness, and curvature movements

$$\frac{\Delta P}{P} \approx -D_L \Delta x_L - D_S \Delta x_S - D_C \Delta x_C$$

callable bond

$$V_{call} = V_{straight} - V_{callable}$$

putable bond

$$V_{putable} = V_{straight} + V_{put}$$

$$V_{put} = V_{putable} - V_{straight}$$

effective duration = $ED = \dfrac{BV_{-\Delta y} - BV_{+\Delta y}}{2 \times BV_0 \times \Delta y}$

effective convexity = $EC = \dfrac{BV_{-\Delta y} + BV_{+\Delta y} - (2 \times BV_0)}{BV_0 \times \Delta y^2}$

convertible bond

minimum value of convertible bond = greater of conversion value or straight value

$$\text{market conversion price} = \frac{\text{market price of convertible bond}}{\text{conversion ratio}}$$

market conversion premium per share = market conversion price – stock's market price

market conversion premium ratio

$$\text{market conversion premium ratio} = \frac{\text{market conversion premium per share}}{\text{market price of common stock}}$$

$$\text{premium over straight value} = \left(\frac{\text{market price of convertible bond}}{\text{straight value}}\right) - 1$$

callable and putable convertible bond value = straight value of bond
\+ value of call option on stock
– value of call option on bond
\+ value of put option on bond

credit analysis

recovery rate = percentage of money received upon default of the issuer

loss given default (%) = 100 – recovery rate

expected loss = probability of default × loss given default

present value of expected loss
= (value of risk-free bond) – (value of credit-risky bond)

upfront premium % (paid by protection buyer)
≈ (CDS spread – CDS coupon) × duration

price of CDS (per $100 notional) ≈ $100 – upfront premium (%)

profit for protection buyer ≈ change in spread × duration × notional principal

STUDY SESSION 14: DERIVATIVES

forward contract price (cost-of-carry model)

$$FP = S_0 \times (1 + R_f)^T$$

or

$$S_0 = \frac{FP}{(1 + R_f)^T}$$

no-arbitrage price of an equity forward contract with discrete dividends

$$FP(\text{on an equity security}) = (S_0 - PVD) \times (1 + R_f)^T$$

$$FP(\text{on an equity security}) = \left[S_0 \times (1 + R_f)^T\right] - FVD$$

value of the long position in a forward contract on a dividend-paying stock

$$V_t(\text{long position}) = [S_t - PVD_t] - \left[\frac{FP}{(1 + R_f)^{(T-t)}}\right]$$

price of an equity index forward contract with continuous dividends

$$FP(\text{on an equity index}) = S_0 \times e^{\left(R_f^c - \delta^c\right) \times T} = \left(S_0 \times e^{-\delta^c \times T}\right) \times e^{R_f^c \times T}$$

where:
R_f^c = *continuously compounded risk-free rate*
δ^c = *continuously compounded dividend yield*

forward price on a coupon-paying bond:

$$FP(\text{on a fixed income security}) = (S_0 - PVC) \times (1 + R_f)^T$$
or
$$= S_0 \times (1 + R_f)^T - FVC$$

value prior to expiration of a forward contract on a coupon-paying bond:

$$V_t(\text{long position}) = [S_t - PVC_t] - \left[\frac{FP}{(1 + R_f)^{(T-t)}}\right]$$

price of a bond futures contract:

$$FP = \left[(\text{full price})(1 + R_f)^T - AI_T - FVC\right]$$

quoted bond futures price based on conversion factor (CF):

$$QFP = FP / CF = \left[(\text{full price})(1 + R_f)^T - AI_T - FVC\right]\left(\frac{1}{CF}\right)$$

price of a currency forward contract:

$$F_T(\text{currency forward contract}) = S_0 \times \frac{(1 + R_{PC})^T}{(1 + R_{BC})^T}$$

value of a currency forward contract

$$V_t(\text{long base currency}) = V_t = \frac{[FP_t - FP]}{(1 + r_{PC})^{(T-t)}}$$

price and value for a currency forward contract (continuous time):

$$F_T = (\text{currency forward contract}) = S_0 \times e^{\left(R_{PC}^c - R_{BC}^c\right) \times T}$$

swap fixed rate:

$$\text{SFR}(\text{periodic}) = \frac{1 - \text{last discount factor}}{\text{sum of discount factors}}$$

$$\text{swap fixed rate (annual)} = \text{SFR}(\text{periodic}) \times \text{number of settlement periods per year}$$

value of plain vanilla interest rate swap (to payer) after inception

$$\text{value to the payer} = \sum \text{DF} \times (\text{SFR}_{\text{New}} - \text{SFR}_{\text{Old}}) \times \frac{\text{days}}{360} \times \text{notional principal}$$

probability of an up-move or down-move in a binomial stock tree:

$$\pi_U = \text{probability of an up move} = \pi_U = \frac{1 + R_f - D}{U - D}$$

$$\pi_D = \text{probability of a down move} = (1 - \pi_U)$$

put-call parity:

$$S_0 + P_0 = C_0 + PV(X)$$

put-call parity when the stock pays dividends:

$$P_0 + S_0 e^{-\delta T} = C_0 + e^{-rT} X$$

dynamic hedging

$$\text{number of } \textit{short} \text{ call options needed to delta hedge} = \frac{\text{number of shares hedged}}{\text{delta of call option}}$$

$$\text{number of long put options needed to delta hedge} = -\frac{\text{number of shares}}{\text{delta of the put option}}$$

change in option value

$$\Delta C \approx \text{call delta} \times \Delta S + \tfrac{1}{2}\,\text{gamma} \times \Delta S^2$$

$$\Delta P \approx \text{put delta} \times \Delta S + \tfrac{1}{2}\,\text{gamma} \times \Delta S^2$$

Option value using arbitrage-free pricing portfolio

$$C_0 = hS_0 + \frac{(-hS^- + C^-)}{(1+R_f)} = hS_0 + \frac{(-hS^+ + C^+)}{(1+R_f)}$$

$$P_0 = hS_0 + \frac{(-hS^- + P^-)}{(1+R_f)} = hS_0 + \frac{(-hS^+ + P^+)}{(1+R_f)}$$

BSM model

$$C_0 = S_0e^{-\delta T}N(d_1) - e^{-rT}XN(d_2)$$

$$P_0 = e^{-rT}XN(-d_2) - S_0e^{-\delta T}N(-d_1)$$

breakeven price analytics; volatility needed to break even:

$$\sigma_{annual} = \%\Delta P \times \sqrt{\frac{252}{\text{trading days until maturity}}}$$

$$\textit{where } \%\Delta P = \frac{|\text{breakeven price} - \text{current price}|}{\text{current price}}$$

Index

T

U

V

Y

Z

Notes

Notes

Notes

Notes